THREE CENTURIES OF AMERICAN
HYMNODY

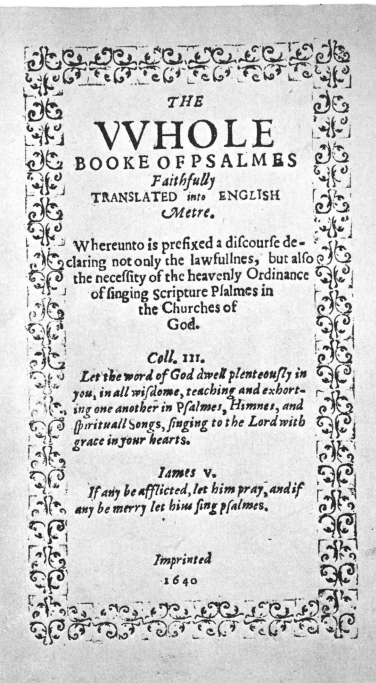

THE
VVHOLE
BOOKE OF PSALMES
Faithfully
TRANSLATED *into* ENGLISH
Metre.

Whereunto is prefixed a difcourfe declaring not only the lawfullnes, but alfo
the neceffity of the heavenly Ordinance
of finging Scripture Pfalmes in
the Churches of
God.

Coll. III.
*Let the word of God dwell plenteoufly in
you, in all wifdome, teaching and exhort-
ing one another in Pfalmes, Himnes, and
fpirituall Songs, finging to the Lord with
grace in your hearts.*

Iames v.
*If any be afflicted, let him pray, and if
any be merry let him fing pfalmes.*

Imprinted
·1640

Title page of the first edition of *The Bay Psalm Book*,
from a copy in the New York Public Library

THREE CENTURIES OF AMERICAN HYMNODY

BY

HENRY WILDER FOOTE

Hamden, Connecticut

THE SHOE STRING PRESS, INC.

1961

TO THE MEMORY OF

MY MOTHER

WHOSE GRACIOUS LIFE WAS A SONG OF FAITH

MORE LOVELY THAN THE HYMNS

WHICH SHE SANG WITH HEART AND VOICE

Preface

This volume, which represents a cumulative study of some years, might not have been written but for the stimulus received from an invitation to deliver five lectures on American hymnody at the Harvard Summer School of Theology held in July, 1936, in connection with the Tercentenary of Harvard University. The material there presented has been worked over, rearranged and greatly enlarged in the attempt to present an adequate account of the development of worship song in the United States from the first permanent English settlements to the present time. The three hundredth anniversary of the publication of *The Bay Psalm Book* in 1640, the first book printed in English-speaking North America, is an appropriate moment to issue a survey of the great and ever-broadening stream of hymnody of which that crudely printed little book is the fountainhead.

My indebtedness to many other writers will appear on every page, even when not indicated by footnotes. Two sources are of primary importance: Julian's great *Dictionary of Hymnology*, which, though no longer up to date, is indispensable; and Louis F. Benson's masterly book, *The English Hymn*, which is the most inclusive and reliable treatise on the subject. Particularly valuable is Dr. Benson's study of American hymnbooks and of the religious tendencies which they exhibit. This rich vein of information which he uncovered had hardly been touched by earlier writers on hymnology, who had, for the most part, limited themselves to biographical sketches of hymn writers and anecdotal accounts of well-known hymns. I have sought to find a *via media* between Dr. Benson's erudite but involved method and the purely anecdotal treatment of hymns and hymn writers, which so quickly degenerates into a catalogue of names to which are appended stories for homiletical use. While it is true that one can hardly overestimate the influence of a few great hymn writers such as Ambrose of Milan, Martin Luther, Isaac Watts and Charles Wesley, a too exclusive attention to the individual tends to shut out the view of the great stream of religious thought and practice which finds expression in the hymnbooks used by successive generations. The story of this constantly changing and developing stream is far more significant than the contribution of any single individual, and the religious thought and feeling of earlier generations can be traced more clearly by an examination of the hymnody which they used than in almost any other way. That is the reason for the inclusion in these pages of what some readers may find a wearisomely detailed account of psalmbooks and hymnbooks long since forgotten even by the descendants of those who used them. They are mirrors which faithfully reflect the beliefs and practices of their time. As the late Dr. Benson put it, "The collection and classification of old psalm-books [and hymnbooks], which are the remains and record of the spiritual life of contemporaneous Christians, is just as scientific as the collection and classification of old fossil shells, which are the remains and record of the animal life of contemporaneous mollusca."

It is inevitable that in such a study as this some attention should be paid to the music to which the psalms and the later hymns have been sung, and to the successive revivals of singing in the American churches. My treatment of that phase of the subject has, however, been purely incidental. I have not attempted to write a history of American church music, nor am I competent to do so. I have been

concerned primarily with the text of psalm and hymn, and
with the thought expressed, as a reflection of the ideas of
the time. The chief sources of information regarding the
musical usages in New England in the seventeenth and
eighteenth centuries have been Mr. Scholes' book, *The
Puritans and Music*, 1934, which is a mine of information
in a hitherto greatly misunderstood field; and Hood's *History
of Music in New England*, 1846, which, though old,
not always accurate, and not well-arranged, contains long
quotations from early sermons and tracts which have generally
been overlooked and are not easily accessible, as
well as accounts of church practices, which I have drawn
upon freely.

Dr. Ninde's popularly written *Story of the American
Hymn* also contains much information, especially about
individual hymn writers. In his Chapters I-IV, covering
the eighteenth century, he goes over the same ground that
I have traversed in my Chapters II-V, and, in some cases,
has given more attention to individuals than I have done,
but he neglects adequately to portray the general movement
in thought and sentiment in the eighteenth century,
and he labors under the current misapprehension of the
Puritan attitude towards music, which appears to me to
be quite mistaken.

Few people today are really acquainted with the usage
of psalmody in the colonial churches, and the story takes
us into a world which seems remote and archaic. Our
colonial ancestors were, however, just as human as we are,
and I have sought to make their practice and their prejudices
intelligible. The story is not without its romance
and its conflicts of taste and opinion, nor does it lack its
humorous episodes. The gradual transition from psalmody
to hymnody during the last half of the eighteenth century
prepared the way for the flood of new hymnbooks and
hymn writers which began about 1800 and which con-

tinues unabated. It is difficult to tell this later story of American hymnody without confusion because of the many parallel rivulets which arose within the diverse denominational boundaries and which at first mingled in the common stream much more slowly than is the case today. For this reason it has seemed better to deal with the hymn writers by denominational groups, unsatisfactory as that method is in many respects. It is only in the present century that such denominational grouping has ceased to have any significance, and that we can apply to American hymnody as a whole the words of a very recent hymn,

> As tranquil streams that meet and merge
> And flow as one to seek the sea,
> Our kindred fellowships unite
> To build a church that shall be free.

It may be doubted whether any previous generation in the United States has witnessed so general and intelligent an interest in hymn singing as prevails at the present time. If this volume can help its readers to a better understanding of the steps which have led to the production of the noble hymnody of today, and to an appreciation of the greatness of our heritage, it will have served its purpose.

I am greatly indebted for counsel and advice to the late Professor Waldo S. Pratt, who read the manuscript of Chapters I and II; to Mr. Percy A. Scholes, who read Chapter III; to Rev. LeTell Douglas Rights, who read Chapter IV; to Rev. Edward P. Daniels, who read large parts of the manuscript; and to my wife, who has read it all.

HENRY WILDER FOOTE

CONTENTS

THREE CENTURIES OF AMERICAN HYMNODY

CHAPTER I

The Heritage of English Psalmody

THE FIRST BOOK printed in the English colonies of
North America was *The Bay Psalm Book*, published
in 1640 at Cambridge, Massachusetts. Its publication marks
the beginning of American hymnody, if we accept St. Augustine's famous definition of hymnody as "praise to God
with song," and so include psalmody, consisting of more
or less faithful metrical versions of the psalms, as well as
hymns in the more restricted sense of lyrical verse intended to be sung in public worship and recognized as the
original composition of the writer.

For nearly a century and a quarter psalmody alone was
used in the churches of the English-speaking colonies, save
for the brief experiment by John Wesley in Georgia in
1737. The German-speaking settlers, who came to Pennsylvania between about 1690 and about 1750, brought with
them a different tradition, that of Lutheran hymnody,
under the influence of which they produced a considerable
number of both hymns and tunes, the earliest of which
date from the opening years of the eighteenth, if not from
the closing years of the seventeenth, century. These were
the first original hymns or tunes to be produced in the
North American colonies, but some of them remained in
manuscript and have only recently been discovered, and
the use of those which were printed was closely limited
to the German-speaking groups who dwelt as small, self-
contained enclaves among the preponderant English-
speaking population to whom the Lutheran tradition was

quite alien. This early German-American hymnody, therefore, though in itself an interesting phenomenon, had no influence whatever on the development of the hymnody in the English tongue, which is what we ordinarily mean when we speak of American hymnody. With the exception of Wesley's experiment there was, before the middle of the eighteenth century, no such thing as American hymnody in the form of original compositions written in English and published on American soil, and few hymns of American authorship came into any general use here before the end of that century, less than one hundred and fifty years ago. Therefore, to gain a true understanding of the soil from which the rich flowering of nineteenth-century hymnody sprang, it is necessary first to survey the background of psalmody which the English-speaking settlers brought to these shores from the mother country, and the variations from that early psalmody which developed out of the conditions of their life here.

It must also be remembered that American hymnody, from its beginning to the present hour, has been powerfully influenced by English usage. Hymn writing in England, apart from psalmody, may for practical purposes be dated from Isaac Watts, and he and many others stimulated by his example had been at work for half a century or more before any American writers seriously began to follow their example. The compilers of our earlier hymn-books were for several decades almost wholly dependent upon English sources, and their books were modelled on English examples, in form, arrangement and content. It was not until the middle of the nineteenth century that the number of hymns written in this country became fairly large, or that the hymns themselves acquired any distinctive character. By the end of that century the volume of American hymns had attained large proportions and included many notable examples, but it still remains true that, of the whole vast body of hymns in the English language, those written in England greatly outnumber those written in this country. Our worship is still largely dependent upon this treasury of English hymns, though it is also true that with the passing years American hymns find their way in steadily increasing numbers into English books. The interaction and merging of these two parallel streams of hymnody must be constantly borne in mind.

Turning back, then, to the story of English psalmody, let us consider its rise in sixteenth century England. For many centuries prior to the Reformation the only hymns used in that country in the worship of the church had been, of course, the Latin ones of the Roman rite. The usage in different localities varied in some measure,[1] but there was a great body of worship-song which was the common heritage of Catholics throughout western Europe, and the Latin hymnody, with its musical settings, was one of the great treasures of the church. This Latin hymnody was definitely liturgical in character, the hymns having their designated places within the framework of the various offices of worship, and they were sung only by the clergy, choirs, or members of a monastic body. The laity in the congregations neither were expected nor were able to sing them, and congregational singing in church had for centuries been discountenanced.

There was, however, in private use a certain amount of religious poetry in the vernacular, such as carols and other semi-religious songs, chiefly for Christmastide, but in

---

[1] The divergence was greatest in the hymns for the Proper of Saints, which made provision for many festivals of purely local interest; the maximum uniformity was in the Office Hymns for the week, which were substantially the same over wide areas. These variations of usage prevailed throughout a large part of western Europe until the Council of Trent required the abandonment of the old local uses and the adoption of the Breviary according to the Roman Use.

smaller numbers for Easter and other seasons. The earliest surviving English carols date from the fifteenth century, but carols originated in France two hundred years earlier in songs to be sung with dancing. Carols were intended for household or social use rather than for public worship, though they were sometimes permitted in church in connection with Christmas festivities, but it is only within very recent times that they have found any place in hymnbooks.

Neither the liturgical Latin hymns nor the popular carols of pre-Reformation England had any influence upon the later English (or American) hymnody until the revival of interest in both which came about the middle of the nineteenth century. Both were for the most part forgotten in the seventeenth and eighteenth centuries. Outside of the closed circles of Roman Catholic families the Latin hymns would have been regarded as "Popish" if their existence had been recognized. And the carols survived chiefly as the picturesque repertoire of rustic waits, or as quaint relics of a period which had lacked the elevating influence of classic elegance. Protestant hymnody is, therefore, the expression of a fresh and democratic religious impulse, originating in the Reformation, which gave back to the people psalms and hymns in their own tongue to be sung by all in common worship, even as had been done in the early Church.

When the Reformation began in Germany, Luther, who was himself both a musician and a poet, who loved the old German folk song, and who was well versed in the music and hymnody of the Roman Church, immediately turned to congregational song in the vernacular as an effective means of spreading the doctrines of the Reformation. He had before him the examples of the "Laudi Spirituali," an Italian vernacular and non-ecclesiastical hymnody associated with the Franciscan movement in the fourteenth and fifteenth centuries, with its joyful melodies; and of the Bohemian Brethren, the followers of John Hus, who in 1501 had published their first book of hymns.² In Germany also, as in England, there was already in existence a considerable body of popular semi-sacred song, intended, like the English carols, for domestic or social use.³ Luther saw no objection to the Roman custom of using hymns, or to making very free paraphrases of the psalms, of which "Ein' feste Burg" is a classic example, instead of limiting himself to closely translated metrical versions of sacred Scripture. Nor did he hesitate to draw his tunes from any available source, whether within the church tradition or outside it. Therefore German Protestantism began immediately the development of that great body of original sacred song which for two centuries was its crowning glory, although, broadly speaking, the words of the hymns had less permanent value than the music.

Calvin, on the other hand, seems to have been by temperament at least indifferent to the music and poetry of the Roman Church, and actively hostile to the light songs popular among the French. He would have nothing sung in public worship at Geneva except the words of sacred Scripture, turned into as close and accurate translations as was humanly possible, and set to grave but beautiful music. Thus psalm singing soon became as characteristic of the Reformed Church as hymn singing was characteristic of Lutheranism.

The beginnings of Calvinistic psalmody are traced to a little book published at Strasbourg in 1539 under the title *Aulcuns pseaulmes et cantiques mys en chant*, containing

---

² See Chap. IV for the influence of the Bohemian hymnody in the German-speaking settlements in the Colonies.

³ Philipp Wackernagle, *Das deutsche Kirchenlied*, Leipzig, 1864, includes 1448 religious lyrics in German composed between 868 and 1518. Many of these are poems and folk hymns, but some are fitted for use in public worship.

metrical versions of thirteen psalms by Marot and six sometimes attributed to Calvin. Calvin returned to Geneva in 1541 and probably introduced the book to his congregation there. Clément Marot was a well-educated French poet, who had been valet-de-chambre at the court of Marguerite of Valois, and later at that of François I. He translated into French verse some thirty psalms which were circulated in manuscript. Singing them to ballad tunes became the fashion at court until their publication in 1542 brought down on Marot the wrath of the Sorbonne and he was obliged to flee to Geneva. He stayed there only a year before going to Turin, where he died in 1544, but in that year he produced for Calvin a book containing fifty psalms, Calvin's versions being replaced with fresh ones by Marot. In 1548 Théodore de Béze (Beza) arrived in Geneva and was commissioned to continue the work. An edition containing thirty more psalms appeared in 1551; another enlarged but still incomplete one in 1554; and the complete French Genevan Psalter in 1562, containing forty-nine psalms by Marot and one hundred and one by Théodore de Béze. The psalms were carefully translated from the Hebrew in a great variety of metres, and the literary standards were much better than those of the contemporary English psalmbooks, because the authors were both better scholars and better poets.

In the preparation of this French Genevan Psalter Calvin was as fortunate in his musicians as in his poets. He probably had at first the assistance of Goudimel, but from 1542 to 1557 the tunes were arranged by Louis Bourgeois, though it is not known which of them he composed and which he derived from other sources. When he left Geneva in 1557 eighty-eight psalms had been provided with tunes. The complete Psalter of 1562 contains 125 tunes, the finest being those arranged by Bourgeois.[4] The tunes are noble

[4] See Waldo Selden Pratt, *The Music of the French Psalter of 1562*, New York, 1939, for an authoritative account of this important book.

and dignified, vigorous and often profoundly moving, very varied in metre, to match the verse. Originally they were printed with only the melody line and were probably sung in unison, but editions with other parts were soon published. No small part of Calvin's success at Geneva was due to the enthusiasm with which Bourgeois' melodies were sung.

Their use spread rapidly to other countries. The Dutch adopted Calvinism at an early date, and took over the French Genevan Psalter entire, merely translating the psalms into their own language. The French Huguenots, of course, sang the Genevan psalm tunes, which also penetrated Germany to some extent. The earliest use of metrical psalmody in America was in the Huguenot settlements of 1564 and 1565 on the coast of Florida and South Carolina. These settlements were soon extinguished by the Spaniards, but not before the neighboring Indians had learned some of the psalm tunes, which they are said to have sung long afterwards. This is the earliest recorded instance of the fondness of the North American Indians for music, of which there are many later accounts. When the first church was organized in New Amsterdam in 1628 the French and Dutch joined in using the same tunes to the versions of the psalms in the two languages.

In the first years of the Reformation the English were open to the influence of both Luther and Calvin, and for a brief time under Henry VIII the Lutheran influence seemed likely to prevail, but presently the English churchmen turned from it towards Calvinism, and it left no mark on English hymnody. In 1531 Myles Coverdale issued his *Goostly Psalmes and Spirituall Songes drawen out of the holy Scripture*, which was strongly influenced by Luther's example, but it had small success and was prohibited in 1546. About the same time the three brothers named Wedderburn issued in Scotland their *Gude and Godlie Ballatis*, also based on Lutheran models, with more success. But when Queen Mary Tudor came to the throne, and the more outspoken English Protestants fled to the Continent, they came under the influence of Calvin. In 1556 they issued at Geneva their *One and Fifty Psalmes of David in English Metre*, each provided with a tune, on the model of the French Genevan Psalter, and this was followed by enlarged Anglo-Genevan editions in 1558 and 1561. When, with the accession of Elizabeth and the establishment of the reformed faith in England and Scotland they returned to those countries, they brought back with them both the music and the forms of psalmody which they had learned in exile and which thereafter formed the model for the succeeding psalters in both countries. The Lutheran hymnody, so far as it had been known at all, was speedily forgotten and was wholly ignored by the English-speaking world until John Wesley, nearly a century and three-quarters later, translated a few of the hymns he had learned from the Moravians. Even then no other English authors awoke to any real comprehension of the treasures of German hymnody until well on in the nineteenth century, by which time the English had at last wholeheartedly abandoned psalmody for hymnody.

Two notes should be made at this point. First, Calvin did not originate the doctrine that only psalms (or other Scripture canticles) should be sung in worship, for the admissibility of hymns had long been a debatable question. In Spain the first Council of Braga, in 561, forbade the use in public worship of any poetical compositions "outside of the psalms . . . of the Old and New Testaments." This decree remained in force for three-quarters of a century, till it was revoked in 633 by the sixth Council of Toledo, though it seems to have applied only to public worship, and not to the use of office hymns in the monasteries. Perhaps the influence of Gregory the Great in favor of hymnody was decisive. In the second place even

Calvin and his English-speaking disciples did not apply the doctrine with absolute strictness, for they did not actually limit themselves to versions of the psalms. The first edition of Calvin's Genevan Psalter (1542) included metrical versions of the Song of Simeon, the Ten Commandments, the Lord's Prayer and the Creed. And when the printer John Day, in 1562, issued his complete English *Book of Psalms* by Sternhold and Hopkins, eleven hymns, of which four were not scriptural paraphrases, preceded the psalms, and eight hymns, of which six were not paraphrases, followed them, and later four more were added.[5] "Proper," that is, designated tunes were provided. In practice, however, these hymns seem to have been little used in public worship and one by one they all dropped out of later editions of the *Book of Psalms*.

It was John Day (or Daye), "dwelling over Aldersgate" in London, one of the earliest English music-printers, who, after the accession of Elizabeth, promptly undertook the task of supplying Protestant England with psalmbooks and thus began the stream of English psalters, as distinguished from the Anglo-Genevan books which the exiles had printed abroad. Day is believed to have printed an incomplete edition of the *Book of Psalms* with tunes in 1559, but no copy survives and it probably was never issued because Day had neglected to have it licensed. An edition was printed in 1560, and another in 1561, but the complete psalter did not appear until 1562, the same year in which the complete French Genevan Psalter came out.

For our purposes John Day's book of 1562 is of primary importance. Its full title is long and cumbersome: *The whole Booke of Psalmes, collected into English Meter by T. Sternhold, I. Hopkins and others; conferred with the*

---

[5] See L. F. Benson, *The English Hymn*, New York, 1915, pp. 27-37, for a detailed discussion of this additional material; also John Julian, *Dictionary of Hymnology*, London, 1915, pp. 857–866.

Ebrue, with apt Notes to sing them withal, Faithfully perused and alowed according to th'ordre appointed in the Quenes maiesties Iniunctions: Very mete to be vsed of all sortes of people privately for their solace & comfort; laying apart all ungodly Songes and Ballades, which tende only to the norishment of vyce & corruption of youth. . . . An. 1562.

It was the most popular and widely used of all the very numerous English Psalters, until the new version by Tate and Brady, published 134 years later, after a long struggle partially superseded it. Because it was the great forerunner of all later English psalmody, and because of its widespread influence and long-continued use, the dramatic story of its origin and development is an essential feature in the heritage of psalmody which the first settlers brought to the American colonies.

Thomas Sternhold, its primary author, had a career curiously parallel in some respects to that of Clément Marot, and he did his work in the reigns of Henry VIII and Edward VI, before any English exiles went to Geneva. Sternhold was groom of the robes to Henry VIII, and it is possible that at court he had heard of the writings of Clément Marot, though there is no trace of direct influence. He was not so good a poet as Marot, though a more truly religious man. He first wrote his psalms and sang them to organ accompaniment for his own "Godly Solace," then, when they attracted attention, printed nineteen of them before his death in 1549,[6] under the title:

---

[6] Sternhold was not, however, the first person to translate the psalms into English verse. Beside Anglo-Saxon and other early versions, Miles Coverdale had printed his *Goostly Psalmes* in 1539; John Croke, Sir Thomas Wyatt and the Earl of Surrey had each put a few psalms into verse, and Robert Crowley brought out the first complete metrical psalter in English in 1549. Several other more or less complete versions appeared before the complete Sternhold and Hopkins in 1562. The work of these other writers, however, was in the nature of a literary

Certayne Psalms, chosē out of the Psalter of David and drawē into Englishe metre by Thomas Sternhold, grome of ye kynge's Maiesties' roobes.
A second and posthumous edition containing thirty-seven of his psalms appeared in 1549. They were written in the old ballad metre, which was common metre,[7] duple or triple, except for one psalm in double short metre and one in 6.6.6.6.6.6. In 1551, after Sternhold's death, John Hopkins added seven more psalms, though he says in his preface to the third edition that he does not count his versions as "in any parte to be compared with Sternhold's most exquisite doynges." There were two reprints in 1553, before the accession of Queen Mary Tudor put an abrupt stop to such activities and Sternhold's book was banished to Geneva along with the exiles, where it formed the basis of the book of 1556 already referred to.

Because only the names of Thomas Sternhold and John Hopkins appeared on the title page of John Day's Psalter of 1562, the book was commonly spoken of as "Sternhold and Hopkins" until the publication of Tate and Brady's *New Version of the Psalms* (1696) gave rise to the nickname of the Old Version to describe the earlier book. The work of Thomas Sternhold and John Hopkins, however, although it formed the basis of the book, was largely supplemented by the "others" also noted on the title page. There were, in fact, ten other contributors, only a few of whom need be named here. The number of Sternhold's versions is variously estimated at from thirty-seven to forty; those of Hopkins at fifty-six to sixty. William Whittingham, who had been an associate of John Knox at Geneva and his successor as minister of English and Scotch exiles there during the Marian persecutions, con-

---

exercise rather than a contribution to worship, so that Sternhold is rightly regarded as the founder of English metrical psalmody.
[7] This was the metre of *Chevy Chase*, with only two rhymes.

tributed twelve, including the first long metre. After the
accession of Queen Elizabeth he was made Dean of Dur-
ham, where he built up the choir-school and secured "the
best songs and anthems that could be got out of the Queen's
chapell, to furnish the quire with all, himself being skillfull
in musicke." Robert Wisdome, later Archdeacon of Ely,
contributed three versions clearly influenced by Luther's
work: Thomas Norton contributed twenty-six versions;
John Marckant four, and probably the two hymns beginning,

O Lord! turn not away thy face, —

and

O Lord! on whom I do depend.

Edward Grindal, later Archbishop of Canterbury, was
the probable author of the hymn "Da Pacem,"

Give peace in these our daies, O Lord,

a translation of a German hymn. In this, as in Wisdome's
versions, we see a momentary revival of Lutheran influence. William Kethe contributed nine versions, including one of the finest, that of the 104th Psalm.

In all probability Kethe was also the author of the
famous version of the 100th Psalm, beginning,

All people that on earth do dwell, —

set to the tune which we know as "Old Hundredth." This
psalm appears in both the Anglo-Genevan Psalter of 1561
and in Day's incomplete edition of the same year, but,
curiously enough, it was omitted from the complete edition
of 1562. It came back again in the Appendix of the edition
of 1564, and in the body of the book in 1565, and was included in the Scottish Psalter of 1564, and in many succeeding books. The words were probably written for the

tune, which is first found in the French Genevan Psalter of 1551, set to the 134th Psalm, and which was given shape by Louis Bourgeois, although the first line was taken from a secular chanson. When it was taken over for use in the English Psalter the notation of the last line was slightly altered from the Genevan form. It immediately became popular and our forefathers liked it because it was "a jocound and lively" air! We think of it as solemn and stately, rather than as lively, because we are familiar with the form in which it emerged from the eighteenth-century usage. When sung, however, in the early form and in fairly quick time it reveals the almost gay character which made it a fitting setting for the words:

> Sing to the Lord with cheerful voice;
> Him serve with mirth, his praise forth tell;
> Come ye before him and rejoice.

It was the vigor and liveliness of a number of these Genevan psalm tunes that led critics to dub them "Geneva jiggs" or "Hopkins his jiggs." To a writer of a century ago it seemed "strange, indeed, that the very tunes that send us to sleep caused our forefathers to dance." But he was unaware that between the end of the seventeenth and the beginning of the nineteenth century the psalm tunes were deliberately lengthened out by giving their notes equal length, and singing was slowed down in the supposed interest of solemnity.

All the early English psalters contained some tunes, mostly from unknown sources, though others beside "Old Hundredth" were taken from the French Genevan Psalter, but the complete edition of 1562 contained only forty-two, as against the French Psalter's one hundred and twenty-five. Day's *Book of Psalms* was, in this respect, as in the quality of its verse, far inferior to the French Psalter. Most of these forty-two tunes remained long in use, and were known as the "Proper" tunes for the psalms to which they were assigned. At the present time the few which survive in use are distinguished by the adjective "Old" prefixed to the number of the psalm to which they were originally set. Later editions of the book included as "Common Tunes" additional music to which various psalms could be sung.

The poetry of the Old Version, which later generations came to regard as crude and barbarous, was satisfactory to the people for whom it was produced. Perhaps it was as good as could have been written in England at that time. In any case, it is poor taste to sneer at devout men who did their best to meet a great need. And at his best Thomas Sternhold could write fine and vigorous verse, witness these stirring stanzas from his version of the 18th Psalm:

O God my strength and fortitude
    of force I must love thee:
Thou art my castle and defence,
    in my necessitie.

My God, my rocke, in whom I trust,
    the worker of my wealth:
My refuge buckler, and my shield,
    the horne of all my health.

The panges of death did compas me
    and bound me every where:
The flowing waves of wickedness,
    did put me in great feare.

The sly and suttle snares of hell,
    were round about me set:
And for my death there was prepar'd
    a deadly trappyng net.

I thus beset with payne and grief,
    did pray to God for grace:

> And he forthwith did heare my playnt,
> out of hys holy place.

> The Lord descended from above,
> and bowed the heavens hye:
> And underneath hys feete he cast
> the darkness of the skye.

> On Cherubs and on Cherubins,
> full royally he rode:
> And on the winges of all the windes,
> came flying all abroad.

This is certainly the Old Version at its best, for the great bulk of it is in a steady jog trot which soon becomes very monotonous. The average may be illustrated by part of John Hopkins' translation of the 42nd Psalm:

> Like as the hart doth pant and bray,
> The well-springs to obtain;
> So doth my soul desire alway,
> With thee, Lord, to remain.

> My soul doth thirst, and would draw near,
> The living God of might;
> Oh when shall I come and appear,
> In presence of his sight?

And it is difficult to imagine how people could sing the following, by Sternhold:

> And tho' ye were as black as pots,
> Your hue shall pass the dove
> Whose wings and feathers seem to have
> Silver and gold above.

> When in this land God shall triumph
> O'er kings both high and low,
> Then shall it be like Salmon hill,
> As white as is the snow.

Yet consider the task which Sternhold had set himself. That is a version of verses 13 and 14 in the 68th Psalm, which read in the Bible,

Tho ye have lien among the pots yet shall ye be as the wings of a dove covered with silver, and her feathers with yellow gold. When the Almighty scattered kings in it, it was white as snow in Salmon.

The original Hebrew of that passage is obscure and modern Biblical scholars differ as to its precise meaning, but Thomas Sternhold was no Hebraist, and it was not for him to raise any questions as to the inspired words of the Psalmist, or do other than put them into the best verse he could achieve.

Perhaps the worst of the Old Version is Whittingham's versification of the "Creed of S. Athanasius, called Quicunque Vult":

What man soever he be that
  salvation will attayne:
The Catholicke beliefe he must,
  before all thinges retayne.
Which fayth unles he holy keepe,
  and undefiledly:
Without all doubte eternally,
  he shalbe sure to dye.

Nevertheless, when all its limitations have been pointed out, the fact remains that Day's *Book of Psalms* of 1562 was a great success. More than six hundred editions, with few alterations save for the gradual dropping out of the hymns appended to it, were issued in a little over two and a half centuries, the last edition being printed as late as 1828, and the book was in use in remote corners of England until a decade later before being entirely superseded by the rising tide of hymnbooks. Furthermore, it was this book which established the familiar metres of English hymnody, which we know as short, common and long.[8] No other book of worship song in English has had such enduring use or so widespread an influence as the Old Version.

When, after Elizabeth's accession in 1558, the Marian exiles returned, bringing copies of the Anglo-Genevan Psalters with them, and introduced psalm singing into the English churches, it was inevitable that question should arise as to the validity of the practice. One Herbert Thorndike in *Just Weights and Measures* complained of "these Psalms in Rhime being crowded into the Church by meer sufferance and so used without order of law," and denied that they were "the exercise of Christian devotion." A precedent, however, had been established by the Act of 1549 authorizing the First Prayer Book of Edward VI, which allowed it to

be lawful — in churches — chapels or oratories or other places to use openly any Psalme or prayer taken out of the Bible — not letting or omitting thereby the service or any part thereof mentioned in said book.

This was generally held to cover psalm singing, perhaps because of the young king's liking for Sternhold's psalms, the first edition of which had been dedicated to him.

[8] There is a striking similarity between the ballad-like character of the English metrical psalms and the literary form of the earliest surviving hymns of the Roman Church, by St. Ambrose and his followers in the 4th and 5th centuries. The Ambrosian hymns broke away from the old classical metres, and were written in the simpler form of prosody based on accent rather than on quantity, which had probably long been in use in the songs of the people. Ambrose thus established the form of Latin liturgical hymnody after the model of current folk songs, very much as the metrical psalms of the 16th century followed the pattern of the popular folk ballads. Our familiar long metre is practically that of the Ambrosian hymn, in English dress. See C. S. Phillips, *Hymnody Past and Present*, New York, 1937, pp. 53–55.

In June, 1559, the Ecclesiastical Commissioners issued an "injunction" which reaffirmed the provision of the act of ten years earlier, but, be it noted, without limiting the words which were sung to those drawn from the Bible. It provided that:

For the comforting of such as delight in music, it may be permitted that in the beginning or in the end of the Common Prayers, either at morning or evening, there may be sung an hymn or such like song, to the praise of Almighty God, in the best sort of melody and music that may be conveniently devised, having respect that the sentence of the hymn may be understanded and perceived.

A curious incident arose in the following December when a party of men and women from London sang psalms in Exeter Cathedral, thereby disturbing matins. Their singing being prohibited by the Dean and Chapter, they carried the case to Archbishop Parker, who bade the Cathedral authorities to "permit and suffer" congregations "to sing or say the godly prayers set forth and permitted in this Church of England." Here, as in the Act of 1549, it was the psalms which were included in the "godly prayers" which might be sung. Thenceforward both anthems and psalm singing had a recognized place in the church service.

It is evident from the foregoing that the practice of psalm singing which came in with the return of the Marian exiles after the accession of Queen Elizabeth in 1558 was not limited to any one locality or group within the church but that it was definitely permitted and encouraged by the ecclesiastical authorities. It was almost inevitable that such should be the case, for the metrical psalms were the only available resource for singing to fill the gap left by the omission from the Book of Common Prayer of any translations of the old Latin hymns, with the sole exception of the *Veni Creator Spiritus*, incorporated in the services for the Ordination of Priests and for the Consecration of Bishops.[9] This omission is difficult to understand because English versions of some of the Latin hymns had already appeared in the *Sarum Primer*, printed in 1538, and in other places. Cranmer in 1544 had made a draft of a version of the hymn *Salve festa dies*, set to a Gregorian melody, and had sent it to the king, writing,

I have travailed to make the verses in English — I made them only for a proof to see how English would do in song. But, by cause mine English verses want the grace and facility that I would wish they had, your majesty may cause some other to make them again, that can do the same in more pleasant English and phrase.[10]

Cranmer's drafts of his plans for liturgical revision also provided for the retention of a limited number of hymns from the Roman rite. In the preface to his draft he wrote, "We have left only a few hymns which appeared to be more ancient and more beautiful than the rest." But, when published, the Prayer Book failed to include these proposed translations of Latin hymns, perhaps because the ecclesiastical authorities had swung to Calvin's view of the inadmissibility of "man-made" hymns. With the old hymns disappeared the old liturgical music to which they had been sung. It was not the Puritans, who had not yet emerged as a party, who were responsible for the loss from the Church of England of this ancient heritage of Catholic hymnody. The responsibility rests with the same church authorities that issued the Book of Common Prayer and

[9] A dull common metre version was used in the Prayer Book of 1549. In 1661 the "skillfully condensed paraphrase" published by Bishop Cosin in 1627, beginning
"Come Holy Ghost, our souls inspire," —
was substituted for the earlier form.

[10] *Misc. Writings and Letters of Cranmer*, ed. J. E. Cox, Cambridge, England, 1846, p. 412.

reorganized the Church of England on reformed lines. And it was they who had the good sense to permit the use of metrical psalmody as an acceptable substitute for that which they had abandoned.[11]

The people in general were glad enough to substitute the metrical psalms for the Latin hymns of the Roman rite, in the singing of which they had had no voice,[12] both because those hymns were in an unknown tongue not "understanded or perceived" by them, and because the music to which they were sung required special training. Furthermore the Catholic liturgical hymnody, as has already been noted, was almost completely incorporated in the various services of the church other than the Mass, the offices chiefly used in the monasteries. A simple Catholic layman, devout though illiterate, might hear Mass and make his confession regularly at his small parish church without ever hearing, much less understanding, the great medieval office hymns. It was only in the cathedrals, abbeys and great parish churches that the fine church music was to be heard, and even there the traditional plain song had in large measure disappeared, having been superseded by the later polyphonic music which reached its culmination in the sixteenth century. At the end of that century even the Church of Rome had subjected its office hymns to a very drastic rewriting to meet the classical taste of the Renaissance, and had permitted its ancient plain song to be almost forgotten. That music, which a modern author calls "the most complete treasure of antiquity bequeathed to us by

[11] For a more detailed study of this matter see Benson, *The English Hymn*, pp. 37–45.

[12] The Council of Laodicea, held at intervals between 343 and 381, decreed in its 13th Canon: "Besides the appointed singers, who mount the ambo and sing from the book, others shall not sing in the church." This injunction certainly was not immediately or universally followed, but the development of liturgical music eventually and necessarily resulted in the exclusion of congregational singing.

any art," [13] has, for the church at large, only been recovered in recent decades by the long and laborious studies of the Benedictines of Solesmes. These facts offer at least a partial explanation of why the English in the middle of the sixteenth century placed so little value on the Latin hymnody that even the churchmen who necessarily were most familiar with it did not care for it sufficiently to make the effort to perpetuate it in the vernacular services of the reformed Church of England.

Into the gap thus created the metrical psalms fitted admirably. We cannot understand how eagerly they were welcomed unless we realize that it was less than twenty-five years since the English Bible had been opened to the people and copies had been placed in the churches, chained to the lecterns, for any to read who could. And in the metrical psalms the people had fresh versions of the Scripture turned into well-known ballad metres and set to music which was easily learned because framed in a familiar pattern. Here at last were sacred songs which were no longer limited to the clergy and to the "religious" in monasteries, but which were the possession of the whole people. Next to the English Bible and the Book of Common Prayer the metrical psalms were the most influential literary contribution made by the Reformation to the religious life of the English people. No wonder that they were accepted with enthusiasm and spread like wildfire. Strype tells of their introduction at St. Antholin's Church in London before "the new Morning Prayer," when

a Psalm was sung after the Geneva Fashion, all the congregation — men, women and boys, singing together — which custom was about this time brought also into St. Paul's,[14]

[13] Winfred Douglas, *Church Music in History and Practice*, Charles Scribner's Sons, New York, 1937, p. 30. Quoted by permission.
[14] John Strype, *History of Life and Acts of Edmund Grindal*, London,

and John Jewel, afterwards Bishop of Salisbury, wrote on March 5, 1560, a Latin letter which is well-known for its account of the spread of psalmody. He wrote,

Religion is now somewhat more established than it was. The people are everywhere exceedingly inclined to the better part. Ecclesiastical and popular music has very greatly helped it on. For, as soon as they had once commenced singing in public, in only one little church in London, immediately not only the neighboring churches, but even far-distant cities, began to vie with each other in the same practice. You may sometimes see at Paul's Cross, after the sermon, six thousand persons, old men, boys, girls, singing and praising God together. This sadly annoys the mass-priests and the devil. For they perceive that by these means the sacred discourses sink more deeply into the minds of men, and that their kingdom is weakened and shaken at almost every note.[15]

Thus from London the practice of psalm singing spread throughout the country, the people rejoicing in their new-found freedom to sing the Lord's songs in their own tongue.

The modern historian may regret that the Church of England at this critical period turned away from Luther's example to come under the influence of Calvin. English hymnody would have been far richer had translations of some of the old Latin hymns been included in the Prayer Book and had the Elizabethan poets been encouraged by the ecclesiastical authorities to write hymns. Had that been the case England would not have had to wait nearly a century and a half for the beginning of a new English hymnody, and three centuries for a rediscovery of the treasures of medieval hymnody. But vain regrets that his-

---

1710, p. 27. The psalmbook used was the *One and Fiftie Psalms of David*, of 1556.

[15] Quoted in E. F. Hatfield, *The Poets of the Church*, New York, 1884, p. 582, from Jewel's *Works*, Parker Society Edition, IV, 1230.

tory did not take another course should not blind us to
the great service to religion rendered by metrical psalmody.
To say of this period, as a modern writer does, that in the
Church of England "the congregational hymn was practically unknown: *except as barbarously represented by
crude metrical versions of the Psalms*," [16] is as unintelligent
as was the attitude of the eighteenth century in regarding
all medieval forms of art as "gothic," and therefore barbarous. The simple fact is that the metrical psalms of
sixteenth-century England were peculiarly well fitted to
the needs of their time, and another and more understanding writer says of the music to which they were sung that
"for simple dignity and solemnity, combined with grave
sweet melody, it is hard to equal these sixteenth and seventeenth century tunes." [17]

It is true that their authors had slight poetical abilities,
but they wrote before the great outburst of Elizabethan
song,[18] and were preceded by no great English poet except Chaucer, whose English was out-of-date and whose
subject matter was wholly different. Thomas Sternhold
had been a student at Oxford, and both Wood and Fuller
speak of his verse as equal to the best composed in his
day "when poetry was in the non-age." John Playford,
whose edition of Sternhold and Hopkins published in 1677
succeeded that of Thomas Ravenscroft (1621) in having
the best musical settings for the psalms, says, in pointing
out that the translations were then over one hundred years
old and could be improved here and there,

The Authors of this Translation were certainly both learned
and godly men, though I believe their Piety exceeded their

[16] Winfred Douglas, *Church Music in History and Practice*, Charles
Scribner's Sons, pp. 191–192. Quoted by permission. (Italics mine.)
[17] J. R. Fleming, *The Highway of Praise*, Oxford University Press,
London, 1937, p. 25.
[18] Sternhold died three years before the birth of Spenser, fifteen
years before that of Shakespeare.

Poetry: yet such as it was, it was valued with the best English Poesie at that time.[19]

Furthermore, "the psalms should be judged as ballads for the people, rather than as poetry." As compared with contemporary popular ballads, or with the translations of the Latin hymns in the *Primers*, Fuller declares that Sternhold's psalms "go abreast with them." It was, no doubt, their faithfulness to the Bible, their simplicity and their similarity to popular contemporary verse which commended them. Warton admits that "had they been more poetically translated, they would not have been more acceptable to the common people." [20] As it was, they met a great need and rendered a great service.

The widespread popularity and general use of the metrical psalms is one of the most striking features of the Reformation in England. The modern notion that psalm singing was a peculiar Puritan practice has its foundation only in ignorance and prejudice. Psalm singing was, indeed, an exclusively *Protestant* practice, as in France it was limited to the Huguenots after the suppression of Marot's psalms by the Sorbonne, but it was universal among English Protestants of all descriptions (except the Quakers, who did not sing at all) both before and after the Puritans emerged either as a distinctive religious group or as a political party. And the Church of England clung to the metrical psalms long after most of the Nonconformist churches had joyfully accepted the hymnody of Watts and his school. For more than two hundred years the metrical psalms, in one or another version, were commonly bound up with copies of the Bible [21] and the Book of Common Prayer, though without any formal author-

[19] John Playford, *Whole Book of Psalms*, London, 1677, preface.
[20] Julian, *Dictionary of Hymnology*, p. 861[1].
[21] The earliest example appears to have been the Genevan Bible of 1569.

ization of the practice, so that the criticism was made that it was done "rather [by] a connivance than an approbation." The practice clearly indicates the popular reverence with which the psalms were held, as does Heylyn's further complaint of the reading of the lessons and prose psalms "being heard with a covered head, but all men sitting bareheaded when a psalm was sung." Indeed, it was apparently common for men out-of-doors to remove their hats even when they heard a psalm sung at a distance.

We can understand this feeling for the psalms when we realize that those who sang them

were using what was to them not doggerel or mere verbal hack-work, but the sincere effort of scholars & divines to render into verse what they conceived to be the very spirit of the Psalms. And there is no doubt that for the common people a far greater influence resided in the metrical text than in the prose text. This influence was intensified by the association of the verses with the melodies that went with them.[22]

The metrical psalms are, in fact, important both as a literary monument and as a spiritual force which for several generations was second only to that of the Authorized Version of the Bible.

Nor was the use of the psalms limited to the opening and closing of worship in church. Thomas Sternhold had first sung them for his own "Godly solace" and had printed them with no idea of their use in church, but to provide other people with clean and pious songs. The same motive appears on the title page of the 1562 edition, already quoted, *Very mete to be used of all sorts of people privately for their solace and comfort; laying apart all ungodly Songes and Ballades, which tende only to the norishment of vyce, and corrupting of Youthe.*[23]

[22] Waldo S. Pratt, "The Earliest New England Music," Proc., *Unitarian Historical Society*, Vol. I, Pt. II, pp. 37–38.
[23] That does not mean that Sternhold or the publishers of the *Book*

In a word, the primary use of the metrical psalms was in private devotions or at social gatherings, and their use in church was secondary. So they became

the book of song in the castle as well as the cottage; for recreation or at work; for the lady in the hall, the weaver at the loom, the peasant at the plough; the first lesson taught to children, the last words whispered to, or uttered by the dying man.[24]

Roundheads and Cavaliers sangs psalms with equal fervor;[25] Sewall's *Diary* bears witness to the social use of psalms in New England; and Robert Burns' *The Cotter's Saturday Night* is the classic illustration of Scottish usage at a later date.

But, for Americans, perhaps the most surprising and thought-provoking illustration is to be found in the account of Sir Francis Drake's famous voyage round the world, in the fifteen-seventies, written by his chaplain Francis Fletcher. Drake certainly was no Puritan, nor is it likely that any of his seamen were, but there are repeated references to psalm singing on board ship. Since Drake had sailed from England in 1577, only fifteen years after the publication of Day's *Book of Psalms*, it is well-nigh certain that this was the version used. In April, 1579, Drake left the west coast of Guatemala and stood westward far out into the Pacific, and then north, battling against cold and tempestuous northwest winds. He made land again on the California coast, and came to anchor on June 17 in what is now called Drake's Bay, some thirty miles north of San Francisco harbor, the entrance to which he missed. He lay there for five weeks, to repair his ship,

of Psalms were opposed to all secular songs, but only to the indecent ones, of which there were plenty with words unprintable today.

[24] W. Garrett Horder, *The Hymn Lover*, London, 1905, p. 66.
[25] Percy Scholes, *The Puritans and Music*, London, 1934, pp. 272-274.

his men camping ashore behind fortifications built as a protection from the Indians, who, however, proved friendly. Fletcher writes that the Indians visited the camp frequently when services of worship were held, and goes on,

In the time of which prayers, singing of Psalmes, and reading of certaine Chapters in the Bible, they sate very attentively: and observing the end at every pause, with one voice still cried, Oh, as greatly rejoycing in our exercises. Yea they tooke such pleasure in our singing of Psalmes, that whensoever they resorted to us, their first request was commonly this, *Gnaáh*, by which they intreated that we would sing.[26]

It is for most of us a wholly new idea that the metrical psalms in English were first heard not in Virginia, or in Plymouth, or in the Massachusetts Bay Colony, but many years earlier on that far California coast which, to Drake's seamen, must have seemed the uttermost parts of the earth.

A great number of other psalters followed the publication of Sternhold and Hopkins in 1562. Julian lists more than three hundred partial or complete ones, including those of the nineteenth century.[27] One of the most important was the *Scottish Psalter*, that classic of Scotch devotion, which also stemmed from Geneva but developed along its own lines. The interrelationship of these psalters presents a very intricate problem, which happily does not

[26] Quoted from "The World Encompassed by Sir Francis Drake," in *Early English and French Voyages*, ed. II. S. Burrage, New York, 1906, p. 163. See also Scholes, *The Puritans and Music*, p. 257. So far as I am aware, Scholes is the earliest authority to note this first recorded use of English metrical psalms within the limits of the present United States.

[27] Julian, *Dictionary of Hymnology*, pp. 916–932. Of the many books on English psalmody that by H. A. Glass, *The Story of the Psalters*, London, 1888, is one of the best. For a clear analysis of the psalters leading up to that of 1562, and some discussion of later developments, see also *Hymns Ancient and Modern, Historical Edition*, Introduction, London, 1937, pp. xxxvii-lxvi; lxxvi-lxxxii, lc.

concern us, since we need only note those which had an influence on early American usage. In the colonies the only ones which were in use, before the introduction in the eighteenth century of Tate and Brady and of Watts' *Psalms of David Imitated*, were those of Sternhold and Hopkins; Ainsworth's *Book of Psalmes* prepared for the use of the Separatist exiles in Holland and brought by them to Plymouth; and the rival psalters of Francis Rous [28] and William Barton (1644), in use among the Presbyterians in New York and to the South in the eighteenth century.

Henry Ainsworth, who had been a student at Cambridge for four years, was an able writer and a trained Hebrew scholar, whose commentaries on the Old Testament were printed in 1627 and were later republished. Governor Bradford wrote of him that "he had not his better for the Hebrew tongue in the University nor scarce in Europe." He was one of the little group of "Brownists" or Separatists who had gone to Amsterdam and thence to Leyden, and from whose fellowship the Pilgrim Fathers emigrated to Plymouth in 1620. In 1609 Ainsworth had written, in defence of psalm singing in church, "we do content ourselves with joint harmonious singing of the Psalms of Holy Scripture, to the instruction and comforts of our hearts, and praise of our God." In 1612 he brought out his *Book of Psalmes: Englished both in prose and metre*, printed at Amsterdam,[29] the first real rival to Sternhold and Hopkins. It contained a fresh prose translation of each psalm, be-

[28] Rous' *Psalmes of David in English Meeter* appeared in 1643; was revised in 1647. The Scotch Psalter of 1650 is largely based on Rous. It is the finest of all the old popular versions and has held its own in Scotland to the present day. Its music was also of superior quality. In England, however, Rous' version, in spite of its merits, never supplanted Sternhold and Hopkins, and gradually disappeared from use.

[29] *The Book of Psalmes; Englished both in prose and metre. With annotations, opening both the words and sentences, by conference with other scriptures. By H. A. Amsterdam: Giles Thorp, 1612*. Reprinted in metre 1618, 1642; in prose and metre 1644; in metre 1644 and 1690.

side which was printed a metrical form which varied from the prose only so far as the exigencies of the verse required, with annotations below. Forty-eight tunes are also printed, of which nine are duplicates, so that the actual number of different tunes is thirty-nine. As was the custom, the melodies only are given, in a single line without bars, in the old diamond-shaped notes. The ancient Hebrew music being unknown, Ainsworth felt at liberty to use the current "man-made" tunes. He writes,

Tunes for the Psalms I find none set of God; so that each people is to use the most grave, decent and comfortable manner of singing that they know . . . The singing notes, therefore, I have most taken from our former English Psalms, where they will fit the measure of the verse. And for the other long verses I have also taken (for the most part) the gravest and easiest tunes of the French and Dutch psalmes.

About half the tunes are thus taken from Sternhold and Hopkins, but the rest are the longer and finer French and Dutch tunes, in a greater variety of metres than Sternhold and Hopkins had employed, one of them running to twelve lines. The result is that Ainsworth's book is much more interesting and less monotonous in its music than Sternhold and Hopkins'. It is unfortunate that his use of the longer and finer French tunes did not prevail over Sternhold and Hopkins' more limited restriction to shorter metres, but they gradually dropped out, and almost the only one now generally known is Old 124th (*Toulon*), and that in a four-line rather than in the original five-line form.

Ainsworth's *Book of Psalmes* had some use in England, as well as in Holland by the congregation of Separatists for whom it was prepared. In Plymouth the Pilgrims and their descendants used it till 1692, and it was adopted in Salem, presumably through the influence of the Plymouth physician, Dr. Samuel Fuller, where it was used until 1667. It had, however, no influence which we can trace on the later development of American psalmody. For us its sole importance lies in its association with the Pilgrims. Longfellow was quite correct when he pictured John Alden's visit to Priscilla:

Open wide on her lap lay the well-worn psalm-book of
 Ainsworth,
Printed in Amsterdam, the words and the music together,
Rough-hewn, angular notes, like stones in the walls of a
 churchyard,
Darkened and overhung by the running vine of the verses.[30]

In 1921 Professor Pratt published an admirable little study of Ainsworth's *Book of Psalmes*,[31] with the tunes harmonized and printed in modern notation. Anyone who harbors the notion that the music which the Pilgrims sang was dull, uninteresting, or unduly difficult will have his opinion changed if he will examine these tunes. And the verse, rugged though it is, goes well to the music. It takes only a little imagination to conceive with what profound emotion the exiles in Holland sang the 32nd Psalm:

Jehovah's song how sing shal wee
Within a foreign people's land?
Jerusalem, if I doo thee
Forget, forget let my right hand.
Cleav let my tongue to my palat,
If I doo not in mind thee bear,
If I Jerusalem doo not
Above my chiefest joy prefer.

[30] *Courtship of Miles Standish*, Boston, 1859.
[31] Waldo S. Pratt, *The Music of the Pilgrims*, Boston, 1921. See also S. Lothrop Thorndike, "The Psalmodies of Plymouth and Massachusetts Bay," *Col. Soc. of Mass. Trans.*, I, 228–238, 1892–1894. These two writers are almost the only ones that I have come across who give an intelligent and understanding report of the subject.

And when they had taken the wings of the morning and had come to what must have seemed the uttermost parts of the sea breaking in thunder upon the Plymouth shore, where cold, hunger, danger and death confronted them, their faith found strength in the 139th Psalm.

> Behind and 'fore Thou doost me strayt inclose;
> Upon me also doost thy hand impose.
>   This knowledge is too marvelous for me;
>   It's high, to reach I shal not able be.
> O whither shall I from Thy spirit goe?
> And whither shall I flee Thy presence fro?
>   If I clime up the heav'ns, Thou art there;
>   Or make my bed in hel, loe, Thou art There.

Such, then, was the great heritage of English psalmody which the first settlers brought with them to this country. The Pilgrims had their recently published Ainsworth. The Puritans and the English settlers in the southern colonies had Sternhold and Hopkins, already in use for some seventy-five years. But the Puritans of the Bay Colony were soon to seek songs still better suited to their taste.

CHAPTER II

The Reign of the Bay Psalm Book

FROM THE EARLY DAYS of psalmody in England there had existed two distinct and divergent tendencies. On the one hand there was the desire for strict adherence to the literal text of inspired Scripture, the closest possible approximation to the original Hebrew passage which could be achieved in metrical translations set to simple tunes. It was the perfectly logical outcome of the accepted belief in the plenary inspiration of the Bible. The psalms were conceived to be the literal word of God, therefore they were superior to any hymns of "humane composure," and any translator who detracted from, added to, or departed from the true meaning of the original was tampering with the revealed Word. This was the logic of Calvin's position, and, to those who adhered strictly to it, the literary quality of the psalms in English was of small consequence compared with the accuracy of the translation.

It was this extreme devotion to the exact meaning of the Hebrew text which was the basic reason for the literary poverty of the older English versions. It is difficult enough to translate any poetry into the poetical forms of another language and yet preserve its exact shades of meaning. But the ancient Hebrew poetry, with its rhythmical parallelism and wholly alien verse form, while easy to translate into the majestic rhythm of the non-metrical Psalms of the Bible, was well-nigh impossible to fit into the measured stanzas of English verse without any variations from the words or ideas in the original Hebrew text. The translators, even if they had been much better poets than was the case, would have found their muse hamstrung by the dogma which required them to make a "close-fitting" translation. Better poets than Sternhold and Hopkins did try their hands at the task, without much greater success, as when Milton turned nine psalms into English verse. It was not until Isaac Watts, following Dr. Patrick's lead, frankly abandoned the dogma and used the psalms as the basis for paraphrases cast in the mould of hymnody, that English psalmody took on any considerable degree of literary excellence. It required a century and a half to bring about this development, and during that period the theory of adherence to the exact text of inspired Scripture was dominant, not only in America, but also, for the most part, in Great Britain, and there are religious bodies which adhere to it today.

But on the other hand, there existed the natural human impulse to expression in forms of beauty. This had found utterance in the prose alike of the Bible and of the Book of Common Prayer, and the contrast between the sonorous and majestic prose which people heard in the service and the psalms which they were called upon to sing became increasingly evident to sensitive ears with the passing decades. The century which followed the publication of Sternhold and Hopkins was one of immense literary activity, and English poetry rose to heights undreamed of in 1562. With this rapid development of literary culture, with the change in taste which is represented by the contrast between Shakespeare and Addison, and with the relegation of the old popular ballads to the more rustic members of the community, the sixteenth-century versions of the Psalms came increasingly to be regarded as archaic and uncouth. Fuller says, with truth, of Sternhold and Hopkins,

Their piety was better than their poetry . . . they had drunk more of Jordan than of Helicon. . . . Sometimes they make the Maker of the tongue speak little better than barbarism, and have in many verses such poor rhymes that two hammers on a smith's anvil would make better music.

Owing to this changing taste there gradually grew up a demand for metrical psalms of more poetical quality. To those who made this demand the question of literal adherence to the original text of Scripture was of much less importance than a well-ordered and flowing verse. Thus Richard Baxter in the preface to his own version of the Psalms (1692), justified his experiment by remarking, "The Ear desireth greater melody than strict versions will allow." We have so completely accepted this latter point of view, and judge a hymn or psalm so largely by literary standards of excellence, that it is difficult for us to understand the devotion of worshippers to the more literal versions of the Psalms.

The many different psalters published in England and Scotland during the sixteenth and seventeenth centuries are the expression of these divergent tendencies. They were attempts to produce either a more exact or a more poetical version of the Psalms than that of Sternhold and Hopkins, or else to introduce a wider range of tunes, as in the case of Este's, Ravenscroft's and Playford's *Psalters*. In Scotland the demand for a better version culminated in the classic *Scottish Psalter* of 1650. In England it culminated in the *New Version of the Psalms of David, fitted to the tunes used in churches*, by Nahum Tate and Nicholas Brady, published in 1696. Nahum Tate was poet laureate — not a great poet, indeed, but hardly deserving Pope's jibe at "Tate's poor page." We still sing his Christmas hymn:

> While shepherds watched their flocks by night,
> All seated on the ground.

Under his hand and that of his collaborator, who was a royal chaplain, the Psalms became more fluent and singable,

and took on much more of the hymnic character to which
we are accustomed.   Some of them are still to be found in
our hymnbooks, as the version of the 34th Psalm:

> Thro' all the changing scenes of life,

or of the 42nd:

> As pants the hart for cooling streams,

or of the 93rd:

> With glory clad, with strength array'd.

The *New Version* came out with a flourish of trumpets,
for King William [1] accepted the dedication of it, and it was
promptly authorized, by an Order of the King in Council,
as a recognized alternative to the Old Version for use in
public worship. In 1700 a Supplement appeared with a
small selection of hymns. The edition of 1708 provided a
few more, and many new tunes, among which were *Hanover* and Croft's *St. Anne.* Those who desired the psalms
in a smoother and more flowing version than Sternhold and
Hopkins had provided welcomed the *New Version.* The
Lord Bishop of London, in 1698, "persuaded that it may
take off that unhappy objection which has hitherto lain
against the Singing Psalms . . . heartily recommended the
Use of this Version to all his Brethren within his Diocess." [2]

[1] Here and there the translation was tinged with the political coloring of the times. A congregation singing
> "The prince, who slights what God commands,
>   Exposed to scorn, must quit his throne,"

could not fail to note the pointed reference to the dethronement and
exile of James II, only eight years before the publication of the *New
Version.* The application of passages in the psalms to a contemporary
situation has been a common practice in English and American church
life. Watts, in his *Psalms of David Imitated*, was much bolder than the
New Version in "accommodating" the psalms to make them a mouthpiece
for British patriotism.

[2] Benson, *The English Hymn*, pp. 48-50.

So it came about that the *New Version* worked its way into the churches of London and the vicinity. Eventually its use became fairly general, although not universal, in the Church of England, in which both the Old Version and the new remained in use until the introduction of modern hymnody in the nineteenth century. The Nonconformists more commonly held to the Old Version, until they abandoned it for Watts in the eighteenth century. The Episcopal churches in the American colonies were under the jurisdiction of the Bishop of London, and, though some of them may have retained Sternhold and Hopkins until after the Revolution, most of them followed the example of King's Chapel, which in April, 1713, voted to use Tate and Brady. Apparently the first Boston edition of the *New Version* was printed in the same year especially for King's Chapel, for its title page reads *Brady and Tate's Psalms for the Use of His Majesty's Chappell of America. Boston: 1713.*[3] It should be noted, however, that a large and handsome copy of the *Book of Common Prayer*, given as late as 1760 to King's Chapel for use at the reading desk, has the Old Version bound in at the back.

But, while those who desired a more elevated type of poetry for use in worship welcomed the *New Version* and the Lord Bishop of London recommended its use, the more conservative element in the Church of England vehemently denounced its departures from the sacred text and clung to the Old Version as tenaciously as any Puritan could have done. When Nicholas Brady tried to introduce the *New Version* into his own church of St. Catherine Cree, London, the vestry refused it as "an innovation not to be endured," and the plain people were firmly attached to the Old Version. Brady's colleague, Tate, reports that a maid in his brother's household declined to sing the new psalms, saying,

[3] H. W. Foote, *Annals of King's Chapel*, Boston, 1881, I, 206.

"If you must know the plain truth, sir, as long as you sung Jesus Christ's psalms I sung along with ye; but now that you sing psalms of your own invention, ye may sing by yourselves." Samuel Wesley, Sr., father of John and Charles, and himself the writer of hymns in a stiffly classical Addisonian style, could refer to the ballad-like verses of the Old Version as "scandalous doggrell"; but the simple villager who, when asked by his parson why he no longer joined in the singing, replied, "Well, sir, David speaks so plain that us cannot mistake 'un; but as for Mr. Tate and Mr. Brady, they have taken the Lord away," no doubt expressed the thought of multitudes.

Churchmen of distinction also rallied to the support of the Old Version. It was defended in Payne's *The Old Psalm-Book Review'd*, in 1701, and, with greater authority, in 1710, in a *Defence of the Book of Psalms* by Dr. Beveridge, Lord Bishop of St. Asaph, who criticized the *New Version* because of its "fine and modish" character, "flourished with wit and fancy," and because it had not been "conferred with the Hebrew."

In this New Translation [he wrote] there is so much regard had to the Poetry, the Style, the Running of the Verse, and such-like inconsiderable circumstances, that it was almost impossible to avoid going from the Text, and altering the true Sense and Meaning of it.

That is the voice of the party which still demanded above all a close adherence to the literal words of inspired Scripture, and feared even as short a step as Tate and Brady took in the direction of introducing hymns which were the work of mortal men.

This sketch of psalmody in England and Scotland down to a period more than two generations later than the settlement of the American colonies throws a direct light on what happened here. The Puritans had hardly established themselves in Massachusetts Bay before they set about preparing their own psalter. Their motive was the procuring of a version of the Psalms which should adhere even more closely to the original than did that of Sternhold and Hopkins. Cotton Mather, writing in his *Magnalia Christi* about the origin of *The Bay Psalm Book*, says,

Tho' they blessed God for the Religious Endeavours of them who translated the Psalms into the Meetre usually annex'd at the end of the Bible, yet they beheld in the Translation so many Detractions from, Additions to, and Variations of, not only the Text, but the very Sense of the Psalmist, that it was an Offense unto them.[4]

Therefore, in 1636, the same year that Harvard College was founded, the work of producing a fresh metrical translation which should faithfully adhere to the Hebrew text was parcelled out among "thirty pious and learned Ministers . . . the chief Divines in the Country [who] took each of them a Portion to be translated." One is led to wonder whether there are today as many ministers in the vicinity of Boston who are equipped for such a task.

There is no evidence whatever as to how many of the thirty fulfilled their assignment, but, human nature being what it is, we are probably safe in guessing that most of the ministers, being very much occupied with their parishes, did nothing more than offer a few suggestions as to the exact meaning of the Hebrew text. Rev. Richard Mather of Dorchester, and Rev. Thomas Welde and Rev. John Eliot of Roxbury, all of whom had studied at Emmanuel College, Cambridge, seem to have acted as an informal editorial committee, and certainly did most of the versification.[5] This is indicated by Cotton Mather, who says that they

---

[4] C. Mather, *Magnalia Christi*, London, 1702, Book III, 100.

[5] John Josselyn, in his *Account of Two Voyages to New England*, London, 1674, pp. 19–20, states that when he reached Boston in July,

were of so different a Genius for their poetry, that Mr.
Shephard of Cambridge, on the Occasion addressed them to
this Purpose,

"You Roxbury Poets, keep clear of the Crime
Of missing to give us a very good Rhime;
And you of Dorchester, your verses lengthen,
But with the Text's own words, you will them strengthen."

The poets of Dorchester and Roxbury unfortunately
were really not poets at all, though godly and learned men.
It is easy to pick out in *The Bay Psalm Book* verses with
false accents, and it is often difficult to see how they could
be sung at all. Yet it is also easy to exaggerate the uncouth-
ness of the verse, and few people have taken the trouble to
note that there are occasional lines with a rugged beauty of
their own. The following examples are taken from a single
Psalm, the 139th:

vss. 9 and 10   If I take morning's wings, and dwell
                     where utmost sea-coasts bee,
                 E'en there thy hand shall me conduct:
                     and thy right hand hold mee.

                 .   .   .   .

        11   Then shall the night about mee be
                 like to the lightsome day.

                 .   .   .   .

        14   Because that I am fashionéd
                 in fearful wondrous wise;
             And that thy works are marveilous,
                 my soul right well descries.

1638, he delivered to Rev. John Cotton "from Mr. Francis Quarles the
poet, the translation of the 16, 25, 51, 88, 113 and 137 Psalms into English meeter, for his approbation." It does not appear that any of Quarles'
work was incorporated in the new book. Certainly the versions of those
particular psalms are not noticeably superior to the rest of the translations.

Perhaps the 23rd Psalm, which no translator seems able
utterly to ruin, shows the authors of *The Bay Psalm Book*
at their best:

> The Lord to mee a shepheard is,
> want therefore shall not I.
> Hee in the folds of tender-grasse
> doth cause me down to lie:
>
> To waters calme me gently leads
> Restore my soule doth hee:
> he doth in paths of righteousnes:
> for his names sake leade mee.
>
> Yea though in valley of deaths shade
> I walk, none ill I'le feare:
> because thou art with mee, thy rod,
> and staffe my comfort are.
>
> For mee a table thou hast spread,
> in presence of my foes:
> thou dost annoynt my head with oyle,
> my cup it over-flowes.
>
> Goodnes & mercy surely shall
> all my dayes follow mee:
> and in the Lords house I shall dwell
> so long as dayes shall bee.

Our difficulty in imagining how those Psalms could possibly be sung arises more from our unfamiliarity with them
than from defects in the verse itself. A very suggestive
illustration of the point occurred at the memorable service
held at the Harvard Tercentenary, at which the version of
the 78th Psalm from *The Bay Psalm Book* was sung to
York, the tune often called "The Stilt." It is true that the
singing was led by a magnificent choir supported by organ
and orchestra, but the great congregation included men
and women of a world-wide diversity of background, to

practically all of whom both words and music were utterly unknown. Hardly any of them sang the first stanza, but by the time the sixth stanza was reached a great volume of singing arose, for they had discovered not only that the crude old verse could be sung, but that both it and the old tune had a simple dignity and austere beauty all their own. In any event the product of "the Roxbury poets" was eminently satisfactory to New England, which was not then asking for poetry but for a faithful and trustworthy translation of the Psalms. As Cotton Mather wrote of the revised edition of 1651, in his *Magnalia Christi*,[6]

tho' I heartily join with those Gentlemen, who wish that the *Poetry* hereof were mended; yet I must confess, That the Psalms have never yet seen a Translation, that I know of, nearer to the *Hebrew Original*. . . .

It was promptly adopted by almost every congregation in the Massachusetts Bay Colony and therefore was commonly called *The Bay Psalm Book*. The church at Salem clung to Ainsworth until 1667, when it voted that "the Bay psalm book should be made use of together with Ainsworth's," and the church at Plymouth waited until 1692 before deciding "to sing the psalms now used in our neighbor churches in the Bay."

The finished product appeared in 1640 under the title *The Whole Booke of Psalmes faithfully Translated into English Metre. Whereunto is prefixed a discourse declaring not only the lawfullnes, but also the necessity of the heavenly Ordinance of singing Scripture Psalmes in the Churches of God*, [followed by quotations from Col. III and James V] *Imprinted 1640*. The preface was written by Richard Mather,[7] and as is the case with the prefaces of many hymn-

---

[6] C. Mather, *Magnalia Christi*, London, 1702, Book III, 100.

[7] At least a rough draft in Mather's handwriting is preserved among the Prince MSS. in the Boston Public Library. George Parker Winship,

books, provides a key to the purposes of the editors and the problems which they faced. Mather was evidently well aware of the pitfalls in his path, for he begins on a note of conciliation.

The singing of Psalmes, though it breath forth nothing but holy harmony, and melody; yet such is the subtilty of the enemie, and the enmity of our nature against the Lord, and his wayes, that our hearts can find matter of discord in this harmony & crochets of division in this holy melody.

Mather goes on to ask,

First: what psalms are to be sung in Churches? Whether David's and other scripture psalmes, or the psalmes invented by the gifts of godly men in every age in the church. Secondly, if scripture psalms, whether in their owne words, or in such meter as English poetry is wont to run in? Thirdly, by whom are they to be sung? Whether by the whole churches together with their voices? or by one man singing alone and the rest joyning in silence and in the close saying amen.

As we should expect, he advocates the congregational use of the Psalms in English verse. But the version should follow as closely as possible the Hebrew original, so he goes on,

If, therefore, the verses are not always so smooth and elegant as some may desire or expect, let them consider that God's Altar needs not our pollishings; Ex. 20. for we have respected rather a plaine translation, than to smooth our verses with the sweetness of any paraphrase, and so have attended Conscience rather than Elegance, fidelity rather than poetry, in translating the hebrew words into English language, and David's poetry into English meetre: that soe wee may sing in Sion the Lord's

in "Facts and Fancies and the Cambridge Press," in *The Colophon*, Autumn, New York, 1938, pp. 531–557, attributes the preface and the major part of the versification to John Eliot, but on purely conjectural grounds.

songs of praise according to his own will; until hee take us from hence, and wipe away all our tears, and bid us entre our masters joye to sing eternall Halleluiahs.

The book was printed in Cambridge and had, wrote Rev. Thomas Prince, "the Honour of being the *First Book* printed in *North America*," a statement which holds true if we add "north of Mexico." [8]

A good deal of inaccurate legendry is current about the printing press used, but the main facts have been pretty well established by Professor Morison.[9] Rev. Jose Glover, sometime rector of Sutton in Surrey, a man of considerable estate, sailed from England for Massachusetts Bay in 1638, with his wife and children, bringing with him a large amount of personal property, a printing press and a font of type, and a printer, Stephen Day,[10] with three assistants, who were obligated to work out the passage money advanced. Mr. Glover "fell sick of a feaver and dyed" on the voyage over, but his widow and her companions reached Boston sometime between September 7 and October 10 of

[8] A printing press was established in Mexico City as early as 1539, just a century before the Cambridge press. The first book which it is recorded to have printed, but of which no copy survives, was a catechism. The second, of which only one fragment remains, was a *Manual* of theology, dated 1540. About 250 titles were issued by various Mexican presses in the sixteenth century, as large a proportion of them dealing with religion as though they had been printed in Puritan New England.

[9] S. E. Morison, *The Founding of Harvard College*, Cambridge, 1935, pp. 255–256; 379–380; but see also George Parker Winship, "Facts and Fancies and the Cambridge Press," for an account of the press which differs from Morison's in a good many details.

[10] Day spelled his first name either Steven or Stephen, and his surname with or without a final *e*. Winship, "Facts and Fancies and the Cambridge Press," doubts whether Day was a trained printer at all, and thinks that the work of the press was done by others. His son Matthew was certainly a printer, as was Samuel Green who succeeded Stephen Day in charge of the press. Day seems to have been a locksmith and was employed by Governor Winthrop as a prospector for iron ore. Nevertheless the grant of land made to him in 1641, cited below, seems clearly to indicate that he was regarded as the responsible head of the press.

that year, and settled in Cambridge, where she bought the residence of Governor Haynes on the Market Place, which is now the open space bounded by Mt. Auburn, Boylston and Winthrop Streets. There she lived with five men-servants and four maids, in a style which was the talk of the town, until her extravagances ran her into financial difficulties. In 1641 she married Henry Dunster, the first president of Harvard College, who had arrived the preceding August, and two years later she died.

The printing press in which Glover had invested was apparently his own private venture, and he may have believed it could be made profitable by printing here Puritan books and pamphlets which might be disallowed in England. It was a small affair, though adequate for printing *The Bay Psalm Book*. Mrs. Glover had it set up in a shop on Crooked Lane, now Holyoke Street, while Stephen Day was housed near by on the corner of Dunster Street and Massachusetts Avenue, as a modern tablet states. As a printer Day showed serene indifference to trifles like spelling and punctuation, but his work, although crude, was so highly valued that the General Court in 1641 rewarded him as "the first that set upon printing with a grant of 300 acres of land."

An edition of 1700 copies of *The Bay Psalm Book* was printed at a cost of thirty-three pounds for printing and twenty-nine pounds for paper; copies sold for twenty pence apiece; the net receipts were 141 pounds, 13 shillings and 6 pence, leaving a handsome profit of 79 pounds, 13 shillings and 4 pence.[11] The book contained 296 pages, and the printing was probably completed by July, 1640. There is no record of the binder, but the only known bookbinder

[11] These figures are taken from evidence given by Stephen Day and Samuel Green in a lawsuit heard in February, 1655/6, fifteen years after the publication of the book. Winship, *op. cit.*, cites reasons for thinking that they are not altogether accurate.

in the colony was one John Sanders of Boston, who had been admitted freeman in 1636. Only ten copies of the first edition survive, five of which, including Richard Mather's own copy, were, in the middle of the eighteenth century, in the possession of Rev. Thomas Prince, only three of them in perfect condition. They were part of Prince's "New England Library," which he bequeathed in 1758 to the Old South Church in Boston, "to be kept and remain in their Public Library for ever." They remained in the steeple chamber of the church for a century; then three of them, including Mather's copy, passed into private hands through the action of a lieutenant-governor of the Commonwealth who was also a deacon of the Old South, who surrendered these copies in consideration of some modern books which were wanted and of the rebinding of a few old volumes. In 1903 a facsimile reprint of *The Bay Psalm Book* was published with an historical introduction by Wilberforce Eames.[12]

In 1647 a second edition, with a few corrections, was published, of which only two copies survive. But, while the book had met with general approval, it was felt that there was some room for improvement. As Cotton Mather puts it,

It was thought that a little more of Art was to be employed upon them: And for that Cause, they were committed unto Mr. Dunster, who Revised and Refined this Translation; and (with some Assistance from Mr. Richard Lyon . . .) he brought it into the Condition wherein our Churches ever since have used it.[13]

This revised edition by President Dunster and Richard Lyon

[12] *The Bay Psalm Book, being a facsimile reprint of the First Edition, printed by Stephen Daye at Cambridge, in New England in 1640. With an Introduction by Wilberforce Eames. New York, Dodd, Mead & Co., 1903.*
[13] C. Mather, *Magnalia Christi*, London, 1702, Book III, 100.

bore a new title page reading, *The Psalms Hymns and Spiritual Songs of the Old and New Testament, faithfully translated into English meter for the use, edification and comfort of the Saints, in publick and private, especially in New England.* It was printed on Glover's press "by Samuel Green at Cambridge in New England." The only known survivor of the two thousand copies printed in 1651 is in the New York Public Library.

In Julian's *Dictionary of Hymnology* and in *The Story of the Psalters*, by Glass, *The Bay Psalter* of 1640 and the *New England Psalter* of "1650" (*sic*) are listed as two separate and distinct books, and Julian says, of the latter,

This was mainly a revised version of Rous's *Psalter* made by President Dunster of Harvard College, Richard Lyon and thirty others.[14]

Glass, in his book which was published four years ahead of Julian's *Dictionary*, says the same thing in almost the same words.[15] The statement is incorrect in several respects. In the first place the date of publication of the *New England Psalter* was 1651, not 1650. In the second place the "thirty others" who are said to have worked with Dunster and Lyon obviously refers to the thirty learned divines to whom the work was originally committed in 1636. In the third place the assertion that the *New England Psalter* "was mainly a revised version of Rous's *Psalter*" appears to be without foundation.

The *Psalter* by Rous had appeared in 1643 (revised ed. 1647), so that copies presumably had reached New England before Dunster started his version of *The Bay Psalm Book*,

[14] Julian, *Dictionary of Hymnology*, p. 928[1]. The article is signed with the initials of Canon Julian and William T. Brooke.

[15] Glass, *The Story of the Psalters*, p. 90. It is clear either that Glass took his information from the writers of the article in Julian's *Dictionary*, or that they took it from his book, which takes precedence by date of publication, though it may not have been written first. No doubt there was collaboration between them.

but Cotton Mather gives no hint that Dunster was influenced by it.   He says that Dunster

was a very good Hebrician, and for that cause, he bore a great Part in the Metrical Version of the Psalms now used in our Churches.[16]

But more conclusive is a comparison of the texts of *The Bay Psalm Book*, Rous' *Psalter* and *The New England Psalm Book*. A comparison of the three versions of a number of psalms, selected at random, does not reveal a single instance in which Dunster borrowed a line or phrase from Rous. On the other hand it discloses several cases, for example, in Psalms 3 and 139, where Rous seems to have taken lines or phrases, sometimes with slight variations, from *The Bay Psalm Book*. And the concluding paragraph of Rous' preface is strikingly like that with which the preface to *The Bay Psalm Book* ends. It would seem quite clear that Rous knew and used *The Bay Psalm Book*, but there is no evidence that Dunster took anything from Rous.

Whether *The Bay Psalm Book* and *The New England Psalm Book* should be classified as two different publications, or whether the second should be counted as a revised form of the first, though with a different title page, is, perhaps, a technical question for the bibliographer. In New England tradition, however, the two have been regarded as successive editions of the same book, and both have been called *The Bay Psalm Book*. There appears to be no good reason for departing from that tradition, which has been followed in the present volume.

Dunster, with the aid of young Mr. Lyon's supposed gift for poetry, did produce a very substantially improved version of the original translation. The extent of their revision may be indicated by a comparison of the two versions of the opening verses of Psalm 25 and of the whole of Psalm 1.

[16] *Magnalia Christi*, Book III, 100.

B. P. B. 1640

PSALM 25, VSS. 1 & 2

I lift my soul to thee, o Lord
My God I trust in thee,
let me not be asham'd; nor let
My foes joy over mee.

Yea, all that wait on thee shall not,
be fill'd with shamefulness:
but they shall be ashamed all,
who without cause transgresse.

N. E. P. B. 1651

PSALM 25, VSS. 1 & 2

I lift my soul to thee, O Lord,
My God, I trust in thee:
Let me not be asham'd, nor let
my foes joy over me.

Yea, let not them that wait on
Thee,
be fill'd with shamefulness:
But let them all ashamed be,
who carelessly transgress.

B. P. B. 1640

PSALM 1

O Blessed man, that in th' advice
of wicked doth not walk:
nor stand in sinners way, nor sit
in chayre of scornful folk.

But in the law of Iehovah
is his longing delight:
and in his law doth meditate,
by day and eke by night.

And he shall be like to a tree
planted by water-rivers:
that in his season yeilds his fruit,
and his leaf never withers.

And all he doth shall prosper well,
the wicked are not so:
but they are like unto the chaffe,
which winde drives to and fro.

Therefore shall not ungodly men,
rise to stand in the doome,
nor shall the sinners with the just,
in their assemblie *come*.

For of the righteous men, the Lord
acknowledgeth the way:
but the way of ungodly men,
shall utterly decay.

N. E. P. B. 1651

PSALM 1

O Blessed man that walks not in
th' advice of wicked men,
Nor standeth in the sinners way
nor scorners seat sit in,

But he upon Jehovah's law
doth set his whole delight,
And in his law doth meditate
both in the day and night.

He shall be like a planted tree
by water-brooks which shall
In his due season yield his fruit,
whose leaf shall never fall.

And all he doth shall prosper well,
the wicked are not so:
But they are like unto the chaff
which wind drives to and fro.

Therefore shall not ungodly men
in judgment stand upright,
Nor in the assembly of the just
shall stand the sinful wight.

For of the righteous men, the Lord
acknowledgeth the way:
Where as the way of wicked men
shall utterly decay.

As the title of the 1651 edition indicates, metrical versions of other Biblical passages were included in that and in the later editions, although it may be doubted whether they were much used in public worship. Thus in front of the Psalms were printed the Songs of Moses, of Deborah and Barak, and of Hannah, and David's Elegy. After the Psalms were the Song of Solomon; Songs in the Prophet Isaiah (chaps. V, XII, XXV, XXVI and XXXVIII); the Lamentations of Jeremiah (chaps. III and V); the Prayers of Jonah and Habakkuk; the Songs of the blessed Virgin Mary (yes, with this title in a Puritan book!), of Zacharias, of Simeon, of the Four Beasts (Rev. 4:8), of the Elders (Rev. 4:11), of the Church (Rev. 5:9), of the Angels (Rev. 5:12), of All the Creatures (Rev. 5:13), of the Innumerable Multitude of Saints (Rev. 7:10), and of Moses and of the Lamb (Rev. 15:3). Of course the traditional interpretation of the frankly amorous passages in the Song of Solomon was that they portrayed the love of Christ and his church, but nevertheless the inclusion of a metrical version beginning,

> Let him with kisses of his mouth
> be pleasèd me to kiss;
> Because much better than the wine
> thy loving kindness is, —

provided the Puritan youths and maidens of New England with an attractive little group of love songs right in their own psalmbooks!

The early editions of the book contained no music, presumably for lack of anyone capable of engraving it, but the first edition (1640) included at the end, and later editions reprinted, an "Admonition" about the tunes to which the Psalms might be sung, in part as follows:

The verses of these psalmes may be reduced to six kinds, the first whereof may be sung in very neere fourty common tunes;

as they are collected, out of our chief musicians, by *Tho.
Ravenscroft*. The second kinde may be sung in three tunes,
as Ps. 25, 50 and 67 in our English psalme books. The third
may be sung indifferently, as ps. the 51, 100, and ten commandments, in our English psalme books, which three tunes
aforesaid, comprehend almost all this whole book of psalmes,
as being tunes most familiar to us. . . .

Altogether some fifty tunes are referred to in this "Admonition" as being either in Ravenscroft's *Psalter* or in "our
English psalme-books," meaning, presumably, editions of
Sternhold and Hopkins which included music. Three such
editions appeared in England before 1600: Damon's *Psalms
of David* in 1759; Este's *Psalter* in 1592; and Allison's in
1599. *Este* (East) printed his tunes in four-part settings arranged by distinguished musicians, and Allison, who set his
tunes in pure Elizabethan counterpoint, was himself a musician of high standing. His collection of psalm tunes has
been called "on the whole the best that ever appeared." [17]
The title page of Allison's book is suggestive. It runs, *The
Psalms of David in Meter. The plaine song being the common Tunne to be sung and plaide upon the Lute, Orphari-
son, Citterne or Base Violl, severally or altogether for the
use of such as are men of mean skill, and whose leysure least
serveth to practise. By Richard Allison, London, 1599.*
Evidently Allison intended his *Psalter* to be used primarily
at social gatherings, for the pages are printed in large type,
with the several parts facing from four directions. A single
book, placed flat upon a table, would thus serve as many as
eight or more singers grouped about it in a circle, each
singer standing before the part he was to sing. This device,
to enable a number of singers to use a single book, was not
uncommon.

[17] Sir George Grove, *Dictionary of Music*, London, 1890, IV, 277,
art. by H. E. Woodridge.

Ravenscroft's *Psalter* [18] was published in 1621 and contains ninety-seven tunes in all. It was by far the best English selection of tunes available in the seventeenth century. It was no exaggeration to say of it that the music had been collected "out of our chief musicians," for Ravenscroft (himself in the front rank) acknowledges his indebtedness to a score of other musicians of his own, or the immediately preceding, generation, including Dowland, Farnaby, Morley, Tallis and Tomkins, who were the best of their time. His *Psalter* remained the recognized standard setting until the publication of Playford's *Psalter* in 1677. Playford's arrangements lacked the strength and vigor which Ravenscroft's settings had given to the tunes, but, perhaps for that very reason, were more pleasing to the decadent taste of the Restoration period. Ravenscroft's book was evidently well-known to the colonists. The copy which belonged to John Endecott bears his autograph and is owned by the Massachusetts Historical Society. The point to be observed is that the editors of *The Bay Psalm Book* were acquainted with, and recommended to the users of the book, the very best collections of psalm tunes which the age afforded.

An edition of *The Bay Psalm Book* with music is said to have appeared about 1690, but no copy is known, and the ninth edition, 1698, is the first surviving book with music printed in the English colonies of North America. It contains thirteen [19] tunes inserted at the back of the book, with "some few directions for ordering the Voice — without

[18] *The Whole Booke of Psalmes: with the Hymnes Evangelicall, and Songs Spirituall. Composed into four parts by sundry Authors, to such severall Tunes as have beene and are usually sung in England, Scotland, Wales, Germany, Italy, France, and The Nether-lands: Never as yet before in one volume published. Also 1. A briefe Abstract of the Prayse, Efficacie and Vertue of the Psalmes. 2. That all Clarkes of Churches, and the Auditory, may know what Tune each proper Psalme may be sung unto. Newly corrected and enlarged by Tho. Ravenscroft — Bachelor of Musicke. London. 1621.*

[19] In later editions the number ranged from twelve to fourteen, due to

Squeaking above, or *Grumbling* below." The tunes, which were, no doubt, those best remembered and most used in the New England churches at the end of the seventeenth century, are Oxford, Litchfield, Low-Dutch, York, Windsor, Cambridge, St. David's, Martyrs, Hackney, 119th Psalm Tune, 100th Psalm Tune, 115th Psalm Tune, and 148th Psalm Tune. Most of them are in common metre, but Cambridge is short metre, the 100th Psalm Tune is long metre, the 119th Psalm Tune is common metre double, and the 148th Psalm Tune is 6.6.6.6.4.4.4.4. The music, which had been copied, not without mistakes, from an undetermined English source, is in the old diamond-shaped notes, in two-part harmony, bass and treble, without bars except at the end of each line. It was cut on wood, and the result is a very crude piece of printing. In later editions well-executed copper plates were used, and it is difficult to understand why this was not done for the 1698 edition, since there were a number of silversmiths in Boston quite competent to do the work.

The cause of *The Bay Psalm Book* was advanced in the colony by Rev. John Cotton [20] of Boston in his tract published in 1647 entitled *Singing Psalms a Gospel Ordinance*, but it hardly needed such endorsement, for it was an unqualified success. It was what New England wanted, and in its 1651 form it spread all over New England and into other colonies as far south as Philadelphia. Twenty-seven editions were printed in New England, the latest in 1762. Moreover, it was reprinted in England as early as 1647 and, in the revised form, in 1652, and ran through at least twenty

---

the addition of the Ten Commandments Tune and the dropping of Hackney and the 115th Psalm Tune.

[20] John Cotton, b. Derby, England, Dec. 4, 1585; d. Boston, Mass., Oct. 23, 1652. B.A. Cambridge (Trinity College). Lecturer and Dean at Emmanuel College. Rector of St. Botolph's Church, Boston, England, 1613–1633. Ejected from his pulpit he emigrated to Boston in New England, and was minister of the First Church, 1633–1652.

editions, the latest being that of 1754. Thomas Prince says that "in that country" the book was "by some eminent Congregations prefer'd to all others in their Public Worship." It was also reprinted in Scotland half a dozen times between 1732 and 1759, and both the English and Scottish editions were published in a form to be bound up with Bibles of octavo size. Altogether well over fifty editions were printed before it gave place either to the *New Version* or to the rising popularity of Isaac Watts. Of the scores of metrical versions of the Psalms in English, only four — those of Sternhold and Hopkins, of Tate and Brady, the Scottish Version, and that of Watts — exceeded it in the number of editions printed or in widespread and long-continued use.[21]

The Bay Psalm Book reigned supreme in New England, with widespread use elsewhere, for more than a century. But, though it had no rival here, it was not the only psalm-book to be printed in seventeenth-century Massachusetts. There was another, which well deserves honorable mention. This was John Eliot's versification of the psalms in the Indian language, printed by Samuel Green at Cambridge in 1661, under the title *Wame Ketoohomae Uketoohomaongash David*.

John Eliot,[22] who had shared with Mather and Welde the preparation of *The Bay Psalm Book*, had already translated the Bible into the Indian language, and these metrical psalms were bound up with that book. The good "Apostle to the Indians" devoted many years to instructing the Indians and to organizing churches, and on his death there were many "praying Indians" to mourn him. The Indians

[21] The British Museum Library contains 601 editions of Sternhold and Hopkins; 303 of Tate and Brady; 98 of the Scottish Psalter; 97 of Watts. See Horder, *The Hymn Lover*, p. 70.

[22] John Eliot, b. England, 1604; d. Roxbury, Mass., 1690; Cambridge University; emigrated to New England 1631; ordained minister of the First Church in Roxbury 1632; the "Apostle to the Indians," and translator of the Bible into the Indian language.

of Massachusetts, like those of the Pacific coast in the preceding century, and in Pennsylvania later, seem to have taken to psalm singing. Increase Mather wrote in 1687, "The whole congregation of Indians praise God with singing, and some of them are excellent singers"; and in 1705, he wrote to Sir William Ashurst a joint letter with Cotton Mather and Nehemiah Walter in which they mention the "excellent singing of Psalms with most ravishing melody" by the Indians. Nor was this little Indian psalmbook of John Eliot's wholly without influence on American hymnody, for it was an early step in that work of evangelizing the Indians which led in the next century to the conversion of Samson Occom, a full-blooded Mohican who became a hymn writer in English, as we shall later see.

For the first sixty years following its publication no New Englander questioned the worth of *The Bay Psalm Book* but to the generation which grew up in the opening decades of the eighteenth century it became less acceptable, for reasons very similar to those which led to dissatisfaction with Sternhold and Hopkins in England. Even Cotton Mather must have been dissatisfied with his grandfather's work, for in 1718 he published his own *Psalterium Americanum*. This is a very curious book, the only importance of which is that it illustrates the logical outcome of the principle of literal adherence to the text of the psalms in total disregard of the desirability of poetic form. Since it represents the last stand of those who held that theory against the rising demand for something more singable, it is worth examination.

Cotton Mather was a very remarkable man, many-sided, and by no means always consistent. To many minds he typifies the least attractive side of Puritanism, and he was the advocate of an old order which was passing away. Such persons are often underestimated by later generations. But he was a man of great intellectual accomplishments and of

indefatigable industry. In his study he had a placard warning visitors, "Be Brief." We can understand why when
we note that in the single year of 1695, near the beginning
of his career, he published seven books, and that, though
he died at sixty-five, he is credited with a total of more than
450 publications. Many, of course, were slender pamphlets,
but his *Magnalia Christi*, published in 1702, is a massive tome
which must have involved enormous labor. Barrett Wendell says that, though hastily put together, prolix in style,
and loaded with conceits after the manner of the period, it
is nevertheless to be ranked "among the great works of
English literature in the 17th century."

One may marvel that Mather should have found time to
produce a new version of the Psalms, but evidently he
wished to provide the churches with one free from any
taint of the human frailty which found delight in jingling
rhymes. That Mather had great hopes that his book would
be a success is evident from entries in his *Diary*. Under
date of April 10, 1718, he writes:

Having praepared and finished a great Work entituled,
Psalterium Americanum, which is an Essay to render the
Book of *Psalms* (in *Blank* Verse, with Illustrations,) more
accomodated for answering its End, and being the most glorious Book of Devotions in the World. I will now with the
Help of Heaven, seek after the best methods for the Publication; as apprehending therein a singular Service to the Kingdome of *God*.

And again, on June 17:

After many Deliberations, I now at length putt into the
Hands of the Book-sellers, a large Book, from whence I expect
a sensible Service to the Kingdome of God, if ever it shall be
published. In order to the Publication, the Booksellers print
Proposals for Subscriptions; that so the Impression of a Book,
which will be five Shillings price, may be courageably carried

on. I am now waiting on my glorious Lord, that I may see how far he will please to accept my poor Offerings to serve His Interests; humbly and wholly submitting to His glorious and sovereign, and wise and just Will concerning all.

The book was published in the fall, with the following title page: *Psalterium Americanum. The Book of Psalms in a Translation Exactly conformed unto the Original; but all in Blank Verse, Fitted unto the Tunes commonly used in our Churches. Which* PURE OFFERING *is accompanied with illustrations, digging for Hidden Treasures in it; And Rules to Employ it upon the Glorious and Various Intentions of it. Whereto are added, Some other Portions of the Sacred Scripture, to Enrich the Cantional. Boston, in N. E. Printed by S. Kneeland, for B. Eliot, S. Gerish, D. Henchman and J. Edwards, and Sold at their Shops, 1718.*

He goes into a long and learned introduction,

to be attentively perused, so that the whole Book may have the Good and Great Ends of it, the more effectively accomplished. . . . Our Poetry has attempted many Versions of the Psalms, in such Numbers and Measures, as might render them capable of being Sung, in those grave Tunes, which have been prepared and received for our Christian Psalmody. But of all the more than twice Seven Versions which I have seen, it must be affirmed, That they *leave out* a vast heap of those rich things, which the Holy SPIRIT of GOD speaks in the Original Hebrew; and that they *put in* as large an Heap of poor Things, which are entirely *their own.* All this has been meerly for the sake of preserving the *Clink* of the Rhime: Which after all, is of small consequence unto a Generous *Poem*; and of none at all unto the Melody of *Singing*; But of how little then, in *Singing unto the Lord!* Some famous pieces of Poetry, which this Refining Age has been treated withal, have been offered us in BLANK VERSE. And in BLANK VERSE we now have the Glorious Book of Psalms presented to us; The Psalms fitted unto the Tunes commonly used in the Assemblies

of our *Zion*; But so fitted, that the *Christian Singer* has his
devotions now supplied, with ALL that the Holy SPIRIT of GOD
has dictated, in this Illustratious and Caelestial Bestowment
upon His Church in the World; and there is NOTHING BESIDES
the pure Dictates of that Holy SPIRIT imposed on him. . . . [The
version] is all in Common Metre eight and six but some of them
are accomodated for a well-known Long Metre by putting in
two Syllables of the Black Letter, which are, without any
Damage to the Truth of the Translation, found enclosed between Two such Crotchets as these [ ] And which being
left out, the Metre, with the Sense yet remaining entire, is
again restored unto the usual Eight and Six.

This ingenious device for using a given psalm with either
a long metre or a common metre tune was not Mather's
own invention, as it had been tried before by no less a person than Richard Baxter. The 23rd Psalm will illustrate
both how it worked and what Mather's idea of blank verse
was:

PSALM XXIII

My Shepherd is th'Eternal God.
I shall not be in [any] want;
In pastures of a tender grass
He [ever] makes me to lie down:
To waters of tranquillities
He gently carries me [along].

.   .   .   .

Yea, when I shall walk in the Vale
Of the dark [dismal] shade of Death,
I'll of no evil be afraid
Because thou [ever] art with me.
Thy rod and thy staff, these are what
Yield [constant] comfort unto me.

.   .   .   .

It is perhaps needless to say that not even Mather's justly great prestige among his contemporaries could make his psalter a success, and it remains only as a curious monument to a slowly dying theory of worship song. That Mather should have gone to the labor of producing it is the more extraordinary in view of his familiarity with Tate and Brady and with Watts' *Hymns*. Copies of the *New Version*, published in England in 1696, had reached these shores, and the earliest American editions, "Fitted to the Tunes used in Churches," were printed in New York in 1710 and 1725, and in Boston in 1713 and 1720, and all of Watts' poetical works quickly found their way to Boston, where they were received with enthusiasm. So a good many people had discovered that other and more poetical versions of the psalms were in use in England, and, such is the frailty of sinful man, their ears were tickled by "the running of the verse," "the clink of the rhyme," "and such inconsiderable circumstances."

It was a growing acquaintance with these then very modern forms of worship song, as well as with the "polite literature" of the Addisonian school, which made *The Bay Psalm Book* seem uncouth and archaic to the better educated of the young generation which was arising before Cotton Mather's eyes, and their distaste for the old book was enhanced by the dreadful condition to which the singing in the churches had sunk. Before dealing with this rising tide of dissatisfaction, however, it is necessary for a moment to turn back half a century to England, and to understand how Watts came to exert so potent an influence.

In 1679, seventeen years before Tate and Brady issued the *New Version*, Rev. John Patrick, Preacher to the Charter House, London, undertook to raise the level of psalmody in the Church of England by substituting his *Century of Select Psalms and portions of the Psalms of David* for Sternhold and Hopkins. His work proved more acceptable to

Nonconformists than to his fellow churchmen. The importance of Patrick's book in no small part consisted in the fact that he abandoned the Calvinistic principle of using the psalms in their entirety, literally translated, and, instead, undertook to select from the psalms those which he thought most fit for Christian worship and to present them in paraphrases, with a Christian coloring, rather than in close translations. This was precisely what Watts did forty years later, following Patrick's example, and Charles Wesley also at a still later date. In his preface to *The Psalms of David Imitated*, London, 1719, Watts wrote of Patrick:

". . . he hath made use of the present language of *Christianity* in several Psalms, and left out many of the Judaisms. This is the Thing that hath introduced him into the Favour of so many religious Assemblies. Even those very Persons that have an Aversion to sing anything in Worship but David's Psalms have been led insensibly to fall in with Dr. Patrick's performance by a Relish of pious Pleasure; never considering that his work is by no means a just Translation, but a Paraphrase; and there are scarce any that have departed farther from the inspired *words of Scripture* than he hath often done, in order to suit his Thoughts to the state and worship of Christianity. This I esteem his peculiar Excellency in those Psalms wherein he has practis'd it."

Watts proceeded to carry out his announced intention to "exceed" Dr. Patrick in the application of the latter's method, and frankly put the psalms into free paraphrases with no pretense of adhering closely to the words or ideas of the original Hebrew text. He says in his preface that he has "brought down the royal author into the common affairs of the Christian life, and led the Psalmist of Israel into the Church of Christ without anything of the Jew about him"! The idea of King David sitting down to write the psalms in the mood of an eighteenth-century English Nonconformist parson may strike us as not a little ludicrous, but Watts was on the right track for the improvement of congregational worship.

It is true that when Watts began to write there was already a considerable body of English hymns in existence, aside from the many versions of the psalms, but most of them were expressions of private devotion or were for special use, like Bishop Ken's famous hymns for morning, evening and midnight, written for the scholars at Winchester College. From this body of religious verse it would have been possible, towards the end of the seventeenth century, to compile a small but attractive collection of good hymns, largely from Anglican writers, had anybody cared to do it.[23] But the Church of England was now firmly attached to psalmody. John Mason, an Anglican who died in 1694, was, "perhaps, the first Englishman . . . to produce hymns for actual use in worship," and his work, with that of others, appeared in 1681, in Barton's *Psalms and Hymns*, and "formed the thin edge of the wedge by means of which, at last, hymn singing found its way into the services of the Independents, who, therefore, are the true pioneers of hymn singing in England." [24] But even Barton's book, which was

[23] George Wither (1588–1667) had published in 1623 a book entitled *Hymnes and Songs of the Church*, the entire contents of which he had himself written, with tunes arranged by Orlando Gibbons. There were hymns for each day of the week, based on the story of Creation in Genesis; for the seasons, for festivals, special occasions, etc. One or two of his hymns have had some modern use. The best is,

"Come, O come in pious lays,
Sound we God Almighty's praise."

The book had a passing popularity, but more opposition. The Church of England was not then ready to substitute hymns for psalms. Wither's attempt also proved, as had Abelard's *Hymnarium* in the Middle Ages, how impossible it is for one man, however gifted, to write a whole hymnbook.

[24] Horder, *The Hymn Lover*, p. 85. Before 1700 the Calvinistic Baptists in England had begun to use Benjamin Keach's *Spiritual Melody*, London, 1691, and the Independents to use a *Collection of Divine Hymns*, London, 1694, ed. by the Earl of Roscommon and others.

known to Watts, had done no more than point the way to the possible future development, which only took practical form when Watts began to write.

It is true also that Watts drew more largely on Patrick than was known to be the case before Benson published his great book on *The English Hymn*, for Watts borrowed many lines and even whole stanzas from Patrick and from other writers. Nevertheless there is good reason for the tradition which calls Watts the father of English hymnody. Under his hands the psalms were practically transformed into hymns. And to them Watts added many hymns of his own composition.

The great bulk of his work has now dropped out of use because it is tinctured with a theology no longer acceptable, or has been superseded by later and better hymns on similar themes, and there is a tendency to underestimate his importance as well as the excellence of much of his verse. But in his own day Watts was a daring innovator who succeeded, where his predecessors had failed, in persuading the English-speaking world to regard "man-made" hymns as an acceptable part of public worship. Because we cannot put ourselves in the place of worshippers who had known only Sternhold and Hopkins, or even Tate and Brady, we cannot fully realize how thrilling it was to come for the first time upon Watts' stirring lines,

> Our God, our help in ages past,
> Our hope for years to come, —

nor know how deeply moving seemed his hymn on the Crucifixion,

> When I survey the wondrous cross
> On which the Prince of glory died,
> My richest gain I count but loss,
> And pour contempt on all my pride, —

or those other lovely verses,

> There is a land of pure delight,
> Where saints immortal reign;
> Infinite day excludes the night,
> And pleasures banish pain.

To exchange the rugged lines of the Old Version for such hymns was to make a great advance in worship song.

Watts' hymns and hymnic versions of the psalms were quickly taken up by the Independents, and from them passed to other Nonconformist churches. They also inspired many other writers, especially Doddridge and the Wesleys, to follow his lead, so that by the middle of the eighteenth century hymn singing had become a common usage among most Nonconformist groups. The Church of England paid small heed to this development, except to express disapproval of it. As late as 1775 Rev. William Romaine, rector of St. Anne's, Blackfriars, London, in the *Essay on Psalmody* which he prefixed to his *Collection out of the Book of Psalms*, denounced "Watts's Whims," and wrote,

My concern is to see Christian congregations shut out the divinely inspired psalms, and take in Dr. Watts's flights of fancy. . . . Why should Dr. Watts, or any other hymnmaker, not only take precedence over the Holy Ghost, but also thrust him utterly out of the church?

Not even Cotton Mather, half a century earlier, had stated the conservative position so strongly. Romaine, however, although he was the mouthpiece for one element in the Church of England, is not a fair representative of the whole church, for other groups were in his day actually introducing hymns into use, without finding that thereby they were "thrusting the Holy Ghost utterly out of the church." In 1776 Toplady brought out his *Psalms &*

Hymns, the source of his own famous hymn, "Rock of Ages," and in 1779 John Newton and William Cowper published their *Olney Hymns*, the source book for all the hymns by either of them. In this latter volume the Church of England at last had a collection by two churchmen which was in some measure comparable to the collections which the Nonconformists had been using for half a century.

Now the influence of Watts reached New England at a very early date. We must remember that he was not only a hymn writer, but a voluminous author in other fields, and the outstanding Nonconformist theologian of his day. His educational manuals and his *Logic* remained in use for a century at the English universities and at Harvard. His *Horae Lyricae*, published in 1706, became a favorite book of religious poetry and was included in a series of *Sacred Classics* as late as 1834. In 1707 he published his *Hymns*, which took the Nonconformists by storm. In 1715 he published his *Divine Songs*, later issued as *Divine and Moral Songs*, the first hymns for children ever issued in English, if not in the whole history of the Christian Church, which ran through a hundred editions in the course of a century.

Among his other activities he carried on a large correspondence with various New England divines. In the unpublished correspondence of Rev. Benjamin Colman [25] of the Brattle Square Church in Boston are some fifty letters from Watts, mostly about literary and theological questions and religious happenings. Cotton Mather was also one of his correspondents.

As early as December 2, 1711, we find this entry in Mather's *Diary*:

By the gracious Providence of God, it is come to pass, that the religious, ingenious and sweet-spirited *Isaac Watts*, hath sent me the new Edition of his *Hymns*; wherein the Interest

[25] Colman MSS. at Massachusetts Historical Society, Boston.

of Piety are most admirably suited. I receive them as a Recruit and a Supply sent from Heaven for the Devotions of my Family. There will I sing them, and endeavour to bring my Family in Love with them. I would also procure our Booksellers to send for a Number of them: and perswade my well-disposed Neighbours to furnish themselves with them; and in this way promote Piety among them.[26]

And on December 25 of the same year, Benjamin Colman wrote to Mather, enclosing verses of his own composition:

Mr. Watts is a great Master in Poetry, and a burning Light and Ornament of the Age. . . . I am highly pleas'd at his undertaking the Psalms, and the length he's already got. . . . You will forgive me that I emulate, and have dared to imitate, his Muse in the Inclosed; its flame, brevity and Metre. Be candid, and think not that I name 'em with the least of His. Yet I have succeeded better, I confess, than I expected. But you shall correct me. What Watt's has taught us of charity will secure me from your Censure.[27]

In 1717, when Watts was preparing for publication his *Psalms of David Imitated* (at the same time that Mather was finishing his *Psalterium Americanum*), he sent to Mather copies of some of his verses for criticism, and a "little Essay" which must have been a draft of his preface. His letter reads:

To my honoured & very dear ffriend
Dr. Mather of New-england.

Rev^d & Dear Sir,

I may persuade my self of a hearty acceptance in this little present I make you: They are ye fruits of some easy hours this past year, wherein I have not sought Poetic flourish, but

[26] *Diary of Cotton Mather*, Massachusetts Historical Society Collection, 7th Series, VIII, 142.
[27] *Diary of Cotton Mather*, Massachusetts Historical Society Collection, 7th Series, VIII, 142.

simplicity of style and verse, for y° use of Vulgar Christians.
Tis not a Translation of David yᵗ I pretend; but an imitation
of him so nearly in Christian Hymns, yᵗ y° Jewish Psalmist
may plainly appear, yet leave Judaism behind. My Little
Essay yᵗ attend this *mst.* will render some of my Reasons for
this way of introducing y° ancient Psalms in y° wording of
the N. T. The Notes I have frequently inserted at y° end are
chiefly to render y° words a reason for y° particular Libertys
I assume in Each Psalm. If I may be so happy as to have your
free Censure and Judgmᵗ of 'em, it will help me in Correcting
others of them.

I entreat you, Sir, that none of them may steal out into
publick. If God allow me one year more even under al[l my
pre]sent weaknesses I hope he will enable me to finish my
design. To him be all y° Glory, Amen.

Yoʳ most affectionate Lover
& obliged ffriend

London, March
1717/8   I. Watts

The manuscript copies of several psalms which came
with this letter show slight variant readings from the final
printed forms. To his paraphrase of the 107th Psalm he
affixed the title "A Psalm for New England."

Mather in turn wrote to Watts about his *Psalterium
Americanum*, though he did not send on any samples for
criticism. Watts replied,

London, Feb. 11ᵗʰ 1719/20

A few months agoe I received your Letter with the friendly
pacquet of Books which you sent me, wherein I find the same
Spirit of holy zeal and practical Piety breathing as in all your
writings. . . . I thank you for the account you give me of your
Psalterium Americanum and tho you tell me I could not have
much approved ye Poesy of it, yet I should have rejoyced
to have seen the Turns of thought and the Illustrations that a
person of your learning and piety would have made upon so
admirable a peece of Sacred Devotion.

To the modern hymn lover it seems inexplicable that a man of Cotton Mather's high intelligence, who was already acquainted with Watts' *Hymns* and had seen in manuscript some of the *Psalms of David Imitated*, could have proceeded with the publication of so sterile and unpoetical a work as his *Psalterium Americanum*. We are likely to think that it was only an inordinate conceit which led Mather to imagine that his work was in any way comparable to that of Watts. Mather undoubtedly had a good opinion of himself, not without justification, but to put that interpretation upon his action is wholly to misunderstand it. He accepted the dogma that the Psalms had been directly inspired by the Holy Ghost, "being the most glorious Book of Devotions in the World," and that only the Psalms or other canticles from holy Scripture, in the closest possible translation, were fit to be used in public worship. As we have seen, he highly appreciated the lyrical beauty and religious fervor of Watts' *Hymns*, and was eager to introduce them for private or family devotions, but he could not allow them to displace the metrical psalms in church. His position should be easily understood by any good Catholic who finds comfort and inspiration in various books of devotional literature which he would not expect his priest to introduce into the ritual of his church. It is true that Mather's enthusiasm for Watts was greatly diminished at a later date, when the latter published his *Disquisitions*. Mather's conservative soul was alarmed by Watts' theological liberalism, and on January 28th, 1726/7, he wrote to Thomas Prince, the then youthful minister of the Old South, denouncing Watts as "a very Disqualified person," and "too shallow" to deal with theology, and warning Prince to beware of him. And, from his point of view, he was right, for in that work Watts took an Arian position and was headed straight down the road which led, a generation or two later, to early English Unitarianism.

The strong disapproval of Watts' theological views on the part of the conservative Mather does not appear to have been very widely shared among the Boston ministers. Mather died a little over a year later, and in any case Watts' poetry had already had a small but appreciative public in Boston for at least fifteen years. Acquaintance with it no doubt helped to intensify the dissatisfaction with the old metrical psalmody felt by the more sophisticated of the young generation which, in the first quarter of the eighteenth century, was entering upon its place in the world. It so happens that this young generation found a spokesman in Cotton Mather's own nephew, Mather Byles, whom he had for the most part brought up. Byles admirably represents the interest in literature and art which was beginning to stir the community now that the pioneering days, at least in the immediate vicinity of Boston, were pretty well past, a development which faintly foretold "the flowering of New England" a century later.

Mather Byles [28] was a brilliant and vivacious youth who graduated from Harvard in 1725 and was ordained in 1732 as the first minister of the newly organized Hollis Street Church in Boston. He was ousted from his pastorate in 1776 because of his strong Tory proclivities, his parishioners being equally ardent patriots, and spent a pathetic and embittered old age in the town of his birth until he died in his eighty-second year. His uncontrolled facility as a punster has detracted from his reputation as the best writer of his period in New England, and as a preacher of imposing presence and acknowledged distinction in style and

[28] Mather Byles (grandson of Increase Mather), b. Boston, March 15, 1706/7; d. Boston, July 5, 1788. He issued a volume of (32) *Poems on Several Occasions*, without his name, in 1744, in the preface to which he "bids adieu to the airy Muse." He received an honorary degree of Doctor of Divinity from Aberdeen in 1765. He inherited the best part of the fine libraries of both Increase and Cotton Mather. See Arthur W. H. Eaton, *The Famous Dr. Mather Byles*, Boston, 1914.

substance. In his youth he aspired to be a poet and he produced high-flown odes upon the death of George I, the coming of Governor Burnet to Boston, and similar occasions. The little coterie of aspirants to literary fame of which he was the leader published in 1744 a *Collection of Poems by Several Hands* which contains a poem describing Byles as

> Harvard's honour and New England's hope,

who

> Bids fair to rise and sing and rival Pope.

As early as 1727 Byles had addressed some admiring verses to Isaac Watts. A few of the stanzas are worth quoting to show Byles' style and to reveal the impression made by Watts on the provincial youth.

> Say, smiling Muse, what heav'nly Strain
>   Forbids the waves to roar;
> Comes gently gliding o'er the Main
>   And charms our list'ning Shore!

> What Angel strikes the tremb'ling Strings;
>   And whence the golden Sound!
> Or is it Watts — or Gabriel sings
>   From yon celestial Ground?

> 'Tis Thou, Seraphic Watts, thy Lyre
>   Plays soft along the Floods;
> Thy notes the ans'ring Hills inspire,
>   And bend the waving Woods.

> .   .   .   .

> When thy fair Soul shall on the Wings
>   Of shouting Seraphs rise,
> And with superior Sweetness sings
>   Amid thy native Skies;

Still shall thy lofty Numbers flow,
Melodious and divine;
And Choirs above, and Saints below,
A deathless Chorus join! [29]

Byles first ventured to write to Watts the next year, and he also wrote to Pope, who did not reply but did send a copy of his *Odyssey*, which Byles cherished as one of his dearest treasures.[30]

Now it so happened that in March, 1730, John Smibert, the Scottish portrait painter who had recently come to Boston, gave an exhibition of pictures, the first in that city.[31] Byles saw the exhibition and was inspired by it to write a poem addressed "To Mr. Smibert, on Viewing his Pictures," [32] in which he rather cockily offered to join the

[29] It should be noted that "divine" and "join" did not make a false rhyme, since the common speech of the day pronounced the latter word "jine," as can be shown by many examples.

[30] If further evidence is needed of the vogue which Watts enjoyed in New England, it may be noted that the Massachusetts Historical Society owns a copy of his *Hymns and Spiritual Songs*, 5th ed., London, 1716, with the autograph of John Winthrop, A.B. Harvard 1700, scientist and astronomer, who was the second of his name to become a member of the Royal Society. See also the letter from Jonathan Belcher to Watts, dated "Whitehall, Jan. 8, 1730," as follows: "In New England I have often regaled myself with your ingenious pieces, and I can assure you (without a compliment) all Dr. Watts's works are had in great esteem and honour amongst us." Quoted in Thomas Milner's *Life, Times and Correspondence of the Rev. Isaac Watts, D.D.*, London, 1845. When Watts' *Psalms of David Imitated* appeared in print, Rev. Stephen Micks (Mix) of Wethersfield, Connecticut, who had graduated from Harvard in 1690, wrote to Benjamin Colman, August 2, 1721, "I am wonderfully pleased with Mr. Watts's Psalm Book, wish it were here in the press and ordinarily used."

[31] Smibert was not the first portrait painter to work in Boston, but he was the first artist with a European reputation. He was soon followed by other painters of British or native origin, culminating in Copley, all of whom found in Boston better patronage than elsewhere in the colonies.

[32] Byles, or Smibert, or some friend sent a copy to London where it was printed, without the author's name, in the London *Courant*, April 14, 1730. It was reprinted in Byles' *Poems on Several Occasions*, 1744, under

painter in the introduction of art and polite literature to inelegant New England. Looking back to the arrival of John Winthrop in Boston in 1630, he wrote:

> An hundred Journeys now the Earth has run
> In annual circles round the central Sun,
> Since the first Ship th'unpolished Letters bore
> Thro the wide Ocean, to the barb'rous shore.
>
> .   .   .   .
>
> No moving Rhet'rick rais'd the ravish't Soul,
> Flourish't in flames or heard its Thunders roll;
> Rough, horrid verse, harsh, grated thro' the Ear,
> And jarring Discords tore the tortur'd Air.
> Solid, and grave, and plain the Country stood,
> Inelegant, and rigorously good.

Now the "rough, horrid verse" which "grated thro' the Ear" was nothing less than the contents of *The Bay Psalm Book*, in which Byles' own great-grandfather, Richard Mather, had taken a hand, and the "jarring Discords" were the tunes to which they were sung. (We can only hope, with a good many doubts, that Byles had had sufficient tact to refrain from expressing an opinion of his uncle Cotton's *Psalterium Americanum!*) In Byles we hear the frank voice of the "polite" members of the young generation, who were nurtured on Addison and to whom Pope was the outstanding living poet.[33]

---

the title "To Picturio," with slight alterations, chiefly substituting classical names for those of the Boston worthies named in the original form. I am indebted to Miss Anne Allison for the identification of the authorship of this poem, and for other points bearing upon Byles' career.

[33] Mather Byles was so strongly under their influence that this very poem is, in several passages, clearly adapted from Addison's "An Account of the Greatest English Poets," written in 1694, which begins on the same note,

> "Long had our dull forefathers slept supine,
> Nor felt the raptures of the tuneful Nine,

Perhaps few others had the temerity to speak out so boldly, or their criticisms passed unheeded. Most of them had to wait until they were old men before the reign of *The Bay Psalm Book* came to an end, for the churches clung to it. The slow transition from psalmody to hymnody in the course of the eighteenth century must be described in another chapter. But a movement for the improvement of singing had already been started, under the leadership of the young generation, and to its progress we must now give our attention.

————

. . . .
An age [as] yet uncultivate and rude."

The temptation to poke none too friendly fun at Byles was too great for his contemporary rival wit, Joseph Green. Byles had a favorite cat whom he punningly called his "Muse," and when the cat died, Green wrote an ode in Byles' name mourning for the death of his "Muse" and including the lines,

"Oft to the well-known volumes have I gone,
And stole a line from Pope or Addison."

CHAPTER III

The Revival of Singing in Eighteenth-Century New England

IT HAS ALREADY been noted that by the beginning of the eighteenth century the psalm singing in the churches of New England, and everywhere else in the colonies, had sunk to a wretched condition. The statement that at that time the churches were limited to ten tunes, and that few could sing more than five, is repeated again and again. Elson, in his *History of American Music* (p. 2), goes further and says that the Pilgrims and the Puritans "at first used but five tunes for their psalmody." The utter falsity of this statement has been made evident in the passages in Chapter II in which Ainsworth's *Psalter* and the "Admonition" about music in *The Bay Psalm Book* have been discussed.

The "five-and-ten" psalm tune legend was set afloat by a footnote in Palfrey's *History of New England* [1] in which he repeats almost verbatim a passage from Coffin's *History of Newbury*. Coffin, referring to the "daring innovation" of Rev. John Tufts of Newbury in introducing "regular" singing in the second decade of the eighteenth century (whereof we shall hear more presently), says,

As late as 1700, there were not more than four or five tunes known, in many of the congregations of this country, and in

[1] John G. Palfrey, *History of New England*, Boston, 1858, II, 41. See Joshua Coffin, *A Sketch of the History of Newbury*, etc., Boston, 1845, p. 186.

some, not more than two or three, and even those were sung altogether by rote. These tunes were York, Hackney, St. Mary's, Windsor and Martyr's.

Coffin's statement requires some modifications. He should have said, "By 1700," instead of "As late as 1700." And the fact that *The Bay Psalm Book* of 1698 included thirteen printed tunes indicates that more than "four or five" were available and were no doubt used in some places. Nevertheless, it is true that in some isolated congregations singing had almost disappeared with the dying out of the much wider range of psalm tunes which the first settlers had brought with them.

Before taking up the story of the revival of music which began about 1715 it is necessary to consider the musical tradition in which the earliest colonists had been reared. First of all let us disabuse our minds of the vulgar superstition that "the Puritans hated music." The first colonists of New England, like those in Virginia, came from a land which was just passing out of a great period of popular song.[2] In Elizabethan England there had been widespread use of madrigals, motets, catches and canons, many of them by that great group of fine musicians whose work was in later times largely neglected until recently revived. The use of the more elaborate types of this music was necessarily limited to the better-educated classes, but the common people had their ballads, carols and psalms, which were sung with zest and were orally transmitted. There is not the slightest reason to suppose that the men and women of the first migration to the colonies were any different from the people they left behind in their fondness for this music or their ability to sing it. Edward Winslow testified that the Separatist congregation at Leyden sang skillfully and finely

[2] Erasmus in his *Praise of Folly*, 1515, speaking of the particular gifts of different peoples, says that the English boast of being most accomplished in skill in music.

from Ainsworth's *Psalter*. Discussing, in his *Hypocrisie Unmasked* (1646), the departure of the Pilgrims from Holland, he wrote,

They that stayed at Leyden feasted us that were to go at our pastor's house [it] being large; where we refreshed ourselves, after tears, with singing of Psalms, making joyful melody in our hearts as well as with the voyce, there being many in our congregation very expert in music; and indeed it was the sweetest melody that ever mine ears heard.

It is, of course, quite true that the Puritans, both here and in England, discountenanced lewd and indecent songs as tending to "the nourishment of vice and the corruption of youth," [3] — as all decent and self-respecting people do — but they had no objection to good music as such. Milton was a lover of music and we all know his great lines from *Il Penseroso*:

> . . . let the pealing organ blow
> To the full-voiced choir below,
> In service high and anthems clear,
> As may with sweetness, through mine ear,
> Dissolve me into ecstasies,
> And bring all heaven before mine eyes.

Cromwell, as Lord Protector, had much good music at his court.[4] At the marriages of his daughters in 1657 a great orchestra played for mixed dancing until five in the morn-

---

[3] Scholes, *The Puritans and Music*, p. 136, writes, "Any one who has studied seventeenth century catches knows that their words are in many instances unprintable today. The Purcell Society, engaged in the preparation of its costly folio edition of Purcell's catches for the use of serious students, has felt obliged to change the words in many examples."

[4] Scholes, *The Puritans and Music*, p. 144. Mr. Scholes, to whom I am indebted for much information on this subject, has completely demolished the myth that the Puritans hated music, for all who will take the trouble to read his masterly book.

ing, and "pastorals" were presented in the form of musical dialogues. During the eleven years of the Protectorate John Playford brought out no less than seventeen publications of secular music, a list which far exceeds any "that could be made of secular musical publications in England in any preceding period." [5] Nor did the Puritans hesitate to use either stringed instruments or organs.

Naturally, the use of instruments was greater in England than in the colonies. Virginals, lutes, and bass viols were costly, and were probably seldom found even in England outside of London and the larger towns, except in the country houses of the nobility and gentry. Most of the early emigrants to this country came from small towns, villages, or rural districts, and from the middle class. They had to turn their possessions into cash to pay for the voyage and for the essential articles needed for settlement here. The larger musical instruments were too fragile and took up too much precious space on shipboard to permit of their transportation, except in rare instances, in the earliest days of the settlement.

The consequent scarcity in New England of the more highly developed types of musical instruments has misled even authors who should know better into exaggerated and misleading statements. Scholes [6] quotes one such from *The Art of Music*, as follows:

Instrumental music was certainly taboo to them [the Puritans]. As far as we know there was not a musical instrument in New England before the year 1700. If there was it has shown remarkable ingenuity in escaping detection.

This preposterous assertion, as Scholes points out, overlooks the fact that drums, trumpets, and horns were from

[5] Scholes, *The Puritans and Music*, p. 133.
[6] See Scholes, *The Puritans and Music*, p. 8, for this quotation, and pp. 23–24, 33, for his refutation of it.

the beginning in common use in New England for summoning people to church, to give an alarm, and to assist in military training, and that jew's-harps were at an early date imported in quantities, because they were in demand for trade with the Indians.

It is true that records of the presence of musical instruments other than these simple ones are very scarce. That fact does not necessarily mean that such instruments did not exist; it is quite as likely to mean that they were sufficiently familiar to pass unnoted except in an occasional will or inventory. Scholes cites one example in the will of Nathaniell Rogers of Rowley, 1664, which mentions "A treble viall, 10 s." The inventory of the estate of John Foster, who graduated from Harvard in 1667 and who was the first Boston printer and the earliest American engraver, discloses his ownership of a "Gittarue" and a "Viall" (guitar and viol). Another case is that of Rev. Edmund Browne of Sudbury, who died in 1678, leaving a "bass Vyol" and some books of music, and who was reputed to be a good musician.[7] As he was past seventy-one at death and had been ordained in England some years before his emigration in 1638, he no doubt brought his viol and music books with him. On Dec. 1, 1699, Samuel Sewall noted in his *Diary* that he had been to a shop in Boston to inquire about his wife's virginal. It is clear that such instruments were not unknown, though probably relatively scarce, in seventeenth-century New England, and that their use for recreation was not condemned. With improved shipping facilities and the growing prosperity of the opening years of the eighteenth century, the number and variety of musical instruments in the colony rapidly increased.

[7] A. W. Cutting, *An Historical Address delivered in The First Parish of Wayland, Mass., Sunday, June 25, 1911*, Boston, 1911. The "bass Vyol" in this instance, as in other cases in the 17th and 18th centuries, was probably what we should call a violincello, not a double-bass.

The case with organs was somewhat different. They were more cumbersome to transport and were very costly. We must further remember that probably only a minority of the early emigrants to this country had any acquaintance with organ music, because at that period in England organs were to be heard only in the cathedrals, college chapels, or larger parish churches in considerable towns. For example, Scholes states that about the time of the great migration to New England (1630–1640) only one church in York besides the Cathedral possessed an organ.[8]

The essential point to be noted in the Puritan attitude towards all instrumental music, including the use of organs, is the clear distinction which they drew between the use of instrumental music in church, of which they disapproved,[9] and music for social enjoyment, which they approved within reasonable limits. Thus Samuel Sewall, when at Oxford, England, wrote home to his friend Mr. Burbank, on July 22, 1695:

The next Sabbath after the Coronation I heard a service at St. Mary's. I am a lover of Musick to a fault, yet I was uneasy there; and the justling out of the Institution of Singing Psalms, by the boisterous Organ, is that which can never be justified before the great Master of Religious Ceremonies.

[8] Scholes, *The Puritans and Music*, p. 230. See his Chap. XV, "The organ in church and home in Puritan England." The current legend that during the Civil War in England all church organs were systematically destroyed by the Puritans contains only a modicum of truth. Some were deliberately destroyed; some were taken down and sold, either for private use or for the lead in their pipes; but some were suffered to remain in place, though silent. Furthermore, as Scholes points out, there had been a strong movement against organs, and the dismantling of some, within the Church of England between the last days of Henry VIII's reign and the early years of Elizabeth's.

[9] Was it not written in Amos 5:23, "I will not hear the melody of thy viols"? And had not "the sound of the cornet, flute, harp, sackbut, psaltery, dulcimer and all kinds of music" been the accompaniment of Nebuchadnezzar's idolatrous worship in which the people were bidden to join on pain of death? Dan. 3:4–6.

On the other hand, the legitimacy of private music (and also the right of the individual to "frame a Spirituall Song") was recognized by Rev. John Cotton in his *Singing of Psalms a Gospel Ordinance*, 1647, in which he says,

> We grant also, that any private Christian, who hath a gift to frame a Spirituall Song, may both frame it and sing it privately, for his own private comfort, and remembrance of some speciall benefit or deliverance. Nor doe we forbid the private use of any Instrument of musick therewithall; so that attention to the instrument, doe not direct the heart from attention to the matter of the Song. Neither doe wee deny, but that in the publique Thanksgiving of the Church, if the Lord should furnish any of the members of the Church with a spiritual gift to compose a *Psalme* upon any speciall occasion, he may lawfully be allowed to sing it before the church, and the rest hearing it, and approving it, may goe along with him in Spirit, and say Amen to it.

The point at issue is perfectly illustrated by the story of Thomas Brattle's organ, early in the eighteenth century. Thomas Brattle was a Boston citizen of good family and considerable wealth. His brother William was minister of the church in Cambridge, and he himself had been a leader in organizing the "Manifesto" Church in Brattle Square, Boston, of which Rev. Benjamin Colman was minister. As early as 1711 Thomas Brattle had imported an organ and set it up in his house for his own pleasure and the entertainment of his friends, for on May 29 of that year Rev. Joseph Green noted in his *Diary*,

> I was at Mr. Thomas Brattle's; heard ye organs and saw strange things in a microscope.

Observe that Green, though a Puritan minister, had no objection to hearing "ye organs" in Mr. Brattle's house. But when Brattle died in 1713 he bequeathed the organ to the Brattle Square Church, of which he was a leading member, or, should the church refuse it, to King's Chapel, where the Episcopalians worshipped. There was a further provision that the church which accepted the organ should "procure a sober person that can play skillfully thereon with a loud noise." As Brattle had probably foreseen, the Brattle Square congregation, though in many respects a very enlightened one, was not ready for so radical a step as the installation of an organ for use in public worship.[10] So the organ went to King's Chapel,[11] where it was used until 1756. It was then sold to St. Paul's Church, Newburyport, where it was used until 1836, when it was sold to St. John's Church, Portsmouth, New Hampshire, where it still exists in usable condition.

Brattle's organ, however, although both the first to be imported into New England and the first to be permanently installed in a church, was not the earliest instrument of the kind in the North American colonies. As early as 1694 a group of German Pietists settled in the valley of the Wissahickon, near Philadelphia, now a parkway within the city limits. They either brought a small organ with them or imported it soon after, for in November, 1703, when one of their number, Justus Falckner, was ordained as a Lutheran minister in the Swedish church called Gloria Dei, in Philadelphia, they not only provided an orchestra

---

[10] It was not until 1790 that the Brattle Square Church imported an organ from England, and even then one wealthy member of the parish was so disturbed that he offered to pay the entire cost if he might destroy the instrument instead of having it placed in the church.

[11] There is a tradition that the organ remained for seven months in the church porch in the boxes in which it was packed, owing to popular prejudice against its use. It is true that approximately that period elapsed between the vote of the church accepting the organ and the vote "that the organs be forthwith put up." Perhaps the explanation for this lapse of time lies in the probability that some alterations in the church were required to accommodate it, and in the necessity of tedious correspondence with England to secure a competent organist.

for the occasion, but loaned a small organ which was temporarily set up in the gallery of the church. This is the earliest use of an organ in any church in the colonies which can be definitely dated, although these Germans had presumably themselves previously used the organ in their worship. A year later an English organ builder, Dr. Christopher Witt, joined their retreat, and built one or more organs for household use, the earliest to be constructed in this country. It was probably one of these latter instruments which was purchased in 1728 for the use of Christ Church in Philadelphia.[12]

It is true that a claim is made that an organ was imported about 1700 for St. Peter's Church at Port Royal, Virginia. This organ was sold about 1810 to Christ Church, Alexandria; thence went to Shepherdstown, Virginia; and thence in the eighteen-sixties to Hancock, Maryland. It is now in the Smithsonian Institution. There appears to be no substantial evidence to support the claim, so far as the date of importation is concerned. The early registers of St. Peter's Church have been burned, and the earliest documentary evidence relating to this organ seems to be the vote of the vestry of Christ Church, Alexandria, in 1810, that steps be taken "for procuring an organ from a church at Port Royal," followed by another vote in 1815 approving an additional expenditure "for building the organ." It is highly improbable that the Port Royal organ was imported earlier than the middle of the eighteenth century. It was not until late in 1755 that Bruton Parish at Williamsburg, Virginia, the capital and social center of the colony, took the final steps for setting up an organ and appointed the younger Peter Pelham as organist. Port Royal was, at that time, a good deal more important place than it is now, but it was never a rival of Williamsburg and is not likely

---

[12] See Chapter IV.

to have been ahead of the capital of the colony when it came to purchasing an organ.

The second church in the colonies to install an organ seems to have been the Dutch Reformed Church of New York, to which an instrument was presented by Governor Burnet in 1724. The third was Christ Church, Philadelphia (1728), already referred to. In 1733 Trinity Church, Newport, received an organ as a gift from Bishop Berkeley, and retained it in use until 1844 before having it rebuilt. In 1736 Trinity Church and Christ Church, Boston, each imported an organ. In 1737 Trinity Church, New York, set up an organ which was built for the church by Johann Gottfried Klemm, a Moravian organ builder who had shortly before emigrated to America.[13] St. Peter's Church in Salem, Massachusetts, imported one in 1743. In 1746 the Swede, Gustavus Hesselius and J. G. Klemm together built an organ for the Moravians at Bethlehem. In 1761, when St. Michael's Church in Charleston, South Carolina, was opened, an organ was hired for the occasion; a year later another instrument was loaned to the church, and about 1768 an organ was imported from England.

It is quite understandable that among the English-speaking colonists organs should generally have been introduced first into the Episcopal churches. Their congregations usually included a larger proportion of late-comers to America, and their clergymen were mostly of English birth, or, if native-born Americans, had gone to England for ordination and naturally wished to introduce Anglican practices. Even among them, however, the increase in the number of organs was slow because of the cost of the instruments and the difficulty of procuring organists.

Other Protestant groups did not venture on organs until near the end of the century. In 1763 a vigorous, not to say

[13] Trinity Church had voted in 1703 to make inquiry about erecting an organ, but nothing came of it at that time.

tart, writer, who signed himself only "A Presbyterian," printed in Philadelphia a pamphlet on *The Lawfulness, excellency and advantages of instrumental musick in the service of God. — Address'd to all (particularly the Presbyterians and Baptists)* who have *hitherto been taught to look upon the use of instrumental musick in the worship of God as unlawful,* in which he deplores the low state of congregational singing and argues that it would be improved by the introduction of organs. Ezra Stiles, then minister at Newport, later the great president of Yale, records in his *Diary* under date of July 10, 1770,

Last month an Organ of 200 Pipes was set up in the Meetinghouse of the first Congregational Chh. in Providence; and for the first time it was played upon in Divine Service last Ldsday, as Mr. Rowland the pastor tells me. This is the first organ in a dissenting presby. Chh. in America except Jersey College, or Great Britain.[14]

He goes on to suggest that the congregation apply for the bequest of £500 which an Anglican gentleman is alleged to have left to the first dissenting chapel that would install an organ. And under date of May 16, 1785, he writes,

They have lately determined to set up an Organ in Dr. Chauncey's Meetghouse being the old Brick or first Chh. in Bo.[15] founded in 1629. The Doctor was against it, but Mr. Clark, his colleague, and the congreg[n] in general were for it.

[14] *The Literary Diary of Ezra Stiles,* ed. F. B. Dexter, New York, 1901, I, 57. "Jersey College" was the institution at Princeton, New Jersey, which has developed into Princeton University. Stiles goes on to say that the organ there "erected in Nassau Hall perhaps about ten years ago, . . . was never much used" and that "in the year 1754 I saw in the Dutch Calvinist Chh. at New York a small Organ, which was the first there and had been there I doubt not many years." This, presumably was the organ given by Governor Burnet, referred to above.

[15] The building then occupied by the First Church in Boston was commonly called "The Old Brick Church." Rev. Charles Chauncey was minister from 1727 to 1787.

This spring the Meetghouse was repaired and Dr. C. preached a consecr* and farewell sermon on acc° of his great age. The people eager to get an organ waited on the Dr. who told them that it would not be long before he was in his grave, — he knew that before his head was cold there they would have an organ — and they might do as they pleased.

There are said to have been fewer than twenty church organs in all New England as late as 1800, and probably a not much larger number in other parts of the country in proportion to the population. As late as 1814 singing in the Park Street Church, Boston, was supported only by a flute, a bassoon, and bass viol, and in 1845 the Hanover Street Church was still using only a clarinet, an ophicleide, and a double bass. It is clear that similar conditions prevailed throughout the colonies (except among the Moravians in Pennsylvania and North Carolina), and that most other church bodies not only shared the prejudice of the Puritans against using organs in church, but were quite as slow in overcoming it.

As already stated, however, this prejudice did not apply to the use of organs at home or for social purposes, and it is interesting to note that the first organ built in this country by a native-born American was constructed by Edward Bromfield, Jr., of Boston, who was born in 1723, graduated from Harvard in 1742, and died in 1746. Describing his organ, Rev. Thomas Prince wrote:

As he was well skilled in Music, he for exercise and recreation, with his own hands, has made a most accurate Organ, with two rows of keys and many hundred pipes; his intention being twelve hundred, but died before he completed it. The workmanship of the keys and pipes, surprizingly nice and curious, exceeding anything of the kind that ever came here from England: which he designed not merely to refresh his spirits but with harmony to sing, enliven and regulate his vocal and delightful songs to his great Creator, Preserver, Benefactor and

Redeemer. . . . And what is surprising was, that he had but a few times looked into the inside work of two or three organs which came from England.[16]

The Puritans were not, of course, peculiar in their disapproval of instrumental music in church. They could quote Tertullian, Clement of Alexandria, St. Chrysostom, St. Ambrose, St. Augustine, St. Jerome, and others of the early Church Fathers in support of their opinion. The Quakers took an even more extreme position and did not allow any vocal music in their meetings,[17] and as late as the end of the nineteenth century some conservative Friends felt that they could not countenance even hymn singing at home.[18] The

[16] *Panoplist*, II, 194, quoted in G. Hood's *A History of Music in New England*, Boston, 1846. Unfortunately Bromfield's organ was destroyed by fire during the siege of Boston.

[17] The precise phrasing of the regulations and statements regarding music adopted by the Society of Friends has varied in different periods and places, but the following provisions in the *Discipline* adopted by the Philadelphia Yearly Meeting may be regarded as illustrative of the attitude of some groups. In the *Rules of Discipline*, 1806, under "Gaming and Diversions," is the following advice:

"As our time passeth swiftly away, and our delight ought to be in the law of the Lord; it is advised that a watchful care be exercised over our youth, to prevent their going to stage-plays, horse-races, music, dancing, or any such vain sports and pastimes; and being concerned in lotteries, wagering, or other species of gambling."

In 1853 the following "Advice" was issued:

"We would also renewedly caution all our members against indulging in music, or having instruments of music in their houses, believing that the practice tends to promote a light and vain mind, and to disqualify for the serious thoughtfulness, which becomes an accountable being, hastening to his final reckoning."

[18] In the *Rules of Discipline* of 1880, the advice against "indulging music," or "having instruments of music in their houses" was repeated with a warning that offenders were liable to be disowned. The *Discipline* of 1910 contained a much milder "counsel" about "such pastimes as music, card-playing, and other varying forms of social levity." The *Faith and Practice* of 1925–26, and 1932, have altogether dropped all "advice" or "cautions" against music. The present attitude towards music of a large number of Friends in England and America is indicated

Eastern Church has never permitted any instrumental music at its services. The glorious modern music of the Russian Church was written for, and is sung by, unaccompanied choirs. In the Western Church organs were not introduced into churches until the latter part of the Middle Ages, and then only by "permission." To this day in the Pope's own chapel in the Vatican only unaccompanied singing is to be heard. In the three branches of the Presbyterian Church in Scotland the use of organs in public worship was not officially authorized until the latter half of the nineteenth century,[19] and in the Reformed Presbyterian Church in this country instrumental music in worship is still forbidden.

The Puritans were also strongly opposed to any elaborate music which attracted attention to the performers and diverted the mind from the worship of God. Nor were they peculiar in that respect. John Evelyn was no Puritan, but when on Dec. 21, 1662, he attended service at the royal chapel he recorded his disapproval of what he heard there.

One of his Ma^{ty's} chaplains preach'd, after which, instead of ye antient, grave and solemn wind musiq accompanying ye organ, was introduc'd a concert of 24 violins betweene every pause, after ye French fantastical way, better suiting a tavern or a playhouse than a church.[20]

---

by the following quotation from the current English *Book of Discipline*, II, 82: "These natural gifts [for music], whether they be for performance and creation or for general appreciation, deserve the chance of full development, and may demand special and ample training. The technical mastery of an instrument will be of value to those who show a real aptitude, but all may learn in measure to feel the beauty of pure and lovely melodies, and to enter into the glory of the works of the great composers. To many, music is a means of expressing the deepest things in their experience, and of bringing them in touch with God."

[19] In the Established Church in 1866; in the United Presbyterian in 1872; in the Free Church in 1883.

[20] *Diary and Correspondence of John Evelyn, Esq.*, ed. William Bray, new ed., London, 1906, II, 156.

Disapproval of that kind of music in church finds expression again and again in Christian history from the days of St. Augustine down. Scholes has two enlightening quotations from the *Histriomastix* (1633) of the irrepressible William Prynne. The first runs:

Let me speake now of those who, under the show of religion, doe obpalliate the business of pleasure. . . . Whence hath the Church so many Organs and Musicall Instruments? To what purpose, I pray you, is that terrible blowing of Belloes, expressing rather the crakes of Thunder, than the sweetnesse of a Voyce? To what purpose serves that contraction and inflection of the voyce? This man sings a base, that a small meane, another a treble, a fourth divides and cuts asunder, as it were, certain middle notes. One while the voice is strained, anon it is remitted, now it is dashed, and then againe it is enlarged with a lowder sound. Sometimes, which is a shame to speake, it is enforced into a horse's neighings; sometimes, the masculine vigour being laid aside, it is sharpened unto the shrilnesse of a woman's voyce; — Sometimes Thou may'st see a man with an open mouth, not to sing, but as it were, to breathe out his last gaspe, by shutting in his breath, and by a certaine ridiculous interception of his voyce, as it were to threaten silence, and now againe to imitate the agonies of a dying man, or the extasies of such as suffer. — In the meantime, the common people standing by, trembling and astonished, admire the sound of the Organs, the noise of the Cymballs and Musicall Instruments, the harmony of Pipes and Cornets.

That passage undoubtedly expresses the opinion of elaborate church music held by Prynne and his fellow Puritans, but it is Prynne's translation from the Latin treatise of Ethelred, Abbot of Rievaulx Abbey, Yorkshire, in the twelfth century, who was denouncing the abandonment of unison plain song for the new polyphonic music which was coming into fashion. Prynne goes on to describe the musical abuses of his own day in a parallel passage:

But now a-dayes Musicke is grown to such and so great licentiousnesse, that even at the ministration of the holy Sacrament all kinde of Wanton and lewde trifling Songs, with piping of Organs, have their place and course. As for the Divine Service and Common prayer, it is so chaunted and misused and mangled of our costly hired, curious, and nice Musitians (not to instruct the audience withall, nor to stirre up men's mindes unto devotion, but with a whorish harmony to tickle their eares;) that it may justly seeme not to be a noyse made of men, but rather a bleating of bruite beasts; while the Coristers ney descant as it were a sort of Colts; others bellowe a tenour, as it were a company of oxen; others barke a counter-point, as it were a kennell of Dogs; others roar out a treble like a sort of Buls; others grunt out a base as it were a number of Hogs; so that a foule evill favored noyse is made, but as for the wordes and Sentences and the very matter it selfe, nothing is understanded at all; but the authority and power of judgment is taken away both from the minde and from the eares utterly.

Prynne could have supported his objection to music which obliterated any understanding of the words sung by referring to the injunction of 1559 by the Ecclesiastical Commissioners, quoted on p. 20, which permitted "hymns or such-like songs" in church "having respect that the *sentence of the hymn may be understanded and perceived.*" But his point had been made again and again, in many generations. Erasmus, the outstanding exponent of Humanism in the Catholic Church in the sixteenth century, who himself had been a choirboy at Utrecht, makes a similar complaint:

They chant nowadays in our churches in what is an unknown tongue and nothing else, while you will not hear a sermon once in six months telling people to amend their lives. Modern church music is so constructed that the congregation cannot hear one distinct word. The choristers themselves do not understand what they are singing. . . . There was no music in St. Paul's time. Words were then pronounced clearly. Words nowadays mean nothing. . . . Money must be raised to buy organs and train boys to squeal, and learn no other thing that is good for them. . . . They have so much of it in England that the monks attend to nothing else. A set of creatures who ought to be lamenting their sins fancy they can please God by gurgling in their throats. Boys are kept in the English Benedictine colleges solely and simply to sing morning hymns to the Virgin. If they want music let them sing Psalms like rational beings, and not too many of these.[21]

The Puritans clearly had ample precedent as well as good sense to support their objection to elaborate church music. They proposed to "sing Psalms like rational beings," set to simple but noble and beautiful music, and sung in unison without accompaniment. They were for reducing the outward adjuncts of public worship to the lowest terms, that the spirit might be all in all, and they believed that the words sung were the essential thing, to which the tune was subordinate. Therefore, the words must be worthy, and what could be of greater worth than the Psalms? That outstanding modern authority on church music, Canon Winfred Douglas, makes the same point when he says that church music "can only attain its true characteristic excellence in being the faithful and subordinate hand maid of the liturgical words to which it is sung," and cites as an "intolerable corruption of divine service" an Easter service when

I saw a singer rise, face the congregation, his back to the altar: and, alas, I heard him sing a sentimental ditty about "the flowers and the trees, the birds and the bees," in music with the "flavour of an over-ripe banana," to quote Geoffrey Shaw.[22]

[21] For this and the preceding quotations and comment, and for much more to the same effect, see Scholes, *The Puritans and Music*, Chapter xiv, "The Antiquity and Nature of the Objection to Elaborate Church Music."

[22] Winfred Douglas, *Church Music in History and Practice*, pp. 119

The feeling of Canon Douglas on that occasion would have been fully understood and shared by the Puritans, and for precisely the same reasons. The Puritans would, indeed, have rejected as "Popish" the ancient church music which Canon Douglas so ardently and justly admires and seeks to revive, but his own lack of appreciation of the noble psalm tunes which they sang, and of their ideals of worship, is even less excusable. When we remember that at the time of the first migration to America there were people still living in England who could recall the Marian martyrdoms at Smithfield, and the Genevan exile of relatives or acquaintances, it is small wonder that the Puritans, fearful of a recurrence of those evil days under the growing absolutism of Charles I and Archbishop Laud, should have sought to wipe out even the most innocent reminders of the abominations from which they had escaped.

This long digression has been necessary to enable us to understand the attitude of the New England Puritans toward music in general and church music in particular. The rapid decline of ability to sing in the New England churches during the seventeenth and early years of the eighteenth century was not due to an unreasoned dislike of music as such, but was rather the inevitable consequence of the hard conditions of life in all the colonies. There was an unavoidable shrinkage of all cultural values after the disappearance of the emigrant generation, which had brought with it the standards of life of the English middle class of the period. The second and third generations inevitably lacked the cultural background which their parents or grandparents had absorbed in England, not only because the educational and social environment was lacking, but also because they were confronted with the hardships of pioneer life, which left scant time or strength for the cul-

and 140. Quoted by permission of Charles Scribner's Sons, New York, owners of the copyright.

tivation of the finer amenities of life. When men and women are isolated in small communities with slender contacts with the outside world, and are confronted with the heavy labor of felling the forest, preparing stony fields for cultivation, building houses and roads, and setting up a church and state, they have nothing left for poetry or song.

Thus, as the first generation died off the memory of much of the music they had known perished with them. This is clearly brought out by the reasons given for the abandonment in 1692 of Ainsworth's *Psalter* by the church in Plymouth, in favor of *The Bay Psalm Book*. In the church records it is noted that on May 17, 1685,

the Elder stayed the church after the public worship was ended, and moved to sing psalm 130th in another translation, because in Mr. Ainsworth's translation, which we sang, the tune was so difficult few could follow it.

And on June 19, 1692,

the Pastor stayed the church after meeting and propounded that seeing many of the psalms in Mr. Ainsworth's translation, that we now sung, had such difficult tunes, that none in the church could set, that the church would consider of some way of accomodation. . . .

On August 7th the church voted "when the tunes are difficult in the translation we use, we will sing the psalms now used in our neighbor churches in the Bay." [23] Thus the Plymouth congregation, whose forebears on leaving Holland had sung so well the noble but long French and Dutch tunes in Ainsworth's *Psalter*, were forced by the decline in musical culture to substitute for them the limited number of short and simple tunes which the people still could manage.

[23] Quoted from Hood, *History of Music in New England*, p. 54.

There was, indeed, some effort to maintain the standards of singing, though a document apparently written about 1673 states that "There are no musicians by trade" in the colony.[24] No doubt there were no professional musicians here — it would have been rather surprising if there had been — but Thomas Symmes, who graduated from Harvard in 1698, states in his discourse on *The Reasonableness of Regular Singing: or Singing by Note* (1720) (and also in his later *Joco-Serious Dialogue*), that there had been singing schools in the early days of the colony, and accounts for the decline of singing by saying, "Singing schools and singing books being laid aside, there was no way to learn." Music, he goes on to say,

was studied, known and approved of in our College, for many years after its first founding. This is evident from the Musical Theses, which were formerly printed; and from some writings containing some tunes, with directions for *singing by note*, as they are now sung; and these are yet in being though of more than sixty years' standing.

The papers to which he refers as evidence were lost in the fire which destroyed the College Library in 1764, but his statement carries back to at least 1660 the time when music was "studied, known and approved of in our College." But this attempt to keep alive the art of song reached too few persons to have much influence.

A secondary cause for the decline of singing may have

[24] *Copy of a curious Paper concerning the Inhabitants of this Government. Observations made by the curious on New England about the year 1673, which was given to Randolph 1673 for his direction.* This document covers a page and a half in Mass. Hist. Soc. Coll., IV, 216–217, Boston, 1795. C. M. Ayars, in *Contributions to the Art of Music in America by the Music Industries of Boston, 1640–1936*, N. Y., 1937, p. 3, says that "Governor Leverett wrote home in 1673 that there was 'not a musician in the Colony.'" I have not been able to verify this quotation from Leverett. Possibly Miss Ayars took it from the above-mentioned document which she attributed to Leverett.

been the lack of any printed tunes in *The Bay Psalm Book*, previous to the edition of 1698, although a similar decline occurred in the Plymouth Colony, where Ainsworth's *Psalter* with its printed tunes was in use. Perhaps by the end of the century the absence of printed music did not matter very much, since by that time probably few people could read music. The result was that the tunes were transmitted by ear and were subject to endless variations arising from the whims or the incompetence of the leader ("Praecentor," as Samuel Sewall calls him). He was usually a deacon who, in this respect, took the place traditionally held by the parish clerk in England. The congregation were dependent upon his skill for setting the right pitch, and upon his memory and the strength of his voice for holding them to the tune chosen.

The responsibility thus thrown upon the precentor was a heavy one, which many a modern, trained singer would hesitate to accept, and few persons in New England, whether pious deacons or roaring sinners, had any qualifications for musical leadership beyond a good ear and a strong voice. In the *Diary* of Samuel Sewall we find recorded the mishaps which occasionally befell his well-meant efforts to set the tune in the South Meeting House in Boston, and be it remembered that Judge Sewall was fond of singing and was probably better qualified than most deacons.

December 28, 1705. Mr. Willard . . . spoke to me to set the Tune; I intended Windsor and fell into High-Dutch, and then essaying to set another Tune went into a key much too high. So I pray'd Mr. White to set it; which he did well, Litchf. Tune.

July 5, 1713. I try'd to set Low-Dutch Tune and fail'd. Try'd again and fell into the tune of the 119th Psalm.

Feb. 2, 1717/18. Lord's Day. In the Morning I set York Tune,

and in the 2d going over, the Gallery carried it irresistibly to
St. David's which discouraged me very much. I spoke earnestly
to Mr. White to set it in the Afternoon, but he declines it.
p.m̄. The Tune went well.

Such episodes are typical of what must have been frequent occurrences almost everywhere in the colonies, and
at least occasional even in English churches. Furthermore,
there were seldom enough psalmbooks to supply the whole
congregation, and in some communities not all the people
could read. To meet these conditions the practice of lining-
out or "deaconing" the psalms arose in England early in the
seventeenth century and was followed in the colonies as
well. Lining-out meant that in England the parish clerk,
or in America a deacon, read a line or two of a psalm, then
led the people in singing what had been read, and so on
alternately, a line or two at a time until the end of the
psalm was reached.[25]
    It is hardly surprising that under such conditions singing
had become a painful performance, and these conditions
were not, of course, peculiar to New England, but prevailed throughout the colonies, and to some extent in
England, where a writer in 1676 says, " 'Tis sad to hear
what whining, tooting, yelling, or screeking there is in
many country congregations." [26] Sonneck is probably war-
ranted in saying that "if psalmody in America was crude
and amateurish, it was not very much more so than in
England." [27] The flippant Lord Rochester, hearing a parish
clerk singing a psalm, produced the following epigram for
the amusement of Charles II.

[25] For a detailed account of the practice of lining-out see Appendix A.
[26] Thomas Mace, *Musick's Monument*, London, 1676, quoted in Scholes,
The Puritans and Music, p. 268.
[27] O. G. Sonneck, *Early Concert Life in America*, Leipzig, 1907,
pp. 310–311.

Sternhold and Hopkins had great qualms,
When they translated David's psalms,
To make the heart right glad;
But had it been King David's fate
To hear thee sing and them translate,
By God, 'twould set him mad.[28]

We can understand why young Mr. Byles complained that "jarring discords tore the tortured air," or why John Adams, writing many years later but looking back to this period, could say that the "old way" of "singing by rote" had so degenerated that it was little more than "a drawling, quavering discord." Rev. Thomas Walter, of whom more presently, complains that he has heard Oxford Tune sung in three different churches with as many variations as there could be between three different tunes, and as to dragging he says, "I myself have twice in one note paused for breath." The ministers were troubled by the wretched quality of the singing, if we may take Cotton Mather's not infrequent entries in his *Diary* as typical.

Sept. 24, 1716. The Psalmody in our Assembly must be better provided for.

Oct. 13, 1718. The Psalmody is but poorly carried on in my Flock, and in a Variety and Regularity inferior to some others: I would see about it.

June 5, 1721. I must of necessity do something, that the Exercise of *Singing* the sacred *Psalms* in the Flock, may be made more beautiful, and especially have the *Beauties* of *Holiness* more upon it.

[28] Compare "Lines written out of temper on a Pannel in one of the pews in Salem church," and printed in the *American Apollo*, April 20, 1792:

"Could poor King David but for once
To Salem church repair,
And hear his Psalms thus warbled out,
Good Lord, how he would swear!"

Quoted in W. A. Fisher, *Notes on Music in Old Boston*, Boston, 1918, p. 17.

And it was among the ministers, who were for the most part the most progressive and enlightened members of the community,[29] that the first steps were taken for a revival of singing. The lead was taken by a number of the younger ministers, though they were cordially supported by the older men, and took the form of trying to teach people to sing from printed notes instead of by ear. This became known as "the new way" of "regular singing," that is, singing by rule or "by note," as opposed to the "old way" of singing "by rote," that is, from memory or by ear.

The originator of the movement was Rev. John Tufts [30] of Newbury, Massachusetts. About 1712 he published *An Introduction to the Singing of Psalm Tunes in a plain and Easy Method with a Collection of Tunes in Three Parts*,[31] which ran through eleven editions. Early editions contained twenty-eight tunes, later ones had thirty-eight,

---

[29] The widespread belief that the Puritan ministers were harsh, narrow-minded, and bigoted persons who held in check their more broad-minded congregations is a gross perversion of the truth. There was, of course, a wide range of opinion and attitude among them, but, taken as a class, they were the best-educated persons in the community and the natural leaders in intellectual and social matters. For their leadership see Clifford K. Shipton, "The New England Clergy in the Glacial Period," Colonial Society of Mass. *Transactions*, XXII, 24–54. They led in the revival of singing; in the introduction of inoculation for smallpox; in the movement for political freedom which culminated in the Revolution (with the notable exception of Mather Byles and the Episcopal ministers); and some of them kept in touch to a remarkable degree with scientific progress in Europe. With few exceptions they were well in advance of most of the laity in these and kindred matters.

[30] John Tufts, b. Medford, Mass., Feb. 26, 1688/9. A.B. Harvard 1708. Settled on the Second Church in Newbury 1714; later minister of the First Church in West Newbury. He had some difficulties with his parish, and asked for dismission, which was voted March 2, 1737/8. He then removed to Amesbury, set up a shop, and died there August 17, 1750. See John L. Sibley, *Harvard Graduates*, Cambridge, 1873, V, 457–461.

[31] This is the title of the later editions from the fifth on, by which the work is best known. Neither the title nor date (about 1712) of the first edition is known. The third edition, *A Very Plain and Easy Introduction to the Singing of Psalm Tunes*, Boston, 1721, contained only twelve pages.

"Printed from Copper Plates Neatly Engraven," and included Tate and Brady's version of the 149th Psalm so as to bring in the tune, as well as a poem, or hymn, "On the Divine Use of Musick," which Tufts took from John Playford's *Whole Book of Psalms* (1677).[32] Playford's *Psalter* had superseded Ravenscroft's earlier book as the best collection of tunes for the Old Version, from the latter part of the seventeenth century on. Playford made a few alterations in the text of the Psalms and inserted at the end, with a few other hymns, the verses which Tufts borrowed. It is not known who put them into the long-metre form which Playford printed, but the hymn is a largely rewritten variant of a song which had appeared, in 1660, in Ingelo's *Bentivoglio and Urania*. Part of the poem is worth quoting as illustrating current views of the religious use of song.

> We Sing to Thee whose Wisdom form'd
> The curious organ of the Ear;
> And Thou who gav'st us Voices, *Lord*,
> Our grateful Songs in Kindness hear.
>
> .   .   .   .
>
> And whilst We Sing, we'll consecrate,
> That too, too much profanéd Art;
> By off'ring up with Ev'ry Tongue,
> In ev'ry Song a Flaming Heart.

[32] Playford, although his book was prepared for use in the Church of England, has a long preface with abundant quotations from the Bible and Church Fathers to prove the validity of singing in church. Referring to Ravenscroft's *Psalter*, he says he has been asked to bring out a new edition, with tunes in three parts. As regards Sternhold and Hopkins' version of the Psalms he says, "But time and long use hath much abated the wonted reverence and estimation it had for about an hundred years after their establishment. The Reasons whereof, as I conjecture, are chiefly these: 1. The faults that some find with the Translation: 2. The dislike that others have for the Tunes: and, 3, The ill custom of Reading every line by itself before they sing it."

We'll hallow Pleasure, and redeem,
From Vulgar Use our precious Voice;
Those Lips which wantonly have sung
Shall serve our Turn for nobler Joys.

And that above we may be sure,
When we come there, our Part to know;
Whilst we live here; at home and Church,
We'll practise Singing here below.

Tufts' little pamphlet, for it is nothing more, is usually
found bound up with copies of *The Bay Psalm Book*. The
tunes were printed in three parts, not in musical notation
but the notes are indicated by letters on a scale, the length
shown by punctuation marks.[33] His instructions for singing
were derived from Thomas Ravenscroft and John Playford,
but he could not have gone to better sources. Slight as it is,
Tufts' little booklet is noteworthy as the earliest book of
instruction in music to be published in the English colonies
of North America, and it marks the beginning of the revival in singing. Its influence was reinforced by personal
efforts on the part of its author, who travelled about Massachusetts organizing singing schools and lecturing on the
subject. The effect of his activities is most easily traceable
in Boston, because of the fuller record of doings there than
in other places. The redoubtable Cotton Mather went to
work in the good cause. That he should have done so, in
view of the die-hard conservatism of his ill-fated *Psalterium
Americanum*, illustrates the inconsistency of his many-sided
character. On March 16, 1720/21, Samuel Sewall recorded
in his *Diary*,

[33] "The *Fasola* notation which has been the characteristic solmization
of American rural communities since that time is directly traceable to
Tufts." "Notes on the Music" by Carleton Sprague Smith, in program
of *Organ Recital and Three Concerts of Chamber Music*, Harvard Tercentenary, 1936. But Tufts was not the originator of Fasola; he only introduced an old English solmization system.

At night Dr. Mather preaches in the School-House to the young Musicians, from Rev. 14.3. — no man could learn that Song. House was full, and the Singing extraordinarily Excellent, such as has hardly been heard before in Boston. Sung four times out of Tate and Brady.[34]

Mather's text does not seem a very happy one for a congregation of young people who were earnestly trying to learn to sing new songs unto the Lord, but evidently it failed to discourage them. The *New England Courant* under date of September 30, 1723, notes that

On Thursday last a Singing Lecture was held here, when the Rev. Mr. Tufts of Newbury preach'd;

and Sewall on July 27, 1726, "Went to Mr. Toft's Lecture."

The movement thus inaugurated by Tufts was quickly taken in hand by other ministers. The first to publish anything was Rev. Thomas Symmes [35] of Bradford, Mass. No doubt influenced by Tufts, he introduced "regular" singing at an early date, precipitating a controversy. "A great part of the Town had for near half a year, been in a meer flame about it." So he delivered a discourse at a singing meeting in his own parish, and in other places as well, which he printed in 1720 (anonymously), entitled, *The Reasonableness of Regular Singing, or Singing by Note, in*

[34] Cotton Mather's *Diary* contains a briefer record of this occasion. Perhaps it was to this group of young musicians that one Timothy Burbank belonged. He was born in 1703 at Malden, and was a tailor's apprentice in Boston 1717–1724, attending the Brattle Square Church. In his old age at Plymouth, where he died at the age of ninety, he was wont to relate that he attended the first singing school and religious society which introduced singing by note at Boston. G. Hood, *History of Music in New England*, Boston, 1846, p. 141.

[35] Thomas, son of Rev. Zechariah Symmes, b. Bradford, Jan. 31, 1677/8; d. Bradford, Oct. 6, 1725. A.B. Harvard, 1698. He was minister at Boxford 1701–1708; at Bradford, 1708–1725.

an Essay to revive the true and ancient mode of Singing psalm-tunes according to the pattern of our New England psalm-books. In this discourse he points out the "neglect of singing psalms. . . . It is to be feared that singing must be wholly omitted in some places for want of skill if this art is not revived." He goes on to argue that "Singing by note is the most ancient way of singing" and had been in use among the first settlers, and urges ministers and schoolmasters to encourage this "innocent and profitable recreation" which would "divert young people . . . from learning *idle, foolish,* yea *pernicious songs* and *ballads.*"

Symmes followed this discourse with another aimed at the same target, *Concerning Prejudice in Matters of Religion,* in 1722, and in 1723 with a pamphlet, *Utile Dulci or a Joco-Serious Dialogue, concerning Regular Singing: Calculated for a Particular Town, (where it was publicly had, on Friday, Oct. 12, 1722) but may serve some other places in the same Climate, by Thomas Symmes, Philomusicus.* . . . *Of all Beasts, there is none (saith Aelian) that is not delighted with Harmony, but only the Ass. Playf. Introd. Pref. No science but Musick may enter the Doors of the Church. Ven. Beda. Boston: Printed by B. Green, for Samuel Gerrish, near the Brick Meeting House in Cornhill, 1723.*

This *Joco-Serious Dialogue* is easily the most entertaining pamphlet printed in this controversy, and the most illuminating in its revelations of the kind of opposition which confronted a progressive young minister in a country parish. After referring to his earlier printed discourses he says,

it being my purpose to encourage Singing Meetings in the Town in the long winter-Evenings . . . I projected . . . an *Answer* to all the *Objections* I could remember to have heard about this matter, and at a meeting call'd for that purpose to communicate it, to such as would give their Attendance . . .

tho' in all my Conversation with Mankind I have never ob-
serv'd a more Ridiculous and Groundless Controversy. . . .

He says that the discussion had reached a point where it was
no longer appropriate for the pulpit, and he proceeds to
put into the mouth of an imaginary antagonist the objections to the "new way" which had reached his ears, and to
answer them with a mingling of good-natured ridicule and
sound common sense. Although his opponent in the debate
is a man of straw, it is obvious that Symmes was listing actual
objections current in his parish. The list is amusing.

1. It is a new way, an unknown tongue.
2. It is not so melodious as the usual way.
3. There are so many tunes we shall never have done learning
   them.
4. The practice creates disturbances and causes people to
   behave indecently and disorderly.
5. It is Quakerish and Popish and introductive of instrumental
   music.
6. The names given to the notes are bawdy, yea blasphemous.
7. It is a needless way, since our fathers got to heaven without it.
8. It is a contrivance to get money.
9. People spend too much time learning it, they tarry out
   nights disorderly.
10. They are a company of young upstarts that fall in with
   this way, and some of them are lewd and loose persons.

Two of Symmes' answers to these objections will illustrate
the temper with which he met them. As to the names of
the notes being blasphemous he says,

Verily, my Friend, Apollo himself, that Laugh'd but once
a year, could never forbear Giggling again, at such Comical
Objections.

As to the "new way" being "Quakerish and Popish," he
replies,

. . . if the Papists sing a better Tune, or with a better Air, than we do, I'd as soon imitate them, and a thousand times sooner, then the Honestest man among you that had no skill in singing. . . . Singing by Rule won't in our Day, introduce Instrumental Musick, much less Quakerism and Popery. . . . Your usual way of Singing, would much sooner, dispose me to fall in with them, Because the Quakers don't Sing at all, and I should be out of the Noise of it; and the Papists sing much better. . . . You may depend upon it, that such as are not willing to be at the Cost of a Bell, to call the People together on the Lord's Day, and of a Man to ring it . . . will never be so extravagant as to lay out their Cash . . . to buy Organs, and pay an artist for playing on 'em.

Useful as were these pamphlets by Symmes, they were less important than the work of Rev. Thomas Walter [36] of Roxbury, who, like Mather Byles, was a grandson of Increase and a nephew of Cotton Mather. Like his cousin Mather Byles, he was a precocious and vivacious youth, but he died early. In 1721 he published a little book, *The Grounds and Rules of Musick Explained*, which went well beyond the ground covered by Tufts. It was fortified by "A Recommendatory Preface" signed by Increase Mather and fourteen other leading ministers of the older generation.[37] The music was printed in diamond notes with bar lines, for the first time in the colonies, and came

[36] Thomas Walter, b. Roxbury, Mass., Dec. 13, 1696; d. Roxbury, Jan. 10, 1724/5. A. B. Harvard, 1713; ordained 1718 as his father's colleague at Roxbury. At the time of the controversy over inoculation against smallpox he and two other young men were inoculated together at his uncle Cotton Mather's house, and some member of the opposing party tossed into their chamber a "granado," which fortunately failed to explode. His early death was a misfortune, for Charles Chauncey wrote of him that he was "one of the first three for extent and strength of genius and power New-England ever produced." I am indebted to Mr. Clifford K. Shipton for access to his unpublished sketch of Thomas Walter, prepared for the forthcoming volume of Sibley's *Harvard Graduates*.

[37] See Proc. Am. Antiq. Soc., XLII, 235–246, for editions.

from the printing press of James Franklin, whose younger brother, Benjamin, was then an apprentice in the shop, learning the printer's trade. The introduction explained the rules for reading music. The little book sold for four shillings, was very popular, and continued in use for forty years, when it was superseded by better publications.

Thomas Walter also preached and lectured in advocacy of "regular singing." The *New England Courant* for March 5, 1722, records that

On Thursday last in the afternoon, a Lecture was held at the New Brick Church, by the Society for Promoting Regular Singing in the Worship of God.[38] The Rev. Thomas Walter of Roxbury preach'd an excellent Sermon on that Occasion, *The Sweet Psalmist of Israel.* The Singing was perform'd in Three Parts (according to Rule) by about Ninety Persons skill'd in that Science, to the great Satisfaction of a Numerous Assembly there Present.

The full title page of this sermon is worth recording for its evidence of a musical organization in Boston. It runs, *The Sweet Psalmist of Israel: A Sermon Preach'd at the Lecture held in Boston, by the Society for promoting Regular and Good Singing, and for reforming the Depravations and Debasements our Psalmody labours under, In order to introduce the proper and true Old Way of Singing. . . . Printed by J. Franklin, for S. Gerrish, near the Brick Meeting House in Cornhill, 1722.* "Music," said the young preacher, "is in its own nature sweet and pleasant," and he goes on with many illustrations, Biblical and classical, to maintain that thesis. Naturally his emphasis is on music in the church, with suggestions for improving it, but there is not a single sentence in condemnation of secular music.

[38] This is the only mention of such a society which I have come across. Perhaps it was the same group as that to which Cotton Mather had preached the preceding year.

The sermon was dedicated to Paul Dudley, son of Governor Joseph Dudley and himself later Chief Justice, who was young Mr. Walter's leading parishioner.

The practical guides to music by these two young ministers, Tufts and Walter, though slight in form and elementary in substance, nevertheless served to reopen for provincial New Englanders the door to the appreciation of music which, in the course of nearly a century, had almost closed upon them. But the pioneer period, with its hardships and limitations which had effectually cut them off from the influence of musical culture, was past. They turned with surprised delight to what was to many of them the revelation of a new art. And that door was to remain open thereafter, giving access to a slowly augmenting love of music, until, in the latter part of the nineteenth century, Boston was the chief musical center in the country and the home of its most distinguished group of composers, the musical counterparts of the New England writers who preceded them by a generation.

The "flame" spread rapidly to other parishes, as the young people eagerly took up with the "new way" of singing. There is no way of telling how many ministers took an active part in promoting the movement by preaching or lecturing, but a great many must have done so when we note that in a dozen years there were published as many pamphlets on the subject, all by ministers, and all advocating "regular" singing. As they repeat many of the same arguments, it is necessary to refer to only a few of the more significant ones.

In 1722 Rev. Solomon Stoddard [39] published his *Cases of*

---

[39] Solomon Stoddard, b. Boston 1643; d. Northampton, Mass., 1729. A.B. Harvard 1662. He remained in Cambridge for eight years after graduation, then preached two years in Barbadoes, before settling in Northampton. He was the maternal grandfather of Jonathan Edwards, who was his colleague and successor.

Conscience about Singing Psalms, and preached a sermon "to stir up young men and maidens to praise the Lord." Inasmuch as most of the more active advocates of "regular" singing were relatively young ministers, it is worth noting that Stoddard was seventy-nine years old at this time.

Cotton Mather, whose sympathy with the movement has already been noted, sought to promote it by publishing his *Accomplished Singer*,[40] in which he complains that

in some of our congregations . . . singing has degenerated into an *odd noise*, that has more of what we want a name for, than any Regular Singing in it;

and he goes on with the true observation,

It is remarkable that when the kingdom of God has been making any new appearance, a mighty zeal for the singing of psalms has attended and assisted it. And may we see our people grow more zealous of this *good work*: what a hopeful sign of the times would be seen in it 'that *the time of singing has come, and the voice of the Turtle is heard in our land.*'

And in 1723 he published a *Pacificatory Letter*, designed to quiet the disturbances which had arisen in a number of parishes, of which we shall hear more presently. Mather reasons with them gently:

Those fond of old tunes should not be too stiff and wilful in their own opinion. . . . As for an *old* tune, or a *new* one, there is no more *Divinity* in one than in the other. It is said, those fond of new tunes, are for bringing indifferent things into the worship of God: it may equally be said, those fond of old tunes are for *continuing* indifferent things in the worship of God. . . . If you say, the most that are for new singing (as it is called) are generally of the younger set of people: what then? If they are willing to take pains

40 See Matt B. Jones, "Some Bibliographical Notes on Cotton Mather's 'The Accomplished Singer,'" Colonial Society of Mass. *Transactions*, XXVIII, 186–193.

and learn, that they may be better able to worship God by singing psalms, would you discourage them from this?

But perhaps the most important of these later writers was Rev. Nathaniel Chauncey,[41] who, on May 12, 1728, preached a very lengthy discourse before the General Association of Connecticut at Hartford. The Association heard, approved, and voted to have printed "Mr. Chauncey's Arguments for Regular Singing . . . Recommending them to the Publick." The sermon came out with the title, *Regular Singing Defended, and Proved to be the Only True Way of Singing the Songs of the Lord, . . . by Nathaniel Chauncey, N. London. 1728.* Evidently progress was being made when a Connecticut minister could argue that the "new way" was the *only true* way of singing in church. Chauncey has a long introduction to prove the usefulness of rules, or sound principles, in any activity, and says that for want of a rule in singing many persons

open not their Mouths to Praise God. And probably many more neglect it in their Families, because they know not how to sing. . . . The Rule being neglected as useless, the Performance is very mean. . . . It is as a flat Drink, compared with that which is lively, brisk and full of Spirit.

Then, very much in the fashion of Symmes in the *Utile Dulci* pamphlet, he takes up a series of "Objections" to the "new way" of singing, in which we can hear the voice of the conservative old deacons who were opposed to anything new. The "Objections" seem to have been very much the same all over New England, and by this time had been

[41] Nathaniel Chauncey, b. 1681, d. 1756, grandson of Charles Chauncey, second president of Harvard College. He was privately educated by his uncle, Rev. Israel Chauncey, and was in 1702 presented for a degree at the first Commencement of the newly founded Yale College, where an A.M. was granted him. He taught school, but from 1706 on preached at the newly organized town of Denham, Conn., though not ordained until 1711. Fellow of Yale College 1746–1752.

answered again and again. To the objection, "This Practice leads to the Church of England and will bring in Organs quickly," he replies,

There is nothing in the nature of the thing that leads to the Church of *England*. This Argument lies as hard against the common way of Singing, for they pretend to Sing the Tunes of the Church of *England*. Its a very strange thing that our Forefathers had no sense of their Danger and Hazard, but that after they were come into the Country, they should turn the Psalms into new Metre, and annex Rules to them to Sing them by.

Again, to the objection, "The very Original of this way was from the Papists. It came from Rome," he replies,

I deny not but the Gospel it self came from Rome to England, and its very probable that Singing came along with the Gospel. . . . If we must reject Regular Singing on that account, we must by the same reason reject the Gospel too. But as for the Original of Musick, that was before ever there was a Papist, or a Church of Rome in the World. . . . It is plain it was in use in Moses' time, and probably known and used before the Flood.

And finally, to the objection, "It looks very unlikely to be the right way, because that Young People fall in with it; they are not wont to be so forward for anything that is good," he answers,

As Old Men are not always wise, so Young Men are not always Fools. They are generally more free from Prejudices than Elderly People; their present Age disposes them to Mirth, and it should be a very Joyful and Acceptable thing unto Elderly People to see them forward to improve their Mirth according to Scripture directions.

In this, as in other pamphlets in this controversy, the tolerance, good temper and intelligent common sense of the ministers are conspicuous.

This series of publications, reinforced by many other unrecorded lectures and sermons, and by the establishment of singing schools, rapidly converted the New England churches to the "new way" of singing, in spite of bitter controversies in some parishes. But new-fangled ideas about the improvement of church music were as certain to arouse opposition then as they are today, and for the older and less progressive church members in the pews the "old way" was still the sacrosanct traditional New England way of psalm singing, which it was well-nigh blasphemous to alter.

It is impossible to say in how many churches an active controversy arose over this issue, but Cotton Mather wrote on November 5, 1723, to Thomas Hollis, the generous English benefactor of Harvard College:

A mighty Spirit came Lately upon abundance of our people, to Reform their singing which was degenerated in our Assemblies to an Irregularity which made a Jar in the ears of the more curious and skilful singers. Our Ministers generally Encouraged the people, to accomplish themselves for a Regular singing, and a more beautiful Psalmody. Such Numbers of good people, (and Especially young people) became Regular Singers, that they could carry it in the Congregations. But who would beleeve it? Tho' in the more polite City of *Boston*, this Design mett with a General acceptance, in the Countrey, where they have more of the *Rustick*, some Numbers of Elder and Angry people bore zelous Testimonies against these wicked Innovations, and this bringing in of Popery. Their zeal transported some of them so far (on the behalf of Mumpsimus) [42] that they would not only use the most approbrious Terms, and call the Singing of these Christians, a worshipping of the Devil, but also they would run out of the Meetinghouse at the Beginning of the Exercise. The Paroxyms have risen to that Heighth, as to

[42] Mumpsimus = an old fogey, one who clings obstinately to an old error or prejudice.

necessitate the Convening of several Ecclesiastical Councils, for the Composing of the Differences and Annimosities arisen on this occasion.[43]

As Mather says in this letter, the ministers generally advocated "regular" singing, and most of the opposition came from the elderly conservatives in the pews, but in one church, at least, the situation was reversed and, since it led to a vehement controversy, it may serve to illustrate the unhappy divisions which occurred in some other churches as well. Rev. Samuel Niles,[44] the minister at South Braintree, a dozen miles from Boston, was in all things a thoroughgoing conservative, of domineering temper and powerful physique. He was a minister who "customarily rode a horse that no parishioner could sit, and to whom were brought for breaking all the rebellious colts and young religious innovators of Braintree." John Adams recalled him as an "honest, virtuous and pious man," but when a majority of his congregation early in 1722 took up with the "new way" of "regular" singing he strongly opposed it, being the only minister of the day who is recorded as taking that stand. He printed nothing, though he no doubt gave vehement expression to his views from the pulpit, but he got more publicity than could have been pleasant in the columns of *The New England Courant*,[45] which

[43] Massachusetts Historical Society, VIII, 693.

[44] Samuel Niles, b. Block Island, May 1, 1674; d. Braintree, Mass., May 1, 1762; A.B. Harvard 1696; lived for a time at Kingston, R. I.; ordained minister at South Braintree, Mass., May 23, 1711. See Sibley, *Harvard Graduates*, IV, 485–491.

[45] *The New England Courant* was at this time "Printed and sold by Benjamin Franklin, in Queen St., Boston," but the youthful Benjamin was only a blind for his older brother James, the owner of the press, whose escapades as a publisher had led to the temporary suppression of his activities by the authorities. Probably the weekly "Letters to Janus," some of which were very coarse, were by several hands, but the Franklins very likely wrote some of them. There was a smouldering feud between the members of the Mather family and the Franklins, who had,

noted the progress of the controversy not only in legitimate news items but in its weekly satirical "Letters to Janus." [46]

By the end of the third decade of the century the excitement over "regular" singing had died down. The "new way" was generally accepted and, through the singing schools, it produced a real revival of singing in New England, and an awakening of interest in other forms of music as well.

The reasons for the lack of musical instruments in early New England have already been pointed out. But by 1700 growing prosperity and better means for shipment had led to the importation of an increasing number of such articles. In April, 1716, the *Boston News-Letter* contained the following advertisement:

This is to give notice that there is lately sent over from London a choice collection of Musickal Instruments, consisting of Flageolets, Flutes, Haut-Boys, Bass-Viols, Violins, Bows, Strings, Reeds for Haut-Boys, Books of Instructions for all these Instruments, Books of Ruled Paper. To be sold at the Dancing School of Mr. Enstone [47] in Sudbury Street near the Orange Tree, Boston.

Note. Any person may have all Instruments of Musick mended, or Virginalls and Spinnets Strung and Tuned at a reasonable Rate, and likewise may be taught to Play on any of these Instruments above mentioned; dancing taught by a true and easier method than has been heretofore.

This advertisement leaves no doubt that by 1716 there were "Virginalls and Spinnets" in Boston to be tuned, or that

---

among other things, attacked Cotton Mather for his promotion of the practice of inoculation for smallpox. In *A Collection of Poems by Several Hands*, published in Boston in 1744, partly the work of Mather Byles, there are two satirical poems on "The Death of Old Janus," celebrating the disappearance of *The New England Courant*.

[46] For the details of this tempest in a teapot the reader is referred to Appendix B.

[47] Edward Enstone was organist at King's Chapel at this time.

young people might learn to dance, without let or hindrance, presumably to the fiddle of the dancing master.

The earliest record of a public concert in any of the English-speaking American colonies appeared in the *Boston News-Letter* for December 16–23, 1731, and was followed by others at not infrequent intervals. Generally the proceeds went to charity. Thus in 1744 "a number of gentlemen" requested "the Use of Faneuil Hall for a Concert of Musick . . . The benefit arising by the Tickets to be for the Use of the Poor of the Town as the Select men shall direct." The program has not been preserved so we do not know whether the music was choral or orchestral, but the occasion must have been highly popular for the "Benefit arising by the Tickets" came to the astonishing sum of £205.5.0.[48]

The awakening of interest in instrumental music had no immediate effect upon the churches, yet to it, and to the singing schools, was no doubt due the introduction first of pitch pipes, and then of bass viols to support the singing. In church the congregation might be reluctant to admit the all too evident need of such aids in setting the right pitch, in spite of the frequent and lamentable failures of the precentor, but when the singing school met in the schoolhouse there was no objection to the use of a pitch pipe to set the pitch or of a bass viol to support the singing. But the young people, once accustomed to such instrumental support, naturally desired it when they sat in the singers' gallery in church. So the pitch pipe was introduced, almost by stealth perhaps, and then, usually, the bass viol — "the Lord's fiddle," because it became so much associated with psalm singing, whereas the violin had secular associations with dancing.

---

[48] For a more detailed account of the development of secular music in Boston see O. G. Sonneck, *Early Concert Life in America*, pp. 250–323, and H. W. Foote, *Musical Life in Boston in the Eighteenth Century*. Proc. American Antiquarian Society, October, 1939.

There was, of course, opposition of the same sort that had been made to "regular" singing, and meetinghouses in which bass viols were used were derided as "catgut churches." Sometimes members of a congregation would leave the meetinghouse in indignation when the instrument was introduced. But by the latter part of the century such instrumental accompaniment of singing became general, and in some instances the church or the town bought and kept in the meetinghouse a bass viol for use at the Sunday services, until eventually it bought an organ. Thus the town of Bedford, Massachusetts, in the late eighteenth century, owned a tuning pipe keyed on A; in 1798 it appropriated $20 for the singing school; and in 1815 the "town's viol" was placed in the hands of Deacon James Wright "for the purpose of assisting in taking the lead in sacred music." In 1818 the town voted to employ Leander Hosmer "to perform sacred music for said town for ten dollars per year, on a Bass Viol, and furnish himself with a Viol." A viol, said to be the one used by Hosmer, is still preserved at the church, and was used to supplement a small organ as late as about 1880.

So long as the churches clung to *The Bay Psalm Book* and the old psalm tunes of the sixteenth and seventeenth centuries they continued to use the booklets by Tufts and Walter. An edition of Walter's *Introduction* was printed as late as 1764, but by that date it had been superseded by far better compilations. The first of these was: *Urania: Or a choice collection of Psalm Tunes, Anthems or Hymns, from the most approved authors, with some entirely new: In two, three, and four parts; The whole peculiarly adapted to the use of churches and families. To which are prefaced the plainest and most necessary Rules of Psalmody. By James Lyon, A.B. Philadelphia, Price 15 S. 1762.*

This was the first book in the interest of better church music to be published outside of Boston, or as a commercial venture rather than under ministerial auspices, although

Lyon later became a Presbyterian minister, but it contains a dedication appealing for patronage addressed "To the Clergy of Every Denomination in America." There were twelve pages of instruction, and some two hundred pages of handsomely engraved music, ninety of which were given to anthems. Six tunes were by James Lyon, the editor, who missed being our first native-born American composer only because his contemporary and fellow townsman, Francis Hopkinson, published a few songs some months before *Urania* appeared. About half the psalm tunes were in the old style; the rest in the lighter and fuguing style which was coming into vogue in England. This was the first appearance of tunes in this style printed in America. The musical editing, however, was bad.

Two years later Josiah Flagg [49] produced a Boston rival to *Urania* entitled: *A Collection of the best Psalm Tunes, in two, three and four parts; from the most approved authors, fitted to all measures, and approved of by the best masters in Boston, New England; to which are added some Hymns and Anthems; the greater part of them never before printed in America. By Josiah Flagg. Engraved by Paul Revere: Printed and sold by him and Josiah Flagg, Boston, 1764.*

This book was somewhat smaller than *Urania*, containing one hundred and sixteen tunes and two anthems, from varied sources, mostly English, but some American. The music was engraved on copper plates by Paul Revere, and, as in *Urania*, was badly harmonized. In view of the fact that *Urania* was the only other American book in the field printed since Walter's *Musick Explained*, published forty-

---

[49] Flagg was not only a compiler and publisher of music; he also was manager for both vocal and instrumental concerts, who included in his programs music by Bach and Handel. See C. M. Ayars, *Contribution to the Art of Music in America by the Music Industries of Boston, 1640–1936*, New York, 1937, p. 4.

three years earlier, it is curious that Flagg should have "thought necessary, that some apology should be made, for offering the public, a new collection of Psalm-tunes, at a time when there are already so many among us." The rising tide of patriotism in Boston is perhaps indicated by the fact that the publishers used paper made in America. Flagg wrote:

It is hoped, it will not diminish the value of the book in the estimation of any, but may in some degree commend it, even to those who have no peculiar relish for the music, that however we are obliged to the other side of the Atlantic chiefly, for our tunes, the paper on which they are printed, is the manufacture of our own country.

In the same year Daniel Bayley of Newburyport brought out a smaller book, with thirty-four tunes, mostly in the old style, yet three editions were called for in the year of publication.

With the publication of *Urania* a new epoch in church music had begun, and a flood of music books began which continued to the middle of the next century. It coincided with, and was, no doubt, in part due to the passing of *The Bay Psalm Book* and the adoption of Watts' *Psalms* and *Hymns*, which will be discussed in Chapter V. The rapidity with which the number of music books increased is indicated by the fact that Hood prints in his *History of Music in New England* (1846), a list of about forty such books issued between 1774 and 1799, mostly from Boston, though a few were published elsewhere.

The story of these publications, and of the far greater number which followed in the early years of the nineteenth century, belongs to the history of American music rather than of hymnody, and the theme has been pursued thus far only to trace the development from the early psalmody to the music which accompanied the introduction of hymn singing. But before taking up the transition from psalmody to hymnody it is worth while to glance for a moment at a picturesque figure who played a leading part in the musical life of New England in the Revolutionary period. Williams Billings,[50] a Boston tanner, was an enthusiastic though self-taught musician with a stentorian voice, unbounded energy, and a patriotic spirit which was determined to liberate America from slavish adherence to the music of the Old World. She should produce her own music, and he would help her to do it. He wrote his first tunes with chalk on the walls of the building in which he worked, while tending the mill which ground bark for tanning. Presently he began to travel about, putting new enthusiasm into the singing schools and amazing the country folk by a magical ability not only to conceive new tunes in his own head but to put them down on paper so that other people could sing them. He was rather vaguely aware that there were rules of musical composition which were followed in Europe, but he preferred to ignore them. His peculiar views are indicated in his remarks "To all Musicall Practitioners" in the preface of his first book.

Perhaps it may be expected by some, that I should say something concerning Rules of Composition; to these I answer that *Nature is the best Dictator*, for all the hard dry studied rules that ever were prescribed, will not enable any person to form an air, any more than the bare knowledge of the four and twenty letters, and strict grammatical Rules will qualify a Scholar for composing a piece of Poetry . . . For my part, as I don't think myself confined to any Rules for Composition laid down by any that went before me, neither should I think (were I to pretend to lay down rules) that any who come after me were in any ways obliged to adhere to them,

[50] William Billings, b. Oct. 17, 1748, at Boston; d. Sept. 26, 1800, at Boston.

any further than they should think proper: So in fact I think it best that Every Composer should be his own Carver.

Being enamored with the effects of the florid counterpoint which had come into use in the Handelian era, he broke away from staid tradition of New England psalmody and introduced his pupils to what he called "fuguing" tunes, though they were not really fugues at all, but are more properly described as "imitative counterpoint." The entire contents of both his books were hymn tunes or anthems of his own composition. He is credited with some 260 compositions, and they were sometimes set to novel words, as his piece,

Swift as an Indian arrow flies.

It is true that his music was "melodic and cheerful; it was strongly rhythmic, and, for all its 'fuguing' was easily memorized; it was not above the heads of his public." [51] In his first preface he claimed for his music,

It has more than twenty times the power of the old slow tunes, each part straining for mastery and victory, the audience entertained and delighted, their minds surpassingly agitated and extremely fluctuated, sometimes declaring for one part, and sometimes for another. Now the solemn bass demands their attention, next the manly tenor; now the lofty counter, now the volatile treble. Now here, now there; now here again, — O ecstatic! Rush on, you sons of harmony!

It was in 1770 that Billings brought out his first book, *The New England Psalm-Singer, or American Chorister, Containing a number of Psalm-Tunes, Anthems and Canons. In Four and Five Parts (never before published). Composed by William Billings, a Native of Boston, in New England.*

[51] Louis C. Elson, *History of American Music*, New York, 1925 ed., pp. 12, 19.

Math. 21¹⁶ Out of the Mouth of Babes and Sucklings hast thou perfected Praise. James 5¹³ Is any Merry? Let him sing Psalms.

> *O, praise the Lord with one consent,*
> *And in this grand design,*
> *Let Britain and the Colonies*
> *Unanimously join.*

Boston in New England. Printed by Edes and Gill.

The frontispiece was engraved by Paul Revere and shows six men sitting about a table, led by a seventh, and was entitled, "A Canon of 6 in One with a Ground, the Words by Yᵉ Rev'd Dr. Byles: Set to Music by W. Billings." It was surrounded by a strip of music with the first stanza of a hymn. This book includes Byles', "New England Hymn," of which the first and last stanzas run,

> To Thee the tuneful Anthem soars,
>   To Thee, our Fathers' God, and ours;
> The Wilderness we chose our Seat;
> To Rights secur'd by Equal Laws
> From Persecution's Iron Claws,
>   Here we have sought our calm Retreat.
>
> .   .   .   .
>
> Lord, guard thy favours; Lord, extend
>   Where farther Western Suns descend;
> Nor Southern Seas the Blessings bound;
> Till Freedom lift her cheerful Head,
> Till pure Religion onward spread,
>   And beaming, wrap the Globe around.

Byles seems to have been as eager to assist his fellow townsman in the promotion of the new type of music as he had been to aid Smibert in the introduction of art forty years earlier, for the book also includes a poem "from a miscellany of the Rev. Dr. Byles," descriptive of the "fuguing" tunes, in which Byles put into sonorous verse the claims which Billings had made in his preface.

> Down steers the *Bass* with grave majestic air,
> And up the *Treble* mounts with shrill career;
> With softer Sounds, in mild Melodious Maze,
> Warbling between, the *Tenor* gently Plays:
> But if th' aspiring *Altus* join in Force,
> See! like the Lark, it Wings its Tow'ring Course;
> Through Harmony's sublimest Sphere it flies,
> And to Angelic Accents seems to rise;
> From the bold Height it hails the echoing *Bass*,
> Which swells to meet, and mix in close embrace.
> Tho' diff'rent Systems all the Parts divide,
> With Music's Chords the distant Notes are ty'd;
> And Sympathetic Strains enchanting winde
> Their restless Race, till all the Parts are join'd:
> Then rolls the Rapture thro' the air around
> In the full Magic Melody of Sound.

Billings' tunes had a vogue during the Revolutionary period which may perhaps be compared with that of the gospel songs a hundred years later. His tune *Chester* was more sung during the Revolution than any other music, for the words to which it was set expressed the patriotic fervor:

> Let tyrants shake their iron rod,
> And slavery clank her galling chains,
> We fear them not, we trust in God,
> New England's God forever reigns.
>
> .   .   .   .
>
> The foe comes on with haughty stride,
> Our troops advance with martial noise,
> Their Vet'runs flee before our Youth,
> And Generals yield to beardless Boys.

Almost as well-known was his imitation of the 137th Psalm, written at the time of the siege of Boston:

> By the Rivers of Watertown we sat down and wept,
> When we remembered thee, O Boston,
>
> .   .   .   .
>
> A voice was heard in Roxbury,
> Which echoed through the continent,
> Weeping for Boston, because of their danger.

It will be guessed that Billings, though not in the army, was no milksop pacifist.

It is needless to say that Billings' music, though immensely popular, seems shockingly illiterate to the modern trained musician. Billings himself recognized some of its weaknesses. When in 1778 he brought out his even more influential book, *The Singing-Master's Assistant*, he referred to his first book as "this infant production of my own Numb-Skull" and said, "I have discovered that many of the pieces in that book were never worth my printing, or your inspection." Nevertheless he did a great deal to stimulate the second revival of singing in eighteenth-century New England. He insisted upon the use of a pitch pipe to set the tune, and of the bass viol to aid the singing, and was strongly opposed to "lining-out," which was indeed impossible with his own lively "fuguing" melodies. His influence and the character of his music gave the finishing touch to that old custom, which, whatever its early justification, had long outlived its usefulness. The singing school which he established in Stoughton, Massachusetts, in 1774, developed into the Stoughton Musical Society, which is now the oldest musical association in this country. And it learned to sing far greater music than that of its teacher. About 1790 there was a music contest between it and the singers of the First Church in Dorchester, who were supported by a bass viol, but the Stoughton group won when they sang Handel's Hallelujah Chorus without an instrument and without books.

Billings' tunes lasted long in rural New England and spread to the West and South, where some of them survive in the folk hymnody still sung there, but their involved and boisterous character soon produced in Boston a reaction in favor of more staid and musically correct church music. As early as 1791 Samuel Holyoke wrote in the preface to his *Harmonia Americana*,

> Perhaps some may be disappointed that fuguing pieces are in general omitted. But the principle reason why few were inserted was the trifling effect produced by that sort of music; for the parts, falling in one after another, each conveying a different idea, confound the sense, and render the performance a mere jargon of words.

Billings died, it is regrettable to say, in poverty, and is buried in an unmarked grave in the Boston Common Burying-Ground. Two days after his death Rev. William Bentley, of Salem, wrote of him in his *Diary*,

> He may justly be considered as the father of our New England music. Many who have imitated have excelled him, but none of them had better original power. He was a singular man, of moderate size, short of one leg, with one eye, without any address, and with uncommon negligence of person. Still he spake and sang and thought as a man above the common abilities.

The music books by Billings were followed by a number of others, mostly of much higher quality, but only one tune composed by an American of this period survives in modern use. The composer was Oliver Holden,[52] of

---

[52] Oliver Holden, b. Shirley, Mass., Sept. 18, 1765; d. Charlestown, Mass., Sept. 4, 1844. He came to Charlestown as a carpenter, went into real estate, was a representative in the Legislature, owned a music store,

Charlestown, a better musician than Billings. He had a hand in producing *The Massachusetts Compiler*, a collection of tunes published in 1794 or 1795, described by a modern critic (Oscar Sonneck) as "the most progressive work on Psalmody which appeared in America before 1800." In his earlier collection, *The Union Harmony*, 1793, appeared the tune *Coronation*, which he had composed on his little pipe organ, still to be seen in the Old State House in Boston. *Coronation* is the earliest American hymn tune still in general use. Holden was also a hymn writer of considerable ability. His best-known hymn in its original form began,

> All those who seek the throne of grace,

but in *The Springfield Collection* (1835) it was recast in a different metre and in this form had long-continued use in America, and to some extent in England.

> They who seek the throne of grace,
> Find that and more in every place;
> If we live a life of prayer,
> God is present everywhere.
>
> .   .   .   .
>
> Then, my soul, in every strait
> To thy Father come and wait;
> He will answer every prayer;
> God is present everywhere.

Let us summarize the facts which have been discussed in this chapter. We have observed that it was in Puritan Boston — not in New York or Philadelphia, in Virginia or Charleston, South Carolina — that there appeared the first music printed in the English colonies in North America;

---

led singing schools and the choir of the Baptist church, and compiled several singing books.

the first book of instruction in singing; the first book printed with modern musical notation; the first discourses advocating better singing in the churches — a dozen of them between 1720 and 1727, all by Puritan divines. During the same period the earliest American singing schools were established in New England. In all this movement for better singing the ministers took the lead. Furthermore, the first organ imported into the English-speaking colonies came to Boston before 1711; and the first organ made in the colonies by a native-born American was built in Boston before 1746. The earliest concert of instrumental music recorded in any of the colonies was held in Boston in 1731, and thereafter such concerts were more frequent here than in almost any other colonial center. In the last forty years of the eighteenth century by far the larger part of the many music books which introduced into this country the new music of the Handelian era were published in Boston. In view of these facts is it not time that the groundless slander that "the Puritans hated music" should be allowed to die an unlamented death?

CHAPTER IV

The Early Hymns and Tunes of the German Settlers in Pennsylvania

A STRIKING CONTRAST to the general decline of
singing and the meagre musical resources in all the
English-speaking colonies down to at least the second quarter of the eighteenth century is found among the Swedish,
and, in much more notable degree, among the German-
speaking settlers in Pennsylvania. Some of these, conspicuously the Moravians at Bethlehem, were remarkable for
their singing, orchestral music and hymnbooks. Their
example had, however, curiously little influence upon their
English-speaking neighbors, and hardly any discernible
effect upon American hymnody in general. It is, nevertheless, a notable and commonly overlooked phase of
colonial life which richly deserves to be recorded.[1]

Swedish Lutherans (with some Finns) settled New
Sweden at Fort Christina, within the present limits of Wil-
mington, on the Delaware River, in 1638. In 1655 the
Dutch from New Amsterdam annexed the colony, and
were in turn superseded by the English in 1664. The
Swedish settlers were undisturbed in their possessions and
religious practices and before 1700 had two churches, of
which the more important was the Gloria Dei Church at

[1] The best account is to be found in *Church Music and Musical Life
in Pennsylvania in the Eighteenth Century*, prepared by the Committee on
Historical Research of the Pennsylvania Society of the Colonial Dames of
America, Philadelphia, 1927, from which the information summarized in
this chapter has been drawn.

Wicaco, still standing, in what is now Philadelphia. In the early years their ministry was supplied by occasional Swedish missionaries sent out from the home-land. When Gloria Dei Church was consecrated in 1700 it had no organ, but there were fifty copies of the "Upsala Hymn Book," sent out by the King of Sweden in 1696. There was another royal gift of three hundred "Swedish psalm-books" in 1704, and a third of four hundred books in 1712, intended for distribution among other Swedish churches in the colony. Services were conducted in Swedish, German and English. In 1743 a visitor reported that the Swedes sang their hymns "astonishingly well."

In 1700 one Justus Falckner [2] emigrated from Germany to Pennsylvania. While at Halle he had been associated with the Pietist August Hermann Francke, who had included several of Falckner's hymns in his *Geistreiches Gesang Buch* (Halle, 1697). The most noted of these hymns, set to the tune *Meine Hoffnung*, is described as "a stirring composition" beginning,

> Auf! ihr Christen, Christi Gleider.

It came into extended use both in Germany and among Germans in America and is still included in Lutheran hymnbooks in both countries. [3]

Soon after he reached Philadelphia he and his brother David joined the Pietists at Wissahickon. The year after his arrival he wrote a letter back to Germany reporting his observations. This letter was printed and a unique copy is preserved in the archives of the University of Rostock. In the course of it he pleads that an organ be

[2] Justus Falckner, b. at Langenreinsdorf, Saxony, 1672, son and grandson of Lutheran pastors. Studied at the universities of Leipzig and Halle; emigrated in 1700; d. at Philadelphia, 1723. *Church Music and Musical Life in Pennsylvania*, I, 166–183.

[3] Translated as, "Rise, ye children of salvation," it appeared in several English hymnbooks, and in *Laudes Domini*, New York, 1884.

sent out for use in Gloria Dei Church. Among his arguments he says,

> It would not only attract and civilize the wild Indian, but it would do much good in spreading the Gospel truths among the sects and others by attracting them. . . . Thus a well-sounding organ would prove of great profit, to say nothing of the fact that the Indians would come running from far and near to listen to such unknown melody, and upon that account might become willing to accept our language and teaching, and remain with people who had such agreeable things; for they are said to come ever so far to listen to one who plays even upon a reed-pipe; such an extraordinary love have they for any melodious and ringing sound.

This comment upon the Indians' fondness for music is an interesting corroboration of the observations of Francis Drake's chaplain on the Pacific Coast and of the Puritans in New England.

On Nov. 24, 1703, Falckner was ordained as a Lutheran minister in Gloria Dei Church,[4] according to the Swedish ritual, with all the ceremony that the colonists could muster. Falckner's friends at Wissahickon provided music with viols, hautboys, trumpets and kettledrums, and a small organ. Since the records of Gloria Dei Church make no mention of an organ having been received in response to Falckner's letter of two years earlier, it seems probable that the organ was loaned for the occasion by the Ger-

---

[4] On the two-hundredth anniversary of this occasion Dr. Sachse gave an address with the following title: *Justus Falckner, Mystic and Scholar, Devout Pietist in Germany, Hermit on the Wissahickon, Missionary on the Hudson. A Bi-Centennial Memorial of the First Regular Ordination of an Orthodox Pastor in America, done November 24, 1703, at Gloria Dei, the Swedish Lutheran Church at Wicaco, Philadelphia.*

The claim that Falckner was the first "orthodox pastor" to receive "regular ordination" in America is, of course, quite untenable, unless the words "in the Lutheran Church" are understood or added.

mans. In any case, this appears to be the earliest definite record of the use of an organ in any church in the colonies on the North Atlantic coast.

The German-speaking settlers came in several small groups and represented several sects. Mennonites settled Germantown in 1683; Labadists settled in New Castle County in 1684; a group of Pietists settled in 1694 in the Wissahickon valley, now a parkway within the limits of Philadelphia but then several miles from the city; Dunkards (German Baptists) appeared at Germantown in 1719; the Ephrata Community, which soon absorbed many of the Pietists of Wissahickon, was established in 1720 on the Cocalico; the Schwenkfelders arrived in 1734; and the Moravians, the first of whom had emigrated to Savannah, Georgia, in 1735, moved to Philadelphia in 1740 and thence to their wilderness settlement at Bethlehem, Pennsylvania, in 1741. Of these small groups of German sectarians the most interesting musical activity is found among the Mennonites, the Pietists of Wissahickon, the Ephrata Community, the Schwenkfelders and the Moravians.

All of these groups presumably brought with them the German hymnbooks which they were accustomed to use, and they had been bred in the great tradition of some two centuries of Lutheran hymnody, whereas the English colonists were limited by the narrow Calvinistic tradition to the use of psalmody alone. They came from a land where instrumental music was far more general among all classes than was the case in England a century (more or less) earlier at the time of the emigration of the first English settlers. And shipping facilities were better, so that space was not too precious to allow them to bring their musical instruments with them. Later arrivals brought to them a steady stream of both new instruments and new musical scores. Furthermore, unlike the first settlers in Virginia, Massachusetts or Connecticut, they did not confront the untamed wilderness immediately upon landing, for they came first to small towns — generally to Philadelphia — which provided some shelter and opportunity to gather up their strength before they went on to establish a new community. Even that task was somewhat easier than for the settlers of New England, for the climate was less severe and the land more fertile. And, finally, although they were people who, having known more or less religious persecution at home, had come in search of religious liberty, and whose lives were as completely dominated by religion as any Puritans, they were accustomed to regard both vocal and instrumental music as fitting expressions of religious emotion as well as their chief source of recreation.[5] All these reasons contributed to the great differences between the musical life of the German-speaking and that of the English-speaking settlers.

The earliest Germans to reach America were the Mennonites who arrived in successive groups between 1683 and 1748, the first group coming from Crefeld on the lower Rhine. They settled chiefly in Philadelphia and Germantown. Their hymnbook was *Das Ausbund: Das ist Etliche Schöne Christliche Lieder*, which had first been published in Schaffhausen, in 1583, and was reprinted at Basle as late as 1838. An edition was printed for them in 1742 by Christopher Saur at Germantown, and again in 1751, 1767, and 1785. Altogether there have been more than a dozen American reprints, and the book is still used by the Amish of Pennsylvania.[6] The Mennonites clung closely to their traditional hymnody and it does not appear

---

[5] The Moravians still like to repeat the story of the New Englander who visited Bethlehem and who criticized the Brethren for using the same instruments for making music at divine worship on Sunday that they used for secular music on Saturday, to which the Brethren replied, "We use the same mouth to eat with on Sunday as on Saturday."

[6] *Church Music and Musical Life in Pennsylvania*, Phila., 1927, II, 14.

that they composed any orginal hymns or tunes in this country.

Perhaps the earliest practical musician to emigrate to America was Johannes Kelpius,[7] who reached Philadelphia in June, 1694, with a small band of Pietists, or Rosicrucians, and soon after settled in the rocky valley of the Wissahickon, near by. He wrote, concerning the voyage to America,

> Our exercises on board the ship consisted in discourses of various kinds and interpretations of Scripture, in which those who felt inclined took part. We also had prayer meetings and sang hymns of praise and joy, several of us accompanying on instruments we had brought from London.[8]

Kelpius left behind him a manuscript book of seventy pages containing twelve German hymns with melodies, which has survived, with English paraphrases attributed to Christopher Witt. It is difficult to determine the exact date of these compositions, or whether, indeed, they are all by Kelpius, since four others of the same group, Heinrich Bernard Köster, Johann Gottfried Seelig, and the brothers David and Justus Falckner, also wrote hymns. In any case this collection by Kelpius appears to contain both the earliest music and the first hymns (as distinguished from paraphrases of the psalms) written in the North American colonies. It was not printed until it was reproduced, in facsimile, in Volume I of *Church Music and Musical Life in Pennsylvania in the Eighteenth Century* (1926). Another collection of manuscript hymns, without music, undoubtedly by the same members of the Hermits of the Wissahickon, is owned by the Historical Society of Pennsylvania. From it nineteen hymns by Kelpius can

[7] Johannes Kelpius, b. in Transylvania, 1763; graduated from the University of Altdorf, 1689; emigrated 1694; d. 1708.

[8] *Op. cit.* I, pp. 10–11.

be identified, though only seven are complete; thirteen are doubtful as to authorship; four are by Seelig. One of Seelig's hymns, "Der einsamen Turtel-tauber," is dated July, 1707, and signed "J. G. S." The simile of the solitary turtledove singing in the silent woods was later used for the title of a hymnbook issuing from the Ephrata Cloister, as we shall presently see.

Kelpius also refers to an organ, which he may have brought with him in 1694, and it is surmised that it may have been this organ which was loaned to Gloria Dei Church for the ordination of Justus Flackner, already referred to. The Wissahickon group also possessed a virginal, as well as other musical instruments, and no doubt furnished most of the orchestral music for the ordination service. Furthermore, Dr. Christopher Witt,[9] who joined the Pietists in 1704, is said to have been an organ builder, and to have constructed an organ while at Wissahickon. Perhaps it was this instrument which was the one installed at Christ Church, Philadelphia, in 1728, and which was purchased from one of the survivors of the group. The vestry minutes report the purchase for £200 from "Sprogel" of "an organ lately arrived here," but the phrase may mean either that the organ had arrived from Europe, or that it had been transported from Wissahickon to Philadelphia.

The Wissahickon settlement lasted about twenty years before dispersal. Some of the group remained in the neighborhood and others joined the Ephrata Cloister. This community, which may be regarded as the successor of the Wissahickon settlement, established itself on the Coca-

---

[9] Christopher Witt, b. in Wiltshire, England, 1675; emigrated 1704; after the abandonment of the Wissahickon settlement he lived in Germantown, where he d. 1765. He was the last survivor of the Hermits of the Wissahickon. He planted a botanical garden at Germantown. He possessed a pipe organ of his own construction; is probably responsible for the English paraphrases of Kelpius' German hymns; and painted a small portrait of Kelpius, now at the Pennsylvania Historical Society.

lico, in Pennsylvania, in 1720. It was a celibate, conventual community of both men and women, not dissimilar to the Shaker Communities in New England a century later. It was remarkable in many respects, not least for the excellence of its singing, for the number and variety of the hymns written by its members, and for the beauty of its hand-written and illuminated hymnbooks, many pages of which are reproduced in *Church Music and Musical Life in Pennsylvania in the Eighteenth Century*. The copying and illuminating were done by women, who worked with speed and great skill, carrying on in America in the eighteenth century the methods and traditions of the medieval monastic scribes. The members of the Ephrata Cloister also edited hymnbooks which were published for them by Benjamin Franklin in 1730 and later, and by Christopher Saur of Germantown in 1739.

In 1747 one of their number, Conrad Beissel,[10] brought out *Das Gesang der einsammen und verlassen Turtel-Taube* (The Song of the solitary and forsaken Turtle-Dove), to which he added instructions on the use of the voice, and a rather crude and inaccurate dissertation on harmony, and in which he included many of his own compositions. The interest of these last lies in the fact that they are among the earliest attempts on American soil to compose sacred music, though Beissel had been preceded at least by Kelpius in this activity. Later he brought out another book, *Paradisisches Wunder-Spiel*, the second edition of which (1766) contained 725 hymns, of which seventy-two are by Beissel, and many others by other members of the community. One of them runs to 215 stanzas! Towards the close of the eighteenth century the Ephrata Cloister came

---

[10] Conrad Beissel, b. Eberbach in the Palatinate, 1690; emigrated 1720; soon after joined the Ephrata Cloister, becoming head of the community; d. July 6, 1768. He is said to have composed 1000 pieces of music and 441 hymns.

to an end, through the dying-off of its members and the failure to recruit new ones. That is the fate of all such celibate conventual communities which do not have a large and strong church behind them.

The Schwenkfelders were a group of some forty families who migrated first from Silesia to Saxony and thence to Pennsylvania in 1734. They appear to have brought with them manuscript collections of hymns, many copies of which are extant. Their first printed hymnbook in this country, *Neu-Eingerichtetes Gesang-Buch*, was published for them by Christopher Saur of Germantown in 1762.

The latest and most important of these successive groups of immigrants were the Moravians. They were members of the *Unitas Fratrum* (United Brethren), which had arisen among the followers of John Hus of Bohemia in the fifteenth century. They were long known as "Bohemian Brethren," and at the time of the Reformation had over four hundred churches in Bohemia, Moravia, and Poland.[11] John Hus had encouraged lay singing in church, had translated Latin hymns into Bohemian, and had written at least six original hymns. He had begun singing as a choirboy, and he died singing in the flames. His followers, therefore, had a stirring tradition behind them.

Their first collection of hymns was published in 1501. It was a small book, of which one imperfect copy remains. A larger book of four hundred hymns, including both original compositions and translations, appeared in 1505, but no copy is extant. Their first hymnbook in Polish appeared in 1554. The first hymnbook of the *Unitas Fratrum* in German appeared in 1561, with the Bohemian hymns freely translated. An enlarged edition, in 1566, included hymns by Luther. After the conquest of Bohemia

[11] For a summary account of this movement see Julian, *Dictionary of Hymnology*, "Bohemian Hymnody," pp. 153–160.

by Austria in 1620, the Brethren were bitterly persecuted and their members were scattered far and wide, maintaining a precarious existence. In 1722 a small group of "the hidden seed" which had kept together in Moravia made their escape to the estate of Count Zinzendorf, at Berthelsdorf, in Saxony, where the colony called Herrnhut was founded. Because this group came from Moravia they were popularly called "Moravian Brethren," and the name has stuck, although a large proportion of later members of the *Unitas Fratrum* were of other nationalities. The first refugees were followed by others during the succeeding nine years, and were joined by other persons from various parts of Germany, and elsewhere, who were attracted by the hope of religious freedom under Zinzendorf's protection. The Count assumed the leadership of the movement and became the second founder of the *Unitas Fratrum*, which he transformed from an almost extinct secret society into a far-flung missionary church with stations in many parts of the world.

Count Zinzendorf [12] was a very remarkable man, of distinguished ancestry and high standing, who had been reared in the German Pietism of the period. He was a prolific hymn writer, his first hymn having been written when he was a boy of twelve, his last only five days before his death at the age of sixty. His first collections of hymns were published between 1725 and 1731, but his contribution to the hymnody of the *Unitas Fratrum* began with his collection of 999 hymns published in 1735. This book, entitled *Gesang-Buch der Gemeine in Herrnhut*, contains

[12] Nicholas Ludwig, Count von Zinzendorf, b. Dresden, 1700; educated at the Paedogogium at Halle, 1710–16, and at the Univ. of Wittenberg, 1716–19. Studied law, but turned to religion. Bishop of the *Unitas Fratrum*, 1734. Exiled from Saxony 1738–47, during which period he travelled extensively, including the West Indies and Pennsylvania (1741–42). Returned to Herrnhut where he died, 1760. See Julian, *Dictionary of Hymnology*, pp. 1301–1305, 1597.

128 hymns by Zinzendorf, and most of the others were drawn from his earlier collections. It is the cornerstone of the later Moravian books, of which the most important, in the eighteenth century, was that published in 1778, by Christian Gregor, *Gesangbuch zum Gebrauch der Evangelischen Bruedergemein.* This last contained no less than 1750 hymns, drawn from many sources.

Zinzendorf was thus not only the second founder of the *Unitas Fratrum,* but must be credited with giving a fresh impulse to the hymnody which has been so marked a characteristic of the Brethren. He wrote with great facility, was very diffuse, and was often very sentimental, but his best hymns have had enduring value. Some of them have been translated, and were introduced into English use, chiefly by James Montgomery in his *Christian Psalmist,* 1825. "The keynote of Zinzendorf's hymns, and of his religious character, was a deep and earnest personal devotion to, and fellowship with the crucified Saviour." [13] He has had a place in Germany hymnody not wholly unlike that of Charles Wesley in English hymnody, but, unfortunately, he lacked a brother John to restrain his too effusive imagination and to prune his exuberant verse. He enters the field of American hymnody not only because of his commanding influence over the Moravian settlements here, but because of the extraordinary coincidence by which the Wesleys sailed to Georgia on the same ship with a band of Moravian missionaries, with very important consequences, and because, when Zinzendorf came to Pennsylvania a few years later, he wrote hymns here as John Wesley had done in Georgia.

The *Unitas Fratrum* at Herrnhut was, from the first, dominated by a powerful missionary motive. As early as 1735 a few members, led by A. G. Spangenberg,[14] sailed

[13] Julian, *Dictionary of Hymnology,* p. 1302.
[14] Augustus Gottlieb Spangenberg, b. 1704, in Prussia; taught at Jena

for Savannah, Georgia. A few months later they were followed by a band of twenty-six others, led by Bishop David Nitschmann.[15] It was with this second group that the Wesleys found themselves associated on shipboard. On their arrival these Moravian missionaries set up a school for Indians, but not finding Georgia satisfactory, they moved to Philadelphia in 1740, and in 1741 established their settlement at Bethlehem, Pennsylvania, on the Lehigh River. They brought with them the hymnbook which Count Zinzendorf had published in the year of their departure, *Das Gesang-Buch der Gemeine in Herrnhut*. In 1742 their first American hymnbook, *Hirten Lieder von Bethlehem*, was printed for them by Christopher Saur of Germantown.

The Moravians not only had a great tradition of hymnody behind them: they also brought wind and string instruments and cultivated music both as an enrichment of their worship and as a recreation. An extraordinary episode is recorded as having taken place as early as Sept. 14, 1745, when at a "love feast," [16] the German hymn "In Dulci Jubilo" was sung simultaneously in thirteen languages [17] to instrumental accompaniment.

and Halle; joined the colony at Herrnhut, 1733; emigrated to Georgia in 1735, going thence to Pennsylvania. He was "the head and heart of Moravian colonization in America." Bishop at Bethlehem, 1744. He returned to Herrnhut after Zinzendorf's death in 1760, and became head of the church there. He wrote Zinzendorf's *Leben* in eight volumes. Died at Herrnhut, 1792. See *Church Music and Musical Life in Pennsylvania in the Eighteenth Century*, II, 144-153.

[15] David Nitschmann, b. Moravia, 1696; d. Bethlehem, 1772.

[16] "Love feasts" were held every Saturday afternoon and on special occasions, as when some special task was undertaken or completed.

[17] Bohemian, Dutch, English, French, German, Greek, Irish, Latin, Mohawk, Mohican, Swedish, Welsh, and Wendish. A Dane, a Pole and a Hungarian were also present, but apparently lacked the facility to turn the words of the hymn into those tongues. See *Church Music and Musical Life in Pennsylvania in the Eighteenth Century*, I, 245 et seq. This occasion illustrates the cosmopolitan character which the Moravian

Early in 1746 an organ was built at Bethlehem by Gustavus Hesselius and his assistant Johann Gottfried Klemm. In 1750 the Moravians organized a Collegium Musicum.[18] In 1754 trombones were introduced from Europe, and ever since the trombone choir has held a peculiar place in Moravian life. Tradition has it that before dawn on Christmas morning, in 1757, a band of hostile Indians, lurking near by with the intention of making an attack, heard the trombone choir and departed. The preceding year Benjamin Franklin had visited Bethlehem as colonel in the militia in an expedition against the Indians. Of this visit he wrote,

I was at their church, where I was entertained with good musick, the organ being accompanied with violins, hautboys, flutes, clarinets, etc.[19]

A little later the Moravians were playing in their settlement in the wilderness some of the best music of the day, within a remarkably short time after its publication in Europe. The claim that the highest level of musical activity in the colonies during the eighteenth century was attained at Bethlehem can hardly be disputed.[20] And they not only played music by Bach, Mozart and Haydn — often from manuscript copies — but also composed much for themselves, generally liturgical music and anthems.

Singing was, from the beginning, an accompaniment of

church rapidly acquired after its refounding at Herrnhut. In this, as in other respects, the Moravian colonists differed from those of the other German settlements.

[18] Collegium Musicum does not mean "an academy of music," but is to be understood as the Latin equivalent of "eine musikalische Zusammenkunft," or music society of the type which had flourished in the German-speaking parts of Europe since about 1600. See Sonneck, *Early Concert Life in America*, p. 2.

[19] *Autobiography*, ed. John Bigelow, Phila., 1868, pp. 324–325.

[20] Philip H. Goepp, ed., *Annals of Music in Philadelphia*, Phila., 1896, p. 24.

the work as well as the worship of the Moravians, and
they had hymns which gave a religious interpretation to
many occupations, as well as "Reislieder," travellers' hymns
for the missionaries to sing upon their journeys. Thus
Bishop Spangenberg wrote a hymn, which is dated Oct.
27, 1746, for the women to sing during their spinning,
which has been translated thus:

> Know, ye sisters, in this way
> Is your work a blessing,
> If for Jesus' sake you spin,
> Toiling without ceasing.
>
> Spin and weave, compelled by love,
> Sew and wash with fervor,
> And the Saviour's grace and love
> Make you glad forever.

Four of Spangenberg's hymns are included, in English
translations, in the current Moravian hymnal.[21] One of
these, which may well have been written in America, since
it is dated 1734, was translated by John Wesley seven
years later as,

> What can we offer thee, O Lord,
> For all the wonders of thy grace?

And another, a noble hymn of the church universal, was
written at Lancaster, Pennsylvania, in 1745. It was translated by Catherine Winkworth, in the nineteenth century,
beginning,

> The Church of Christ, which he hath hallowed here
> To be his house, is scattered far and near
> In North and South, in East and West abroad,
> And yet in earth and heaven, thro Christ her Lord,
> The Church is one.

[21] *Hymnal and Liturgies of the Moravian Church* (*Unitas Fratrum*),
Bethlehem, Pa., 1920.

At least three other eighteenth-century Moravian hymn writers in this country are represented by a single hymn apiece in the same hymnal, but their hymns have a strong otherworldly flavor and have had no general use. It is impossible within the limits of this chapter to go into a detailed study of the stream of hymns which the Moravians produced in Pennsylvania, the use of which was limited to their own group. But it is interesting to note that when visiting the colony in 1742 Count Zinzendorf wrote verses dealing specifically with the American scene. On August 1 of that year he composed a poem of eighteen stanzas in Sickihillehocken, on the west bank of the Schuylkill River, near Philadelphia, one stanza of which runs,

> Hier schreib ich einem Brief,
> Als alles um mich schlief,
> In der finstern Wüsten
> *Sickihillehocken*
> Wo wenig Vöglein nisten,
> Wird ich doch kaum inn'
> Dass die *Schuylkill* rinn
> Ueber Nachbar *Green*.

> [Here I write a letter
>   As all around me sleep,
> In Sickihillihocken
>   Wilderness dark and deep,
> Where scarcely a bird is nesting,
>   And one hardly knows
> That the Schuylkill River
>   By neighbor Green flows.]

And a few months later when Zinzendorf was in the Wyoming valley in Pennsylvania he wrote another hymn, dated "Wyomik im Nov. 1742," containing the following stanzas:

Dort in der Fläche *Wajomik*
Auf einem wüsten Ackerstück,
Da Blaseschlagen nisteten
Und ihre Bläge brüsteten,—

Auf einem Silbererzenen Grund,
Wo's Leibes Leben miszlich stund,
Da dachten wir; — Wir sähen gern,
Das wurd eine Stadt des Herrn.

[There on the plain of Wajomik
In a desert place we're led,
Where the venomous viper [22] lurks
And threatening rears its head.

On this ground that shines like silver,
That naught for life can afford,
There we thought: We gladly plant
A city of the Lord.]

These verses illustrate his capacity for extempore verse
rather than the heights to which his genius sometimes rose,
but it is a moving and unfamiliar idea to most of us that
this great German Pietist and hymn writer thus poured
forth his soul amid the perils and hardships of our American wilderness during that journey which brought great
joy and courage to his fellow missionaries at Bethlehem.

Only a little while after settling Bethlehem the Moravians
pushed down into North Carolina. An entry in an old
diary, dated November 17, 1753, gives a glimpse of their
progress, and of their resort to music on their way.

We drove three miles further on the new road, then turned
to the left and cut a road for two and a half miles to the little

---

[22] *Church Music and Musical Life in Pennsylvania in the Eighteenth
Century,* II, 231. The reference to the "viper" suggests rattlesnakes: the
silver-strewn ground indicates a snowfall.

house that the Brethren found yesterday. We reached it in
the evening, and at once took possession of it, finding it large
enough that we could all lie down around the walls. We at
once made preparation for a little Lovefeast, and rejoiced
heartily with one another. Br. Gottlob began singing, with
the little verse:

> We hold arrival Lovefeast here
>   In Carolina land,
> A company of Brethren true,
>   A little Pilgrim band,
> Called by the Lord to be of those
>   Who through the whole world go,
> To bear Him witness everywhere,
> And naught but Jesus know.[23]

The chief settlement of the Moravians in North Carolina was at Winston-Salem (1766), and there organ-build-
ing, the formation of a trombone choir and the development
of choral singing followed along lines similar to those in
Pennsylvania.

The missionary impulse which had brought the Moravians to America to Christianize the Indians continued
through the eighteenth century. As early as 1763 they had
published a *Harmony of the Gospels* and a collection of
hymns in the language of the Delaware Indians, and in
1803 Rev. David Zeisberger brought out *A Collection of
Hymns, for the Use of the Christian Indians, of the Mission of the United Brethren, in North America*, translated
into the Delaware language.[24]

It is curious and regrettable that the hymnody and music
of these German-speaking colonists had no discernible in-

[23] *Records of the Moravians in North Carolina*, trans. A. L. Fries,
Publ. N. C. Historical Commission, Raleigh, 1922, p. 79.
[24] The English and Delaware title pages are reproduced in *Church
Music and Musical Life in Pennsylvania in the Eighteenth Century*, ed.
Penn. Society of Colonial Dames, Phila., 1926–1928, II, 200–201.

fluence upon their English-speaking neighbors or upon the
later course of American hymnody, except as it has been
transmitted to their descendants and to later German
churches in this country. This is the more remarkable
because their settlements, especially those of the Moravians,
were not in isolated and little-frequented spots. Their
towns were early trade and industrial centers, refuges from
Indian attacks, and the destination of immigrants from
many European lands. English-speaking congregations and
schools were early established, and their music school was
patronized by many who were not members of the *Unitas
Fratrum*. Both the singing and the instrumental music of
the Moravians were favorably known not only to European visitors but to some English-speaking Americans as
well, numbers of whom, besides Benjamin Franklin, recorded their impressions.

There were, however, several reasons for their failure
to stimulate a similar love of church music among the
English of Pennsylvania. In the first place, the music and
hymnody of these German groups were alien to the English
tradition. The Presbyterians and Episcopalians in the
colony, like the Puritans in New England, still clung to
psalmody and denied the legitimacy of "man-made" hymns
in worship. The Quaker element, who might have had
more in common with the pietism of some of the German
groups than the Presbyterians or the Episcopalians would
have had, were strongly opposed to music in any form, as
a dangerous concession to worldliness. Furthermore, there
was the barrier of language, which persisted throughout
the eighteenth century, and to some extent survives today.
Finally, most of these German-speaking colonists were
settled in small, self-contained enclaves, closely knit together by blood, tradition, and tenaciously held peculiarities of religious belief and practice. They maintained a
minimum of social intercourse with outsiders, and not much

more even with neighboring Germans belonging to other sects. Count Zinzendorf tried in vain to bring them into a common fellowship. The result was that what might have become an influence of great value to the religious life of the English-speaking colonists never overflowed the narrow boundaries within which it was so richly cultivated.

CHAPTER V

The Transition from Psalmody to Hymnody

WE MUST now turn back to the point reached in Chapter II and take up the story of the slow transition from psalmody to hymnody. We have noted the early vogue of Watts in New England, and the enthusiasm with which his *Horae Lyricae*, his *Hymns*, and his *Psalms of David Imitated* were welcomed as devotional literature, although their use in public worship was not yet even to be thought of. But the influence of Watts reached the other colonies as well, at a little later date. Benjamin Franklin reprinted Watts' *Psalms* in Philadelphia as early as 1729, but complained two years later that they remained unsold on his shelves. He did not print another edition till 1741, the same year in which the first Boston edition appeared. Watts' *Hymns* were printed first in Boston in 1739, in Philadelphia in 1742, in New York in 1752.[1]

But in 1735 occurred that episode with which the introduction of Watts into the southern colonies is associated. In October of that year John and Charles Wesley sailed as Church of England missionaries for Oglethorpe's newly established colony in Georgia, commissioned by the Society for the Propagation of the Gospel. The Wesleys took with them copies of Tate and Brady's *New Version*, of Watts' *Hymns*, and of his *Psalms of David Imitated*, no doubt to

---

[1] See Benson, *The English Hymn*, pp. 162–163; also for list of later American editions.

supplement the Old Version which was probably in use in such Episcopal churches as had been organized in Georgia. Perhaps John and Charles Wesley shared their father's scornful opinion of the Old Version as "scandalous dog-grell," and had in mind the introduction of better and more modern psalms and hymns.

The story of that memorable voyage is well-known. Twenty-six Moravian colonists were on board, with their bishop, David Nitschmann, and they held daily services with much singing of hymns. On the third day out John Wesley began to study German, that he might talk with his fellow passengers, and soon he took part in their daily worship. He became profoundly impressed with the spiritual possibilities of hymn singing, and eager to further it in his own flock. His *Journal* has an entry for October 25, 1735, "Began *Gesang-Buch*," apparently referring to a study of Count Zinzendorf's *Das Gesang-Buch der Gemeine in Herrnhut*, which the Moravians were using. The spiritual beauty of these hymns was a revelation to Wesley, who probably was the first Englishman to examine them. He very soon began to translate them, and, out of the total of some thirty hymns which he translated from French and Spanish sources as well as from German, the few which remain in use today are generally versions of the hymns which he learned from the Moravians. As a translator he is unsurpassed. Garrett Horder says of him:

John is as great a translator as Charles is as an original hymnist. — [His] are probably the finest translations in the English language, whilst they have the high honour of having opened to us the rich treasures of sacred song which Germany possesses.[2]

Perhaps it is not quite fair to count the translations which he made while in Georgia as belonging to American hym-

[2] W. Garrett Horder, *The Hymn Lover*, p. 114.

nody, since Wesley was but a visitor here, yet it remains
true that they are the earliest English hymns (as distinguished from psalms) written on American soil, and almost
the only ones written here before the end of the eighteenth
century which have had wide and lasting use. It is interesting to reflect that both the beginning of Wesleyan hymnody and the opening to the English-speaking world of
the treasury of German worship-song took place in Georgia
in the fourth decade of the eighteenth century, when that
colony was still only an outpost in the wilderness.

The Wesleys found Georgia little to their liking and
remained there only three years, but during that time John
Wesley prepared his first hymnbook, printed by Lewis
Timothy at Charleston, South Carolina, the first English
hymnbook, as distinguished from psalmbooks, to be printed
on American soil. It was entitled *Collection of Psalms and
Hymns, Charlestown, 1737*, a roughly printed little volume
of seventy-four pages, only two copies of which survive.
It includes seventy hymns, half of them by Watts, seven
from John Austin, six adapted from George Herbert, two
from Addison, five by Samuel Wesley, Sr., the father of
John, five by Samuel Wesley, Jr., John's brother, and five
translated from the German by John himself; none by
Charles Wesley, who had already returned to England.[3]
Wesley's name does not appear in it, but he was undoubtedly known as the compiler, for he had already introduced
the use of some of these hymns at religious gatherings, and
even in church, and in August, 1737, the Grand Jury at
Savannah presented, among other charges against him, the
accusation that he had altered the authorized metrical
psalms and had introduced "into the church and service at
the Altar compositions of psalms and hymns not inspected
or authorized by any proper judicature."

[3] Benson, *The English Hymn*, p. 226.

The following winter John Wesley also returned to England, and in 1738 printed in London his second *Collection of Psalms and Hymns*, which is a not dissimilar collection, with Watts represented by thirty-six out of seventy-six pieces. The first little book which he printed at Charleston is of significance only as marking the beginning of his career as a translator of hymns and editor of hymnbooks, and as the first publication of the sort on this soil, but it had no influence on American hymnody, and was soon forgotten.

Even the later books in the great succession of Wesleyan hymnals had surprisingly little influence here for several decades. When Rev. George Whitefield made his great preaching tour through the colonies, from 1739 to 1741, and spread far and wide that remarkable revival of religion known as "The Great Awakening" which had been started by Jonathan Edwards in Northampton, Massachusetts, in 1734, he brought with him from England copies not only of Watts, but also of John and Charles Wesley's *Hymns and Sacred Poems* (1739), just off the press in London. The Wesleys' book was reprinted in Philadelphia as early as 1740, but we hear little or nothing of the use of Wesleyan hymns until much later, and they only found their way into the hymnbooks of other denominations towards the end of the century, or later. It was not until about 1766 that the first Methodist societies were organized in the colonies. They used current English editions of Wesley's hymnbooks, presumably lining-out the hymns. In 1784 John Wesley sent over the printed sheets of a small collection of psalms and hymns with the sheets of his *Sunday Service of the Methodists in North America*. The same year a Conference which held its closing session in Baltimore discussed, among many other topics, "How shall we reform our singing?" The question was answered by the ruling, "Let all our preachers who have any knowledge in the notes, improve it by learning to sing true themselves, and keeping close to Mr. Wesley's tunes and hymns." [4] The last phrase refers to the struggle which was already beginning among the Methodists between adherents of the high standards of hymnody on which John Wesley insisted, and adherents of a more popular and revivalistic type of song, which led to widespread use of "camp meeting songs" of a very crude type. These diverging tendencies have marked the hymnody of American Methodism down to the present day and may be traced in the *Methodist Hymnal* of 1935.

The small collection which John Wesley sent over in 1784 was soon superseded by the *Pocket Hymn Book*, reprinted here in 1790, and that, in time, by *The Methodist Pocket Hymn Book, revised and improved*, 1802, and by similar volumes. In 1820 the General Conference ordered the publication of *A Collection of Hymns for the use of the Methodist Episcopal Church, principally from the Collection of the Reverend John Wesley*, which appeared the next year in New York, and in revised form in 1832.[5] All of these publications were practically reprints of English Wesleyan hymnbooks, in which the hymns by Charles Wesley overshadowed those of all other writers. Aside from helping to introduce the Wesleyan hymns to editors of other denominational hymnbooks they had no influence on American hymnody, original contributions to which, by Methodists, came only at a much later date.

Whitefield, however, had a very active part in promoting the use here of Watts' *Hymns* and *Psalms*, which he greatly admired, and he was a great believer in the value of singing,

---

[4] Benson, *The English Hymn*, p. 285. See also pp. 280–314 for a detailed statement of the rather complicated situation which developed in Methodist hymnody down to 1850.

[5] See *Our Hymnody*, edited by R. G. McCutchan, New York, 1937, pp. 9–10.

although, unlike his revivalist successors in the nineteenth and twentieth centuries, he had no singing partner to fan the emotions of his hearers. "The Great Awakening" was accompanied from the first by enthusiasm for singing. Jonathan Edwards regarded zeal for singing, especially on the part of the young, as one of the great assets of the revival, and approved of "abounding in singing," whether in or out of the meetinghouses. No doubt he had been greatly influenced by his grandfather, Rev. Solomon Stoddard, whose colleague at Northampton he became in 1727. As has already been pointed out, Stoddard had five years earlier preached and printed in favor of "regular" singing. Edwards, in his account of the early years of "The Great Awakening," refers both to the excellent singing which already prevailed at Northampton and to the added impetus to song given by the revival, saying,

Our public praises were then greatly enlivened: God was then served in our psalmody, in some measure in the *beauty of Holiness*. It has been observable, that there has been scarcely any part of Divine worship, wherein good men amongst us have had grace so drawn forth, and their hearts so uplifted in the ways of God, as in singing his praises. Our congregation excelled all that I ever knew in the external part of the duty before, generally carrying regularly and well, *three parts of music*, and the women a part by themselves. But now they were evidently wont to sing with unusual elevation of heart and voice, which made the duty pleasant indeed.[6]

We might suppose that, as a staunch Calvinist, he would have felt deeply the traditional objection to the use of "man-made hymns" in place of the inspired psalms. But the contrary was the case, for, perhaps influenced by Whitefield, he was willing to give Watts' hymns at least some

[6] "The Revival of Religion in New England before 1740," in *The Christian History for 1743*, quoted in Hood's *History of Music in New England*, p. 138.

place in public worship. Returning to Northampton from a journey in 1742, he found that his congregation had turned to Watts' hymns "and sang nothing else, and neglected the Psalms wholly." He writes that he "disliked not their making some use of the Hymns; but did not like their setting aside of the Psalms." A compromise was arranged. The people were to sing three times on the Sabbath, including both the morning and the afternoon services, and were to use "an Hymn, or part of a Hymn by Dr. Watts' the last time; viz, at the conclusion of afternoon exercise." [7] Whitefield thus found the door already open for the introduction of Watts as he travelled up and down the colonies drawing large crowds by his preaching. It should be noted, however, that neither his methods nor his message won universal approval, especially in Boston, where the more intellectual and progressive ministers either tacitly or openly disapproved, and Rev. Charles Chauncey of the First Church came out vigorously in print against the excesses of the revival.

At a little later date Watts' *Hymns* and *Psalms* were introduced among the Presbyterians in Virginia by a remarkable young pioneer preacher, Rev. Samuel Davies,[8] who, at the age of thirty, in 1753, succeeded Jonathan Edwards as president of the College of New Jersey. In Virginia he drew great crowds of hearers, and when he went to London to raise money for the college, his preach-

[7] Benson, *The English Hymn*, p. 163; see also Massachusetts Historical Society Proceedings, 2nd Ser., vol. X, p. 429.

[8] Samuel Davies, b. Nov. 3, 1723, near Summit Ridge, Newcastle, Del.; d. Feb. 4, 1761, at Princeton, N. J.; privately educated for the Presbyterian ministry; a missionary in Virginia, 1747-1753; president of the College of New Jersey, now Princeton University, 1753-1761. Moses Coit Tyler, in *History of American Literature*, New York, 1878, II, 241, says he was "probably the most brilliant pulpit orator produced in the colonial time, south of New England." For a discussion of him as a hymn writer, see L. F. Benson, *Journal of the Presbyterian Historical Society*, II, no. 6, Sept.–Dec., 1904.

ing attracted such attention that he was invited to preach in the Chapel Royal before George II.

The Presbyterians in the American colonies as a rule clung to the old psalmody of the sixteenth or seventeenth centuries, generally using the versions of Rous or of Barton, but Davies, who was something of a poet, evidently felt at liberty not only to use both the psalms and the hymns of Watts, but to write a considerable number of hymns himself. In both respects he was exceptional, and far in advance of his time. In fact, the singing of hymns was not formally authorized by the synod of the church in which he ministered until twenty-seven years after his death. Some of his hymns were written to form the conclusion to a sermon, the most striking examples being

> How great, how terrible that God
> Who shakes Creation with his Nod! —

appended to a sermon on the Lisbon earthquake of 1755, and

> While o'er our guilty land, O Lord,
> We view the terrors of thy sword, —

following a sermon on Braddock's Defeat in the same year. A few weeks later he preached again before some of the colonial troops who had been under the command of the youthful George Washington, praising their courage and resourcefulness in saving the army from utter rout. When his discourse was printed he added these prophetic words in a footnote: "As a remarkable instance of this, I may point out to the public that heroic youth, Colonel Washington, whom I cannot but hope Providence has hitherto preserved in so signal a manner for some important service to his country." [9]

[9] Quoted in Edward S. Ninde, *Story of the American Hymn*, New York, 1921, p. 46.

After the death of Davies, at the early age of thirty-seven, some of his manuscripts were sent to Dr. Thomas Gibbons, an English Independent minister with whom Davies had formed a close friendship when in England. In 1769 Gibbons published in England a book called *Hymns Adapted to Divine Worship*, mostly of his own composition, but including sixteen by Davies. Seven of these were later included in Rippon's *Selection* of 1787 and are noted in Julian's *Dictionary*. Thus, as Dr. Benson points out, if Davies' hymns "owe their publication to the loyal friendship of Dr. Gibbons, they owe their circulation to Dr. Rippon." Two of these hymns, "Great God of wonders! all thy ways," and "Lord, I am thine, entirely thine," have had long and widespread use, the former particularly in Britain, where it was included in the Scottish *Church Hymnary* as late as 1898, the latter in America, but both have now practically disappeared, and not a single hymn by him is included in the new Presbyterian *Hymnal*. Nevertheless, Davies deserves an honored place in the story of American hymnody as an agent for the introduction of Watts, and as the earliest native-born American hymn writer [10] whose hymns had any general acceptance. It was

[10] Mather Byles, who has been already referred to, was born eighteen years earlier than Davies, and included in his *Poems on Several Occasions*, published in 1744, a number of literary pieces entitled "Hymns." From one of them, "The God of Tempest," a number of stanzas were later taken to form his hymn beginning,

"When wild Confusion wrecks the Air,
   And Tempests rend the Skies,
Whilst blended Ruin, Clouds and Fire
   In harsh Disorder rise;

"Amid the Hurricane I'll stand,
   And strike a tuneful Song;
My Harp all-trembling in my Hand,
   And all inspir'd my Tongue."

This was included in Belknap's *Collection* in 1796, and survived at least as late as Beecher's *Collection* of 1855, but it never had any such wide-

three-quarters of a century before the Presbyterian Church
produced another.

In spite of the influence of Davies the adoption of Watts'
Psalms and *Hymns* by the Presbyterians from New York
to Virginia was slow, and was attended by a controversy
which split the Presbyterians into "Old Side" and "New
Side" groups in 1741. The "Old Side" group, mostly
Scotch and Scotch-Irish, adhered tenaciously to the psalm-
books of Rous or of Barton. The "New Side" group inclined towards Tate and Brady, or Watts. The trustees of
the Presbyterian Church in New York recorded their
views of psalm singing in an undated entry in a journal
which has been preserved in manuscript.

In that period [The Great Awakening] the poetick writings,
particularly the Hymns of the Sweet Singer of our Israel
[Watts], became of excellent service and for the divine relish
which in the use of them had affected many minds. During
that remarkable season, many of the people became desirous
of introducing some one of the New Versians of the Psalms,
into the stated publick worship of the congregation. — After
this matter had been some years under consideration and by
the private use of the New Version, the Old Version had become every day to the Taste of many more and more flat, dull,

---

spread use as Davies' hymns. Byles' *Poems* also included a sentimental
one on the love of Jesus,

> "Where shall I find my Lord, my Love,
> The Sov'reign of my soul?"

and a better hymn of nature, written at sea,

> "Great God, thy works our wonder raise,
> To thee our swelling notes belong;
> Whilst Skies, and Winds, and Rocks, and Sea
> Around shall echo to our Song."

His later "New England Hymn" was included in Billings' *New England
Psalm Singer*, 1770, but was perhaps not used elsewhere. Although Byles
preceded Davies in the composition of his earlier "hymns," he had no
such influence on American hymnody as Davies had, and his name does
not appear in Julian's *Dictionary*.

insipid and undevotional — and it had been judged that no objection could arise against introducing Dr. Watts version but from ignorance of the difference between the old version and that, or from some unreasonable prejudice, the ministers, elders, deacons and trustees with the approbation of the principal part of the congregation — desired that, that version might be proposed to the congregation to be introduced in a month's time unless sufficient reason to the contrary should be signified.[11]

The "Old Side" minority promptly seceded to organize a new Society, but the "New Side" Synod of New York decided in 1754,

Since Dr. Watts's version is introduced in this church, and is well adapted for Christian worship, and received by many Presbyterian congregations, both in America and Great Britain, they can not but judge it best for the well-being of the congregation under their present circumstances, that they should be continued.

Those Presbyterian churches which were newly organized at this time had less difficulty than those with an established usage to overcome. The church at Newburyport, Massachusetts, founded by Whitefield's supporters in 1746, began at once to use Watts' *Psalms of David Imitated*, and the Boston Presbytery recommended the book as "well adapted to the New Testament Church." Its use continued at Hanover, Virginia, after Davies left to go to Princeton, and his successor at Hanover, Rev. John Todd, gave an address in defence of the practice, printed under the title, *An humble attempt towards the improvement of Psalmody; The propriety, necessity and use, of Evangelical Psalms in Christian worship. Delivered at a meeting of*

[11] Quoted from Benson, *The English Hymn*, pp. 179–180. See Benson, pp. 177–196 for details of this movement in the Presbyterian Church.

the Presbytery of Hanover in Virginia. October 6th 1762, in which he said,

I am fully persuaded that the churches in these parts have received very great advantage from Watts's excellent compositions, especially his sacramental hymns.

This struggle between the two factions within the Presbyterian churches was, however, long-continued and is known as "the great Psalmody Controversy." Its echoes reverberated for a century. The Synod of 1787, having already approved of the use of Rous' version to please the "Old Side," also cautiously approved the use of Barlow's *Watts*, leaving the choice to the local parishes. The churches in many of the older settlements in the East, if they were not already using some other edition of Watts, accepted Barlow's book, but in the frontier settlements the heat of controversy split many parishes asunder when confronted with the choice, which was in reality the old issue between the use of "inspired" psalms and the use of "manmade hymns." In the Third Presbyterian Church in Philadelphia the change to Watts was made in 1788; in Carlisle, Pennsylvania, not until 1824. No designated psalmbook was formally authorized for use until 1802, when the General Assembly approved Timothy Dwight's *Psalms of David*, of which we shall hear more presently, and no official Presbyterian hymnal appeared until 1831.

The attempts to improve singing among the Presbyterians, toward the end of the century, also worked for the introduction of Watts, and in "many parish records the giving up of lining and the adoption of Watts are recorded as a single entry." [12] Nevertheless, in many congregations the singing was as wretched as it had ever been in New

---

[12] Benson, *The English Hymn*, p. 193. See also pp. 177–196 for the preceding quotations, and for a review of this whole movement in the Presbyterian Church.

England. The anonymous "Presbyterian" whose pamphlet, published in Philadelphia, in 1763, has been already referred to in Chapter III, complains that "the miserable manner in which this Part of their Worship is droned out, seems rather to imitate the Braying of Asses, than the divine melody so often recommended in Scripture." Another writer describes the congregations as "drolling out the tones of ill-measured dullness, or jarring with harsh discord." And John Adams, in 1774, notes that the psalmody in the "Old Presbyterian Society" in New York is "in the *old way*, as we call it — all the drawling, quavering, discord in the world." Even the publication of *Urania* by James Lyon, in spite of his Presbyterian affiliation, did not help much, although it was supplemented by the organization of singing-schools, and by the activities of a music teacher and publisher, named Andrew Adgate, who brought out in Philadelphia no less than five books on singing in the years 1787 and 1788, among them a small collection of forty *Select Psalms and Hymns for the use of Mr. Adgate's pupils, and proper for all singing-schools*, which included hymns by other authors than Watts.

Another interesting figure of the second half of the eighteenth century was Samson Occom,[13] a full-blooded Mohican Indian, who became a very successful Presbyterian missionary among his own people in New England and New York State. He developed remarkable ability as a preacher, and, when he visited England in 1766–67, created a profound sensation there. The object of his visit was to raise money for the education of the Indians, and he was successful in securing an amount variously estimated

[13] Samson Occom, b. 1723, at Norwich, Conn.; d. 1792; converted during the Great Awakening; ordained as a Presbyterian Missionary among the Indians, 1759. For hymns attributed to him see Julian, *Dictionary*, p. 855. For the most favorable presentation of his claims as a hymn writer see *Samson Occom and the Christian Indians of New England*, W. D. Love, Boston, n. d. (1899), pp. 176–187.

at ten to fifteen thousand pounds. With it he established a school at Hanover, New Hampshire, which was later merged with Dartmouth College. In 1774 he published at New London, Connecticut, his *Choice Collection of Hymns and Spiritual Songs*, chiefly interesting because of its source, and as, in a way, the eighteenth-century successor to John Eliot's version of the psalms in the Indian language. Occom has also been credited, on somewhat insufficient grounds, with being a hymn writer. One of the hymns attributed to him, "Wak'd by the gospel's joyful sound," is quoted in full in Ninde's *Story of the American Hymn*. It had wide use both in this country and in Great Britain, with variant readings for the opening line. The original composition was probably Occom's, but, in the form quoted and commonly used, it is much rewritten.

By mid-century the New England churches were slowly moving away from use of *The Bay Psalm Book*. In 1752 Rev. John Barnard [14] of Marblehead published *A New Version of the Psalms; Fitted to the Tunes Used in the Churches:* with *Several Hymns out of the Old, and New, Testament*. Bound up with it was a neatly engraved collection of forty-nine tunes. In his preface he said:

> Tho' the New-England Version of the Psalms of David, in Meetre, is generally very good, and few of the same Age may be compar'd with it; yet the Flux of Languages has rendered several Phrases in it obsolete, and the Mode of Expression in various Places less acceptable: for which Reasons an Amendment, or New Version, has been long, and greatly, desired, by the most judicious among us.

Barnard frankly abandoned the antiquated verse form of *The Bay Psalm Book* and put his rather free translation into the current style of the mid-eighteenth century. A single

[14] John Barnard, b. Boston, Mass., 1681; d. Marblehead, Mass., 1770; A.B. Harvard, 1700; minister of the First Church, Marblehead, Mass., 1716–1770.

stanza from Psalm 8 will illustrate his conception of an
acceptable mode of expression:

> When I survey the vast Expance,
> Form'd by thy Finger's Might,
> Or view the Moon, and glitt'ring Stars,
> Ordain'd to rule the Night:
> Lord! What is feeble Man! that thou
> Do'st bear him still in Mind?
> And what the Son of Man, whom thou
> To visit art so kind?

Barnard's book does not appear to have been used outside
of Marblehead, but it indicates both the diminishing emphasis on a "close-fitting" translation and the growing desire
for more modern forms of worship song.

The Bay Psalm Book, however, was still dear to many
hearts and did not go out without a last effort to maintain its
prestige. Rev. Thomas Prince,[14a] the distinguished minister of the Old South Church, had urged the introduction
of a more modern book, but his congregation were unwilling to give up *The Bay Psalm Book* altogether, though
they did agree to let him revise it. He did so to the extent
of making what was practically a new book. He was a
thorough scholar, and, if not much of a poet, at least he
could write verse that would scan. His volume was entitled, *The Psalms, Hymns, and Spiritual Songs, of the Old
and New Testaments, Faithfully translated into English
metre. Being the New-England Psalm-Book Revised and
Improved: by an Endeavor after a yet nearer approach to
the inspired original as well as to the Rules of Poetry. With
an addition of Fifty other Hymns on the most important
Subjects of Christianity. . . . Boston: N. E. Printed and
sold by D. Henchman, in Cornhill, and S. Kneeland in
Queen Street, 1758.*

[14a] Thomas Prince, b. Sandwich, Mass., 1687; d. Boston, Oct. 22,
1758; A.B. Harvard, 1707. He spent several years in England but returned
to Boston in 1717, and was minister of the Old South Church 1717–1758.
He rendered invaluable service as historian of early New England.

The preface, unsigned but dated "Boston in N. E. May 26, 1758," begins with praise for the compilers of *The Bay Psalm Book*.

They had not only the happiness of approaching nearer to the *inspired original* than *all other Versions* in *English Rhyme*, but in many places of excelling them in Simplicity of Style and in affecting terms, — On which Accounts I found in *England* it was by some Eminent Congregations prefer'd to all *Others* in their *Public Worship*, even down to 1717, when I last left that Part of the *British* Kingdom.

It seems a Thousand Pities, that such a Version which has more Inspiration, and therefore of Doctrine Authority and Influence on the Heart than others, should on Account of the Flatnesse in Diverse Places, be wholly laid aside.

Prince goes on to describe his method. "I collected all the different versions in English metre I could find, which are above thirty, and I think all but two," and compared them, selecting those that kept closest to the Hebrew. He then read over each psalm in the English Bible, comparing it with the Hebrew and with the versions of the Chaldee and the Septuagint. The result, he claims, is a very considerable rewriting and improvement of the metrical version of *The Bay Psalm Book* from a literary point of view, without sacrifice of closeness to the original. He says, "For grand Ideas I seek the most *majestic* words, for tender *Sentiments*, the *Softest Words*; for *affecting* the most moving; for *wondrous*, the most striking."

Even more significant, however, was his inclusion of "fifty other hymns," all but eight of them by Watts, with a subtitle *Hymns, which are not Versions of the Scriptures, but Pious Songs derived from them By Dr. Watts and Others.*

Among those hymns are the following classics: "My dear Redeemer and my Lord," — "When I survey the wondrous cross," — "Behold the glories of the Lamb," and "Awake our souls, away our fears."

One of them was by Prince himself;

> With Christ and all his shining Train
> Of Saints and Angels, we shall rise
> To pass the glittering Worlds around
> While Heav'n wide opens to our eyes.

The book also contained forty-eight tunes, some of them of recent English origin, engraved in three parts.

Prince had labored on this work for three years, and his thoroughness and scholarship are characteristic of the man. He died just as the book came from the press, and it was used for the first time in the Old South Meeting House on the Sunday following his death, we can imagine with what emotion. It continued in use there until 1789, but was adopted in few, if any, other churches. With it the long reign of *The Bay Psalm Book* came to an end. Prince's inclusion of a supplement of hymns indicates clearly that the inspired psalms (in the most literal translation), as the only songs worthy to be sung in worship, had at last given way to the recognition of the legitimacy of singing lyrics of human authorship. Once embarked on that path the evolution of modern hymnody became possible.

It was not until 1760 that Mather Byles was able to introduce into his own church in Boston an edition of Tate and Brady, with an appendix of 103 hymns, some of which he had selected as additions to the smaller collection which the Brattle Square Church had adopted for use in 1753. Thus the abandonment of *The Bay Psalm Book* in favor of the *New Version*, or of Watts, went slowly forward among the New England churches. The church at Dedham abandoned it in 1751, the New North Church in Boston in 1755, the First Church in Roxbury in 1758, and First Church in Boston in 1761. The First Parish in Ipswich, which had been exceptional in holding to Sternhold and Hopkins until about 1667 before adopting *The Bay Psalm Book*, introduced the *New Version* before 1757, and Watts' *Psalms and Hymns* in 1776.[15]

The following passage, quoted from Benson,[16] describes what was, no doubt, a typical situation:

> The parish at Spencer, Massachusetts — after making trial for some time of *Tate and Brady* — met in June, 1761, and decided to restore *The Bay Psalm Book* for four Sabbaths, then to use Watts' Imitations till September, and finally meet for a decision. At the meeting the vote stood, for *The Bay Psalm Book*, 33; for *Watts*, 14; for *Tate and Brady*, 6. It was agreed to refer the matter to three ministers, who recommended a trial of *Tate and Brady*. . . . There was a dissatisfied minority, and it was agreed to use *The Bay Psalm Book* and *Watts* jointly "till the church and congregation shall come to a better understanding as to what version may be sung." This arrangement continued until October, 1769, when it was agreed to adopt Watts' *Psalms and Hymns*, by a vote of 26 in his favor, and "about 6 votes for the old version." Even so Spencer was years ahead of very many New England parishes.

But one by one the rural parishes moved in the same direction, and often the introduction of Watts' *Psalms and Hymns* was accompanied by an attempt at better singing. Thus the church in Bedford, Massachusetts, voted in 1773 "to bring in Dr. Watts' versions for the present, and to have Messrs. Jeremiah Fitch and James Wright sett in the fore seats in the front gallery, as they are appointed to begin the Psalm or tune." Nevertheless the use of Watts did not become general in New England until the end of the Revolution.

By that time the soil was well prepared for his *Psalms*

[15] *Last Sermon preached in the ancient meeting-house of the First Parish in Ipswich, by David T. Kimball, pastor.* Boston, 1846, p. 14.
[16] Benson, *The English Hymn*, p. 165.

and Hymns, but the Revolution itself made necessary some changes in those passages in which Watts had made King David speak too much like a patriotic Englishman.[17] The earliest revision of Watts which undertook to eliminate references to Great Britain and its king and to substitute for them references suitable to America, was published by John Mycall in Newburyport, Mass., in 1781, and was the work of a committee of ministers cooperating with the publisher. A single example will illustrate their method. Watts had entitled Psalm LXXV, *Power and government from God alone, Apply'd to the Glorious Revolution by King William, or the Happy Ascension of King George to the throne.* Mycall altered this to read, *Applied to the glorious revolution in America, July 4th, 1776.*

Mycall's revision ran through several editions, the latest printed in 1812. It won the approval of President Stiles of Yale and had considerable use. That it was not entirely successful, however, is indicated by the action of the General Association of Connecticut, which, in June, 1784, appointed a committee to confer with Joel Barlow with regard to alterations of Watts' *Psalms* and a collection of hymns to be added to the psalms. The book was published at Hartford the following year as *Doctor Watts' Imitation of the Psalms of David, corrected and enlarged by Joel Barlow. To which is added a Collection of Hymns; the whole applied to the state of the Christian Church in General. Hartford: printed by Barlow and Babcock, M, DCC, LXXXV.* The "Collection of Hymns" included seventy items, mostly by Watts.

"The ingenious Mr. Joel Barlow of Connecticut" was a Yale graduate with literary inclinations, a Revolutionary soldier who turned army chaplain with scanty preparation,

[17] Benson, *The English Hymn,* pp. 164–168; also Benson, "American Revisions of Watts's Psalms," in *Journal of the Presbyterian Historical Society,* 1903.

and later became a lawyer and a diplomat. And he was a poet who composed popular patriotic songs and a pretentious work called *The Columbiad*. He seemed well qualified to edit a hymnbook, but he took too free a hand in revising Watts to please the Congregationalists. Soon after the publication of his book he is said to have met "a roving rhymer, with a peculiar gift for making extemporaneous verses," who promptly struck off the following stanza:

> You've proved yourself a sinful cre'tur';
> You've murdered Watts, and spoilt the metre;
> You've tried the Word of God to alter,
> And for your pains deserve a halter.

And President Stiles in his *Diary* noted that Barlow had made many unnecessary alterations and inserted far too much of his own verse, concluding, "Mr. Barlow is an excellent Poet; yet he cannot retouch Watts to advantage." Nevertheless four editions of Barlow's *Watts* appeared within five years, and, curiously enough, it had wide popularity among the Presbyterians, who continued to use it in considerable measure until the General Assembly of the Presbyterian Church published its own *Psalms and Hymns*, in 1830. In 1788 Barlow went abroad and in France identified himself with radical groups, which led to reports that he had become "an infidel." He and his book thereafter rapidly lost whatever esteem they had enjoyed in Connecticut.

With the rejection of Barlow's *Watts* by the Congregationalists the need of something more acceptable became urgent. In 1799 *The Hartford Selection* appeared, which reached an eighth edition in 1821. It was edited, in cooperation with Abel Flint and Joseph Steward, by Rev. Nathan Strong,[18] who had shared with Timothy Dwight the leadership of the class of 1769 at Yale. It was exten-

[18] Nathan Strong, b. 1748; d. Dec. 25, 1816; A.B. Yale, 1769; Minister of the First Church in Hartford, Conn.

sively used in evangelistic revivals, for which it was better adapted than for more normal forms of church worship. Benson quotes "a competent observer" who in 1833 wrote,

It has been printed in greater numbers, has been diffused more extensively, and has imparted more alarm to the sinner, and more consolation to the saint, than any other compilation of religious odes in this country, during a period of nearly thirty years.[19]

Strong was himself a hymn writer, and included several of his own hymns in the book. One of them, intended "to impart alarm to the sinner," describes the Last Judgment, though in terms more poetic and less lurid than those of many of the current hymns of damnation. His last stanza runs,

> Thus ends the harvest of the earth:
> Angels obey the awful voice;
> They save the wheat, they burn the chaff:
> All heaven approves the sovereign choice.

Strong's two Thanksgiving hymns have had wide use, though they have dropped out of recent hymnbooks. One is a good, though not very original, hymn, beginning,

> Almighty Sovereign of the skies,
> To Thee let songs of gladness rise.

The other betrays the obvious influence of Charles Wesley in the lines

> Hark! the voice of nature sings
> Praises to the King of kings.

Since *The Hartford Selection* did not meet the demand for a version of the psalms "accommodated to America,"

[19] Benson, *The English Hymn*, p. 373.

the Connecticut Association, in 1797, with the concurrence of the General Assembly of the Presbyterian Church in 1798, sponsored a new book, which did not appear until 1801, under the title *The Psalms of David — by I. Watts, D.D. A new edition, in which the Psalms, omitted by Dr. Watts, are versified, local passages are altered, and a number of Psalms are versified anew. By Timothy Dwight, D.D., President of Yale College. At the request of The General Association of Connecticut. To the Psalms is added a Selection of Hymns: Hartford — 1801.*

The vote of the Association requesting Dwight to prepare the book asked "that such passages in Dr. Watts' version of the Psalms as were local and inapplicable to our circumstances [i.e. since the independence of the colonies] might be altered"; and also stated that there was a demand for hymns among "a number of the clergy and laity, of the first respectability." Both requests were met, and the increase in the number of hymns is especially significant. There were 263, of which 168 were from Watts and ninety-five by other writers, mostly of the Watts' school.[20] And this represented a compromise between Dwight, who favored a large collection, and some of his advisers who wanted only a small one.

Dwight's book, which was approved by the General Assembly of the Presbyterian Church in 1802, by contrast to Barlow's took no more liberties with the text of Watts than were deemed permissible, and came from a source of impeccable respectability, since its editor was the great president of Yale, and a grandson of Jonathan Edwards. Dwight [21] was an outstanding man, with a large share of

[20] That only one of Charles Wesley's hymns was included illustrates how slowly the Wesleyan hymnody made its way into American hymnbooks.

[21] Timothy Dwight, b. Northampton, Mass., May 14, 1752; d. Philadelphia, Jan. 11, 1817; A.B. Yale, 1769; schoolteacher; chaplain in the Revolutionary Army; minister of the Congregational Church at Green-

the intellectual brilliance which ran in the Edwards' strain. He had been a precocious youth; a remarkable scholar; a chaplain in the Revolutionary Army; a member of the Massachusetts legislature; and he was now a great college president, with a wide acquaintance among the leaders of his day. Like Barlow, he had acquired a reputation as a poet. At the age of twenty-four he had completed an epic on *The Conquest of Canaan*, which the English poet, William Cowper, is said to have commended. In the army he had written songs for the soldiers, and the popular *Ode to Columbia*. Obviously, he was the ideal man for the work which he was asked to undertake. He included in his book some of his own paraphrases of the psalms, including one of part of Psalm 137:

> I love thy kingdom, Lord,
> The house of thine abode, —

probably the earliest American hymn still in use today. His book was received with general approval and remained in use for a generation.

By the early years of the nineteenth century the more conservative elements in the New England churches had come to regard Watts with almost the same degree of veneration which their forefathers a hundred years earlier had accorded to *The Bay Psalm Book*. The devotion to Watts, however, never here reached such extremes as was the case in England, where, according to Garrett Horder's perhaps overdrawn statement,

For more than a century Watts remained undisputed master of the hymnody of the Independents. No other hymns than his were heard in any of the assemblies. . . . The Independent churches became as superstitiously conservative in clinging to

---

field Hill, Connecticut; president of Yale College from 1795 until his death.

Watts' hymns as their forefathers had been in rejecting them, and using only the Psalms in metre. . . . So venerated were his hymns and psalms, that in this very [i.e. the nineteenth] century there were persons who refused to sing any others, and actually sat down if any others were announced.[22]

There were, however, groups in this country over whom Watts did not hold sway. In spite of John Wesley's attempt in Georgia to introduce hymns into the worship of the Episcopal churches, those churches throughout the colonies were almost wholly unaffected by these developments which we have been tracing. If they had known of Wesley's attempt at all, which is most unlikely in view of the remoteness of Savannah from any other settlement except Charleston, it would have been regarded only as an irregular experiment not "authorized by any proper judicature." The Episcopal parishes clung to the Old Version of Sternhold and Hopkins, or to the *New Version* of Tate and Brady until after the Revolution. In 1786 a convention was held in Philadelphia, attended by delegates from the Episcopal churches in seven of the states, at which the Protestant Episcopal Church of the United States of America was organized. The convention appointed a committee to adapt the *Book of Common Prayer* for American use and adjourned.

The two important members of this committee were Rev. William White, who the following year became the first bishop of Pennsylvania, and Rev. William Smith of Philadelphia. The Committee produced a "Proposed Book," in the preface of which they wrote,

A *Selection* is made of the . . . *singing* Psalms . . . and a collection of hymns are added, upon those *Evangelical* subjects and other heads of christian worship, to which the psalms of *David* are less adapted, or do not generally extend.

[22] Horder, *The Hymn Lover*, p. 100.

Before the collection of fifty-one hymns they inserted a rubric,

Hymns suited to the Feasts and Fasts of the *Church* and other Occasion of public Worship; to be used at the discretion of the Minister.

It is interesting to note that the committee had no precedent for thus including hymns within the Prayer Book, nor had the vote of the convention given them any warrant to do so. In England even the metrical psalms were supplementary to the Prayer Book, and hymns, where used, were introduced by private initiative, except for the few which were attached to the *New Version*. The hymns included in the "Proposed Book" were all selected by William Smith, who was eager for their inclusion. William White, though opposing the plan as "extending their [the Committee's] powers pretty far," gave up his "sentiment respecting ye hymnifying ye Psalms" and yielded reluctant consent. But it is said that never, through a long life, did he give out a hymn in church, unless at Christmas.

The "Proposed Book" failed of adoption, and the convention in 1789 approved another revision, which appeared in 1790 as *The Book of Common Prayer . . . according to the use of the Protestant Episcopal Church in the United States of America*. But it followed the example of the "Proposed Book" in including metrical psalms and hymns, the latter being reduced in number to twenty-seven of William Smith's selection,

set forth and allowed to be sung in all congregations . . . before and after Morning and Evening Prayer; and also before and after sermons, at the discretion of the Minister.

In 1808 thirty more hymns were added, but with a rubric requiring some of the metrical psalms "to be sung at every celebration of divine service."

Thus within the Episcopal Church a cautious transition from psalmody to hymnody was slowly brought about without any open controversy, largely because of the discretion with which two men handled what might have been a thorny problem. From William Smith came the initiative which opened the door to hymn singing, while Bishop White's prudence kept the movement which he regretted from proceeding more rapidly than the churches were prepared to follow.[23]

The Baptists in eighteenth-century America probably at first used *The Bay Psalm Book*, but were less convinced of the necessity of adherence to strict psalmody than were either the "Old Side" Presbyterians or the Congregationalists of New England. In Boston they changed to the *New Version* in 1740, and later in some places to Watts. But there was naturally a demand for hymns giving voice to the tenets which the Baptists especially emphasized; their congregations were satisfied with much lower educational standards in the ministry than were the Congregationalists, Episcopalians or Presbyterians; and they desired more emotional songs than Watts could supply, sung to popular melodies with choruses. The result was a series of hymnbooks adapted to the "popular liking," most of them of very slight literary value, but of interest as showing the readiness of the Baptists to turn from psalmody at an early date, and because in some of them we can trace the rise of American folk-hymnody.

One of the earliest of these Baptist hymn writers was Henry Alline,[24] an evangelist of erratic views who started the Freewill Baptist movement in New England and Nova Scotia. He published an undated collection of four hundred and eighty-seven *Hymns and Spiritual Songs*, every

---

[23] For a more detailed account of this development in the Episcopal Church see Benson, *The English Hymn*, pp. 390–402.

[24] Henry Alline, b. June 14, 1748, Newport, R. I.; d. Feb. 7, 1784.

one of which he had written himself, which ran to at least four editions, the latest appearing in 1802. Only one of his hymns seems to have been used outside the limits of his own following, but his "Amazing sight, the Saviour stands," was adopted by Nettleton for his *Village Hymns* (1824), and thence passed into use among the Presbyterians.

Another Baptist writer of this period was "Elder" John Leland.[25] Most of his hymns were very crude. One of them, written for a baptism in Virginia in 1779 — presumably in winter — was intended to encourage the fainthearted, for it contains the familiar lines,

> Christians, if your hearts are warm,
> Ice and snow can do no harm.

But another, first published in 1792, is of better quality and was long popular for evening services:

> The day is past and gone,
> The evening shades appear;
> O may we all remember well
> The night of death draws near.

> We lay our garments by,
> Upon our beds to rest;
> So death will soon disrobe us all
> Of what we have possessed.

> Lord, keep us safe this night,
> Secure from all our fears;
> May angels guard us while we sleep,
> Till morning light appears.

> And when we early rise,
> And view the unwearied sun,

[25] John Leland, b. May 15, 1754, at Grafton, Mass.; d. Jan. 14, 1841. A restless and eccentric Baptist preacher in Massachusetts and Virginia. His *Sermons, Addresses, Essays and Autobiography* were published in 1845.

May we set out to win the prize,
And after glory run.

And when our days are past,
And we from time remove,
Oh, may we in thy bosom rest,
The bosom of thy love.

This lugubrious emphasis on death is quite alien to modern thought but is very characteristic of much of the hymnody, and particularly of the folk hymns, of the latter part of the eighteenth and the first half of the nineteenth century. In fact Leland's hymn is not only better verse but less melancholy than the majority of such effusions. Compare it, for example, with another hymn of the period:

Hail, ye sighing sons of sorrow,
Learn with me your certain doom:
Learn with me your fate tomorrow,
Dead, perhaps laid in the tomb.

Another example of the naive hymns popular at this period was produced by an anonymous Baptist of Philadelphia for use at immersions in the "Baptisterion" on the banks of the Schuylkill River just outside the city, adjacent to a large stone which was used as a pulpit.

Jesus, Master, O discover
Pleasure in us, now we stand
On this bank of Schuylkill River,
To obey thy great command.

. . . .

Of our vows this stone's a token,
Stone of Witness bear record
'Gainst us, if our vows be broken,
Or if we forsake the Lord.[26]

[26] See Benson, *The English Hymn*, pp. 198–200; Ninde, *Story of the American Hymn*, p. 59.

As Ninde points out, this "Schuylkill Hymn" had the advantage that the name of the river could be changed to suit other localities.

None of these eighteenth-century Baptist compilations made any contribution of permanent value to American hymnody. It was not until early in the nineteenth century that they gave way among the Baptists to two books of real worth: Winchell's *Psalms, Hymns, and Spiritual Songs of Watts, bound up with a Selection of more than three hundred Hymns, from the most approved authors* (1818–1819), published in Boston, and *The Psalms and Hymns of Dr. Watts, arranged by Dr. Rippon: with Rippon's Selection in one Volume*, published in Philadelphia in 1820. In both books the hymns were still supplementary to "Watts entire." The second was only an American reprint of John Rippon's famous *Selection*, first published in London for the Baptists, which ran through many editions over a period of nearly eighty years, in the course of which the selection of hymns was increased from 588 to 1174. Few other hymnbooks of the period were so influential in both England and the colonies.

The folk hymnody which arose in the colonies in the second half of the eighteenth century, and which still survives in the upland and inland South, deserves some further mention here. As already pointed out, it began among the Baptists, and even more conspicuously among the Methodists, who, as has been noted, as early as 1784 found the musical and literary standards of John Wesley too severe for many of their congregations. Information about American folk hymns has only recently been made available. It was an Englishman, Cecil J. Sharp, who early in this century first drew attention to the survival in the rural South of a considerable body of old English folk songs. Mr. Sharp, however, overlooked the hymns of the same region, and it has been left to later writers to uncover an interesting phase of the more primitive religious life of the country.[27]

These early folk hymns were the forerunners of the camp meeting and revival hymns, and of the gospel songs of the latter part of the nineteenth century. These may all be regarded as successive steps to meet the demand for a popular hymnody, running more or less parallel to the more staid and conventional church hymnody and occasionally influencing it. While in general their effect on American hymnody has been neither permanent nor valuable, they do represent sweeping movements which had a large popular appeal and were very characteristic of the place and period in which they occurred. And one type of folk hymnody, the Negro spirituals, constitutes a most significant contribution to our music.

On the musical side the early folk hymns were greatly influenced by William Billings. His "fuguing" tunes, after their brief popularity, passed out of use in the more sophisticated circles, but survived for a considerable period in nineteenth-century rural New England, spread through the singing schools to other parts of the country, and are still in use in the rural South. The folk hymns were also sung to other music of a similar type as well as to traditional tunes inherited from England. The field is one which deserves full investigation, and it is not impossible that some tunes may be recovered from it as available for modern use as the English folk tunes which Mr. R. Vaughan Williams and others have adapted for use in *Songs of Praise*. Indeed, two American tunes of this type, *Convention* and *Pleading Saviour*, have already found place in some modern hymnbooks.

Some of the earliest books of folk hymnody were pro-

---

[27] See George Pullen Jackson, *Spiritual Folk-Songs of Early America*, N. Y., 1927; and Annabel Morris Buchanan, *Folk Hymns of America*, J. Fischer, N. Y., 1938. They give a detailed and interesting account of both words and music used in the South.

duced in New England, but the folk hymn did not long
continue in use in this region, giving way to the rising
standards of church hymnody. The folk hymn was suited
to revivals and social gatherings like out-of-door camp
meetings, and the climatic and social conditions of the
South were much more favorable to such out-of-door camp
meetings than were those of New England. The result was
that most of the collections of this sort, after the early
years of the nineteenth century, are of southern or south-
western origin.

It is not possible to go into a detailed account of the
hymns to be found in these collections, and in any case
they fall outside the main current of American hymnody.
In a few instances the anonymous hymns rise to a genuinely
poetic level, of which the following is perhaps the best
example.

> There is a world we have not seen,
> That time shall never dare destroy,
> Where mortal footstep hath not been,
> Nor ear hath caught its sounds of joy.
> There is a region lovelier far
> Than angels tell, or poets sing,
> Brighter than summer's beauties are,
> And softer than the tints of spring.
>
> There is a world, and oh how blest,
> Fairer than prophets ever told,
> And never did an angel guest
> One half its blessedness unfold;
> It is all holy and serene,
> That land of glory and repose,
> And there to dim the radiant scene,
> The tear of sorrow never flows.
>
> It is not fanned by summer's gale,
> 'Tis not refreshed by vernal showers,

It never needs the moon-beam pale,
For there are known no evening hours.
No: for this world is ever bright,
With a pure radiance all its own;
The streams of uncreated light
Flow 'round it from th' eternal throne.[28]

More often they represent a survival, or an unconscious revival, of the old ballad versification inherited from England. The earliest of such collections is, perhaps, *Divine Hymns, or Spiritual Songs*, published in 1784, in New Hampshire, by Joshua Smith and others. Standard hymns are interspersed with folk hymns, — as is the case with most if not all of these collections, — and Smith's book is to be credited with being the first American hymnbook, outside those of the Methodists, to have included Charles Wesley's "Jesus, Lover of my soul."

For present purposes it is sufficient to examine in some detail another New England publication, which, though it did not appear until after 1800, is typical of the folk hymnody of the end of the eighteenth century, and not essentially different in character from the later books used in the South. It was intended for use in Vermont, where cultural conditions still resembled those of the rural South more than they did those of the older town life of New England. This book is *The Christian Harmony or, Songster's Companion*, compiled by Jeremiah Ingalls and published at "Exeter, Newhampshire," in 1805.[29] Ingalls was a brother of the organist of the Bromfield Street Methodist Church, Boston, who may have helped him. The book has "A Plain and Concise Introduction to Music" in nine lessons, and contains 133 tunes and 140 hymns. The tunes are almost entirely anonymous, for the most part in the "fuguing" style, some gay, some mournful, with many in

[28] A. M. Buchanan, *Folk-Hymns of America*, pp. 80–81.
[29] The preface is dated "Newbury, Vermont, Nov. 1804."

the minor key. The hymns, or songs, vary greatly in length. About a quarter of them are from known sources, Watts, Wesley, and Newton predominating. The authorship of the remainder is unidentified, but many of them are of American origin. There is the usual heavy emphasis on the prospect of death and the wrath to come, with such exhortations to repent as,

> Remember, sinful youth, you must die, you must die,
> Remember sinful youth, you must die.
> Remember sinful youth, who hate the way of Truth,
> And in your pleasure boast, you must die,
> And in your pleasure boast, you must die, —

or

Ye brave and bold, ye brisk and dull, come listen to my story,
I'll tell you things which I have seen, surpassing all vain glory.
When I was young, and brisk and gay, my heart was set on
    pleasure,
And in the wand'ring path of youth, I thought to find a treasure.

One of the most picturesque is the "Lamentation" which describes the death of Judith Brock, in eighteen stanzas.

> She's gone, she's gone, the parents mourn,
> She's gone, the children cry;
> While my affected bowels yearn
> With pangs of sympathy.
>
> .   .   .   .
>
> She had a taste for things divine,
> But not for carnal mirth;
> To those indeed she was inclin'd
> Who knew the heav'nly birth.
>
> .   .   .   .
>
> Where is the mind remains unshock'd?
> Yet view the awful scene:

Her sore distress with her jaws lock'd,
No food could go between.

Thus seventeen days she lay confin'd,
And then her life expir'd:
If she in Jesus was resign'd,
Not life could be desir'd.

But now we hope she is at rest,
Beyond the reach of pain,
We hope she is with Jesus blest,
Upon the blissful plain.

This is no other than a religious ballad of the old English
type. It may be compared with the similar ballad called
"Wicked Polly," written to tell the tragic fate of a less
pious girl and actually sung in a church at Little Rest, R. I.[30]

O young people, hark while I relate
The story of poor Polly's fate!
She was a lady young and fair,
And died a-groaning in despair.

She would go to balls and dance and play,
In spite of all her friends could say;
"I'll turn," said she, "when I am old,
And God will then receive my soul."

One Sabbath morning she fell sick;
Her stubborn heart began to ache.
She cries, "Alas, my days are spent!
It is too late now to repent."

She called her mother to her bed,
Her eyes were rolling in her head;
A ghastly look she did assume;
She cried, "Alas! I am undone.

[30] See Ninde, *Story of the American Hymn*, p. 68.

"My loving father, you I leave;
For wicked Polly do not grieve;
For I must burn forevermore,
When thousand thousand years are o'er.

"Your counsels I have slighted all,
My carnal appetite to fill.
When I am dead, remember well
Your wicked Polly groans in hell."

She [w]rung her hands and groaned and cried,
And gnawed her tongue before she died;
Her nails turned black, her voice did fail,
She died and left this lower vale.

May this a warning be to those
That love the ways that Polly chose.
Turn from your sins, lest you, like her,
Shall leave this world in black despair.

In another folk hymn in *The Christian Harmony*, "The Complainer" aims at a carping spirit not yet extinct.

I set myself against the Lord,
Despised his spirit and his word,
 And wish'd to take his place;
It vex'd me sore that I must die,
And perish too eternally,
 Or else be saved by grace.

Of every preacher I'd complain,
One spoke thro' pride, and one for gain,
 Another's learning's small:
This spoke too fast and that too slow,
One prayed too loud and one too low,
 The others had no call.

With no professors could I join [jine],
Some dress'd too mean and some too fine,
 And some did talk too long:

Some had a tone, some had no gift,
Some talk'd so weak, and some so swift,
That all of them were wrong.

. . . .

Kindred and neighbors all were bad,
And no true friends for to be had —
My rulers were too vile:
At length I was brought for to see,
The fault did mostly lie in me,
And had done all the while.

More cheerful is the better-known "Appletree Hymn," [31]
set to a very gay and lively tune.

The tree of life my soul hath seen,
Laden with fruit and always green;
The trees of nature fruitless be,
Compar'd with Christ the appletree.
This beauty doth all things excel,
By faith I know, but ne'er can tell,
This beauty doth all things excel,
By faith I know, but ne'er can tell
The glory which I now can see
In Jesus Christ the appletree.

. . . .

I'll sit and eat this fruit divine,
It cheers my heart like spir'tual wine;
And now this fruit is sweet to me,
That grows on Christ the appletree.

[31] It had appeared in Joshua Smith's *Divine Hymns*. Ninde, *Story of the American Hymn*, p. 122, says it has been traced to an English magazine of the middle of the eighteenth century, but gives no authority for his statement. Julian's *Dictionary* does not list it. If of English origin it presumably never came into use in that country. It had considerable popularity in this country, and it is so characteristic of New England that it would seem much more probable that it was written here.

The compiler was a loyal Vermonter, and did not hesitate to include in his book patriotic songs and references to contemporary events not dissimilar to those of William Billings. An "Election Hymn" contains these verses:

He call'd our fathers forth, to leave their native land,
And in this western clime, rear'd Freedom's happy band.
>   When we were weak, His goodness gave
>   A Washington, our land to save.

He all our councils rul'd, our troops to conquest led,
While our usurping foes before his banner fled.
>   We'll ne'er forget those vet'rans brave,
>   Who gave their lives, our rights to save.

Warren, on Bunker's Hill, Mercer, on Princeton plain,
Montgom'ry, at Quebec, lie with the mighty slain.
>   High angels guard each Hero's tomb,
>   And on their breasts may flowrets bloom.

Hail, deathless Washington! Columbia's pride and boast,
Whose name a bulwark prov'd, whose counsel was a host,
>   Thy name embalm'd in ev'ry heart,
>   Shall long survive the works of art.

.   .   .   .

May Jefferson, our Chief, in Cabinet and Field,
Check vice and party feud, be Order's friend and shield;
>   In virtue great, as in command,
>   Deal justice with Impartial hand.

And his love of Vermont is shown in his "Honor to the Hills," and even more explicitly in the "Election Ode."

>   Secure upon his well earn'd spot
>   The farmer cultivates his lot;
>   The city's din, and tinkling sounds,
>   Where gladiators walk their rounds,
>   And pirates launching from Algiers,
>   Excite in him no racking fears.

Not fifty years have roll'd away,
Since savage yells spread wild dismay;
Where now rich fields of yellow corn,
The suburbs of our towns adorn;
The maple, screen for Indian darts,
Now yields the wealth of Indies' marts.

Vermont, thy sons are more than blest,
In wealth increasing, public rest:
Thy rulers from the people's choice,
Obedient to the public voice,
Possess the pow'r, the goodness, will,
A nation's interests to fulfill.

. . . .

Ye mountaineers, to you is giv'n,
These favors by propitious heav'n;
Let gratitude employ your themes,
By day your tho'ts, by night your dreams,
Then freedom, like your mountain's scene
Shall flourish in perennial green.

Meanwhile other religious groups, unaffected by the folk
hymnody movement, and not markedly under the influence
of Watts, embarked upon endeavors to produce a hymnody
adapted to their own tastes. The religious movement known
as Universalism had taken root in New England after the
arrival of John Murray in 1770. Murray had been a disciple
of James Relly in England, and Relly had been a convert
of Whitefield's who had moved over to a belief in the universal salvation of mankind. Relly had organized a congregation in London, and as early as 1754 had published
his *Christian Hymns, Poems, and Sacred Songs, sacred to
the praise of God our Saviour*. Since very few of the hymns
current at the time did not include sentiments more or less
repugnant to Relly's views, the contents of the book were

composed by James Relly and his brother John. The verses were very crude and rough, but when John Murray organized the first Universalist Church in this country at Gloucester, Massachusetts, soon after his arrival, Relly's book was the only one available. Music was provided by a barrel organ which ground out ten tunes.

In 1776 an American edition was printed, and it was again reprinted at Portsmouth, New Hampshire, in 1782, with an addition of five hymns by John Murray himself, which were an improvement on most of those in Relly's book. These were the earliest hymns produced in America by a Universalist, but others soon followed, for in 1791 the Universalists in Philadelphia produced *Evangelical Psalms, Hymns and Spiritual Songs, Selected from various authors*, with thirty-five hymns by Silas Ballou, and the next year the Universalists in New England brought out *Psalms, Hymns and Spiritual Songs: selected and original*, containing fifty-two hymns by Rev. George Richards. None of these eighteenth-century Universalist hymns have enough merit to have enabled them to survive in modern use.

More important for the development of American hymnody was the course followed by the churches of the liberal wing of New England Congregationalism, mostly in eastern Massachusetts and centered in Boston, which, in the first quarter of the nineteenth century, were destined to split with the "orthodox" wing and become Unitarian in theology. These churches, while still drawing heavily upon Watts, made rapid progress in the latter part of the eighteenth century toward the production of what were definitely hymnbooks, rather than psalmbooks with a supplement of hymns. In the course of seventy-five years following the Revolution they produced a remarkable succession of books, which, though often of small circulation, stood in the front rank for excellence and for the freedom with which they introduced new hymns from English sources.[32]

The first of these books was a little volume of 166 hymns entitled *A Collection of Hymns, more particularly designed for the use of the West Society in Boston, 1783*, edited by Rev. Simeon Howard. This book dropped most of the psalms and hymns of theological content, though it prints one beginning,

> Shall atheists dare insult the cross
> Of Christ, the Son of God?
> Shall infidels reproach his laws,
> Or trample on his blood?

It includes Watts' "Hark! from the tomb a doleful sound," — as well as his: "I sing th' almighty power of God," — and Wesley's arrangement of "Before Jehovah's awful throne"; — Mrs. Barbauld's "Praise to God, immortal praise"; — Addison's "The spacious firmament on high," — and "The Lord my pasture shall prepare," — and "When all thy mercies, O my God," Doddridge's "See Israel's gentle Shepherd stand," Tate's Christmas hymn, "While shepherds watched their flocks by night," and Thomas Scott's hymn on "Persecution," which, though of English origin, was to find a welcome in a number of post-Revolutionary American books,

> Absurd and vain attempt! to bind
> With iron chains, the free-born mind;
> To force conviction, and reclaim
> The wand'ring by destructive flame.

But while the book does contain a considerable number of fine hymns it also contains a number of quaintly didactic moral songs probably written, like the hymn first quoted,

[32] See H. W. Foote, *A Descriptive Catalogue of American Unitarian Hymnbooks*, Proc. Unitarian Historical Society, Boston, Mass., May, 1938.

by now-forgotten Boston versifiers. One of these, headed
"Against pride in clothes," begins,

> Why should our garments (made to hide
> Our parents' shame) provoke our pride?
> The art of dress did ne'er begin
> Till Eve our mother learnt to sin.

And one on "Temperance" contains an amusing anticlimax.

> Is it a man's divinest good,
> To make his soul a slave to food?
> Vile as the beast, whose spirit dies;
> And has no hope beyond the skies?
>
> .   .   .   .
>
> Can I forget the fatal deed,
> How Eve brought death on all her seed?
> She tasted the forbidden tree,
> Anger'd her God, and ruin'd me.

In these songs the religious liberals of Boston made what
was perhaps their nearest approach to folk hymnody. This
little book, though it lasted, with revisions, for forty years
in the church for which it was prepared, is significant only
as pointing the way to much better hymnbooks in which
religion and ethics were more conspicuous than theology.

A far better book was published, in 1788, by Rev. William Bentley [33] of Salem, containing forty psalms selected
from Tate and Brady and 163 hymns of good quality, including Alexander Pope's

> Father of all! in every age,
> In every clime adored, —

and Beddome's "When Israel through the desert pass'd."

[33] Rev. William Bentley, b. Boston, 1759; d. Salem, Mass., 1819; A.B.
Harvard, 1777. Minister of the East Church, Salem, 1783–1819. Author of
a *Diary* which throws much light on the period between 1784 and 1819.

Bentley was a man of very exceptional intellectual abilities and with wide interests. His *Diary* contains references to the problems of church music, and he notes that the young people in the singing school often took "extraordinary liberties." The history of New England was one of his hobbies and he furnished his correspondent, Professor Eberling of Hamburg, with much information for the latter's history of the United States. In Bentley's *Diary* under date of April 3, 1801, is the following entry, which is interesting as recording what is probably the earliest historical survey of New England psalmody.

Wrote to Eberling the history of our Psalmody. From the single part in our old Bibles, and the Tunes to every Psalm in Sternhold & Hopkins till the New England version, then mentioning Increase Mather's measured prose, Prince's poetic version & Barnard's of Marblehead. The introduction of Tate and Brady by Dr. Colman and of Watts by Mather Byles. The Collection for West Boston by Dr. Howard, my own Collection in Salem, Dr. Belknap's Collection in Boston, introduced into several churches. Relly's Hymns among the Universalists & the Scotch version among the Sandemanians. I then noticed the progress of music from the single part to Tenor, bass and medius. The work of Tansur and the improvement by Williams. The singing of appropriate tunes to Psalms interrupted by the new Version. The Selection of Tunes. The change by Billings, his Reuben and other books. The works of Holyoke, Kimball & Holden, and the numberless publications which have appeared in New England, which I did not presume to enumerate. I mentioned the compilation of Holyoke and Holden for Instrumental music and the expected publication of political songs. This is the outline of a long history which I wrote to him.

Eberling's papers were purchased after his death for the Harvard Library, and Bentley's were deposited in the collections of the American Antiquarian Society at Worcester, but, unfortunately, Bentley's historical sketch is not to be found in either collection.

Much more important and influential was *Sacred Poetry. Consisting of Psalms and Hymns adapted to Christian devotion in public and private. Selected from the best authors, with variations and additions Boston, 1795,* edited by Rev. Jeremy Belknap, Channing's immediate predecessor in the Federal Street Church, in Boston. Belknap's aim was to produce a book which should be satisfactory to both the liberal and the conservative wing of New England Congregationalism. In this he failed, for he was too far in advance of his time to meet the approval of the orthodox Calvinists. Among the Unitarians, however, the book was generally used for the next forty years, and when, in 1808, the vestry of Trinity Church, Boston, impatient at the delay of the General Convention of the Protestant Episcopal Church in getting out a satisfactory hymnal, prepared one for the use of the Trinity Church, they drew heavily on Belknap's, saying in their preface, "In this selection we are chiefly indebted to Dr. Belknap, whose book unquestionably contains the best specimens of sacred poetry extant."

This was hardly an exaggerated estimate of Belknap's book. In addition to a large number of psalms taken from various sources, often with "variations," it contained 300 hymns, chiefly from Watts, Doddridge, Anne Steele, Addison, and from various English collections. It also included Helen Maria Williams' hymn, "While thee I seek, protecting Power."

The hymn by Mather Byles (whose great-nephew Belknap was), "When wild confusion rends the air," — appears to be the only hymn of American authorship in the book. Belknap was particularly pleased with his introduction of Anne Steele's hymns to American usage.

In 1799, Rev. James Freeman, assisted by a layman of

his parish, Joseph May, brought out *A Collection of Psalms and Hymns* for King's Chapel, where it superseded the *New Version* which had been used there for eighty-six years. This collection was "principally from Tate and Brady," supplemented by a selection of ninety hymns. In quality it was quite inferior to Belknap's, and it is noteworthy only as another indication of the transition from psalmody to hymnody.

With the nineteenth century we enter a new era. It is true that psalmody, in the modified form in which it was presented in the various compilations from Watts, with more or less adequate supplements of hymns, long survived in the more conservative bodies, but the issue of denominational hymnals soon began, and presently swelled into a flood of new books in which appeared a steadily increasing number of hymns of distinctive quality and worth by American authors.

CHAPTER VI

The Opening of a New Era, 1800-1830

WITH THE OPENING of the nineteenth century we enter upon a new era. The rough and stony field which had been so slowly prepared was at last ready to produce its crop of hymns of permanent value by native American authors. The tongue of the dumb began to sing, and waters broke out in the wilderness and streams in the desert. To the few and scattered voices lifted in the eighteenth century was added an ever-increasing chorus of song.

With the substitution of Watts for the old psalmody of the Puritan days, and the introduction of new types of music (including both the eighteenth-century English hymn tunes and the popular and exuberant, though less admirable, American tunes of Billings and his followers), came also the use of hymns, at first generally inserted unobtrusively as "Supplements" to Watts. These supplements, in books of the better type, were almost exclusively composed of hymns drawn from the later eighteenth-century English hymn writers and "Collections." But the books of a more popular type, especially those intended for evangelistic work, included also hymns by American authors, often anonymous, most of which rose little above the level of doggerel, while the music was of similar character.

In the first quarter of the century, indeed down to about 1840, the book most widely used among the more conservative Congregationalists and the Presbyterians was

the one, already referred to, which had been edited by
Timothy Dwight, and was commonly called *Dwight's
Watts.*

In 1815 appeared another book which, in its revised
form, was destined to be a rival of Dwight's in orthodox
Congregational circles. It was prepared by Rev. Samuel
Worcester of Salem, Massachusetts, and was called *Christian
Psalmody, in four parts: Comprising Dr. Watts' Psalms
abridged: Select Hymns from other sources; and select
Harmonies.* It was an excellent selection, the "fourth part"
consisting of eighty-two good tunes at the back of the book.
Unfortunately, Worcester had underestimated the attach-
ment of the churches to Watts, for he had made room for
new hymns by dropping some of Watts' psalms, and
shortening others. Immediately a clamor arose against
"mangling" and "amputating" and "robbing" Watts, and
a demand for "Watts entire." [1] So, against his better judgment, Worcester brought out in 1819 a second and inferior
book which contained the complete *Psalms and Hymns*
by Watts, with other selected hymns, but without music.
This book, entitled *The Psalms, Hymns and Spiritual Songs
of the Reverend Isaac Watts, to which are added Select
Hymns from other authors*, but commonly called *Watts
and Select*, had a lasting vogue, especially in the churches
which were inclined to dispute the right of any other
authors to trespass on the sacred field where Watts now
reigned supreme.

By 1820, a desire for a wider range of hymnody for
evangelistic services began to make itself manifest among
the Congregational and Presbyterian churches of Connecticut and New York. In that year the General Association
of Connecticut proposed "A New Selection of Hymns,"
for which the Albany Presbytery reported an "imperious

[1] Benson, *The English Hymn*, p. 168. See also Ninde, *Story of the
American Hymn*, pp. 111-114.

and pressing" demand, "very extensively in the West and South." [2]

This demand was met in 1824 by the publication of *Village Hymns for Social worship. Selected and original. Designed as a Supplement to the Psalms and Hymns of Dr. Watts. By Asahel Nettleton,*[3] although the book was not formally authorized by either the Congregationalists or the Presbyterians. Nettleton was a young Congregational evangelist, a graduate of Yale, who had worked in both New England and New York. His book contained six hundred hymns, and was based chiefly on Strong's *Hartford Selection,* Worcester's *Select Hymns,* and a little book of Leonard Bacon's published the previous year. Nettleton, says Benson, knew a good hymn when he saw it, and produced the finest evangelical hymnbook yet made in America. He had the good taste to reject the cheaper type of revival hymn as "unfit for the ordinary purpose of devotion, as prescriptions, salutary in sickness are laid aside on the restoration of health." He introduced about fifty missionary hymns, including Reginald Heber's "From Greenland's icy mountains" — which had been printed in two American periodicals the preceding year; a great many items from the *Olney Hymns* (1779) of John Newton and William Cowper, which had played so important a part in the evangelical revival in the Church of England; several hymns by Charles Wesley; some by James Montgomery; many by Anne Steele. A large proportion of these were new to the users of his book, and some were included for the first time in any American hymnbook. He also included hymns by a number of American authors, of whom at least three were represented for the first time in a hymnbook. Of these, Abby B. Hyde's nine contribu-

[2] Benson, *The English Hymn*, p. 376.
[3] Asahel Nettleton, b. April 21, 1783, at North Killingworth, Conn.; d. 1843; A.B. Yale, 1809; ordained 1817, but never settled in a parish;

tions have passed out of use, though her "Dear Saviour, if these lambs should stray," was long popular. But Phoebe Brown's [4] "I love to steal awhile away," is still a favorite with the Methodists, as is William B. Tappan's [5] hymn, "'Tis midnight, and on Olive's brow."

Nettleton met the problem of supplying appropriate music not merely by printing at the head of each hymn the names of one or more tunes to which it might be sung, but by taking the further step of publishing a companion tune-book, called *Zion's Harp*, containing all the tunes recommended. This tune-book was in a general way similar to many others which had been published, mostly in Boston, in the preceding fifty years,[6] but it had the particular advantage of being arranged for use with *Village Hymns*, and was at least a short step in the direction of the modern practice of providing each hymn with its own tune. But it still left the congregation with only the printed words, and the singers had to manipulate two books, unless they knew either the words or music by heart.[7] It was not till

---

an evangelist in Massachusetts, Connecticut, New York and Virginia; visited Great Britain in 1831.

[4] Phoebe (Hinsdale) Brown, b. Canaan, N. Y., 1783; d. Marshall, Ill., Dec., 1861. She had a harsh upbringing, did not learn to write until eighteen years old, and had only three months' schooling in all. Nevertheless she wrote many hymns of which this is the sole survivor. For an account of its origin see *Our Hymnody*, by R. G. McCutchan, pp. 83–84, or C. S. Nutter's and W. F. Tillett's *Hymns and Hymn Writers of the Church*, New York, 1911.

[5] William Bingham Tappan, b. Oct. 24, 1794, Beverly, Mass.; d. West Needham, Mass., June 18, 1849; a clock-maker who became a Congregational minister and evangelist. Author of ten volumes of commonplace verse, this hymn being taken from *Poems, 1822*. Its long-continued popularity is due in no small part to William B. Bradbury's tune *Olive's Brow*, published in 1853.

[6] Over 140 tune-books were published in New England between 1780 and 1820. Fisher, *Ye Olde New England Tunes*, p. XIII.

[7] Ainsworth's *Psalter* had printed the tunes with the words, as had some other seventeenth-century psalters, but generally only a few tunes

1855 that Beecher's famous *Plymouth Collection* first printed the tune immediately above the words. *Village Hymns*, with its accompanying music, won immediate popularity, and ran through seven editions in three years. And it proved a valuable source book for the editors of later books.

Among the Presbyterians the embers of "the great Psalmody Controversy" were still glowing. The conservatives clung to the old metrical psalms; the more progressive congregations used *Dwight's Watts*, or Worcester's *Watts and Select*, with *Village Hymns* for revival meetings. The Baptists in New England used Winchell's *Watts and Select*; in the Middle West they used *Watts and Rippon*; elsewhere they sang songs of the revival type. The Lutherans, the German Reformed Church and the Dutch Reformed Church gradually turned from psalms or hymns in the language of the mother country which they had brought with them to the use of English in public worship, as a generation grew up for whom English was the mother tongue. Some of them clung closely to strict psalmody. Others brought out collections largely influenced by the evangelical hymnody of their neighboring English-speaking churches. None of them, at this period, made any original contributions of value to American hymnody, though the Lutheran Paul Henkel of Virginia produced a *Church Hymn Book* with a large number of hymns from his own pen which Benson describes as "nothing more than didactic

---

were printed in the back of the book, as in *The Bay Psalm Book* of 1698. Even this inclusion of tunes had died out later, and the music was supplied by separate tune-books. The leader of the singing was obliged to pick out an appropriate tune for each psalm or hymn chosen by the minister. This was the common practice in England also, where collections of several hundred tunes were brought together, without the words of hymns, in volumes such as the *Bristol Tune-Book*, one of the best-known British examples in the middle of the nineteenth century.

prose broken up into short phrases that serve as lines of verse." [8]

The Universalists, meanwhile, were busy producing books which represented the somewhat divergent views of the two groups centered, respectively, in Philadelphia and in New England. One of these, *Hymns composed by different authors, by order of the General Convention of Universalists of the New England States and others* (1808), consisted of hymns by the editors, Hosea Ballou, Abner Kneeland, and Edward Turner, rather than a collection from varied sources, which was what the Convention had intended. But a later volume, *The Universalists' Hymn Book* (1821), more nearly met the original intention. None of these original hymns has had any general acceptance, though one or two by Hosea Ballou are still in use among the Universalists, more by virtue of his repute among them than because of the excellence of his verse.[9]

The only really notable hymns of high literary quality and permanent value written during the first three decades of the century came from the Episcopalians centered about New York and Philadelphia, and the Unitarians centered about Boston.

We have seen in the preceding chapter how the Protestant Episcopal Church made the transition from psalmody to hymnody when it approved hymn singing in principle by including a selection of twenty-seven hymns within the covers of the Prayer Book of 1790. Thirty more were added in 1808, but this enlarged though still very limited selection soon proved unsatisfactory to Episcopalians interested in good singing, and it compared unfavorably with the resources then available in several other denominations. As has already been noted, Trinity Church, in Boston, put

[8] For an account of the movement in these churches see Benson, *The English Hymn*, pp. 402–420.
[9] See Benson, *The English Hymn*, pp. 421–425.

out its own hymnbook in 1808, adapted from Belknap's *Sacred Poetry*. A few years later Rev. William A. Mühlenberg,[10] then a young man, wrote *A Plea for Christian Hymns* (1821), which he followed with a collection entitled *Church Poetry: being portions of the Psalms in verse, and Hymns suited to the festivals and fasts, and various occasions of the church. Selected and arranged from various Authors. By William Augustus Mühlenberg, associate rector of St. James's Church, Lancaster* (1823). The book represented the taste of the evangelical wing of the Church of England, and drew largely on Cotterill's *Selection*, published in England in 1819. Mühlenberg at once introduced it into his own church, and it was adopted by some other neighboring parishes.

An immediate result of the publication of *Church Poetry* was to stimulate the General Convention of 1823 to appoint a committee, of which Mühlenberg was a member, to prepare a hymnbook for the Church, although Bishop White put forth a pamphlet expressing his disapproval. Notwithstanding the doubts of the conservatives, who were still satisfied with Tate and Brady, the Convention in 1826 approved a collection of 212 hymns prepared by Mühlenberg and Rev. H. U. Onderdonck, which was published in 1827 under the title, *Hymns of the Protestant Episcopal Church, in the United States of America*. In 1833 a revised edition of the metrical psalms, mostly from Tate and Brady, was published and bound up with the hymns. This combined book, commonly called the *Prayer Book Collection* because often bound with the Prayer Book, continued in use until 1872, as the authorized hymnal of the Episcopal Church.

[10] William Augustus Mühlenberg (grandson of Henry Melchior Mühlenberg, the patriarch of Lutheranism in America), b. Philadelphia, Sept. 16, 1796; A.B. Univ. of Pennsylvania, 1814; ordained 1817; rector of churches in Lancaster, Pa., and in New York City; died April 6, 1877.

The hymns were chiefly the eighteenth-century productions of Watts, Doddridge, Anne Steele, and Charles Wesley, with a sprinkling of other writers. The editors seem either to have been unaware of, or to have been influenced in surprisingly small degree by the new currents in the hymnody of the Church of England. These currents dated from about the time of the publication, in 1779, of the *Olney Hymns* by Newton and Cowper, and moved towards the publication of Heber's *Hymns* in 1827, of which Mühlenberg had some knowledge in advance. But Mühlenberg appears to have been suspicious of Heber's desire to promote hymns of a more definitely literary and liturgical character. Benson calls the *Prayer Book Collection* "decidedly evangelical and quite colorless in Ecclesiastical and Sacramental directions," [11] but it was noteworthy in its inclusion of hymns by five American Episcopalians whose work has survived. No other single book published in the first third of the nineteenth century included so important a contribution to American hymnody. The nearest approach was Nettleton's *Village Hymns*, a very different type of book, and the original American hymns which Nettleton included were of inferior quality and of less permanent value.

Mühlenberg himself contributed five hymns to this collection, including his baptismal hymn, "Saviour, who thy flock art feeding" — the Christmas hymn "Shout the glad tidings, exultingly sing" — which he wrote to go to the tune *Avison*, which Thomas Moore's song, "Sound the loud timbrel," had made popular, and that "classic of evangelical otherworldliness," "I would not live alway." This last one has not lived, though once widely popular, and Dr. Mühlenberg did not desire that it should. He wrote it in a mood of deep depression when a very young man; it was included originally because he was a member of the

[11] Benson, *The English Hymn*, p. 400.

committee which prepared the book; and he later came to think its sentiment unhealthy and to regret that it had been published.

Rev. Henry U. Onderdonck,[12] who had assisted Mühlenberg in preparing the collection, contributed nine hymns, but only one of them, "How wondrous and great are thy works," survives in the present *Hymnal*, and perhaps nowhere outside its covers.

More important was the contribution of Rev. George Washington Doane,[13] later bishop of New Jersey. Bishop Doane was eminent for his abilities and force of character, and was a minor poet of considerable skill. From the volume of verse which he had already published were taken two of the three hymns by which he is now remembered, "Softly now the light of day" — and "Thou art the way, by thee alone." His third hymn, "Fling out the banner, let it float" was not written until many years later. These three have had wide use in both England and America, but his remaining hymns, sixteen in number, have disappeared.

The other two new American authors represented in the *Prayer Book Collection* were Rev. James Wallis Eastbourne, whose hymns have not survived, and a layman, Francis Scott Key, better known as the author of "The Star-Spangled Banner." The one hymn by him which has had wide use, "Lord, with glowing heart I'll praise thee," was included in Mühlenberg's *Church Poetry*, and was thence taken over into the *Prayer Book Collection*. That book, limited and timidly conservative though it was in its

[12] Henry Ustick Onderdonck, b. New York, March 16, 1789; Columbia College; rector of St. Anne's Church, Brooklyn; assistant bishop of Pennsylvania 1827–1836; bishop 1844, in succession to Bishop White; d. Philadelphia, Dec. 6, 1858.

[13] George Washington Doane, b. Trenton, N. J., May 27, 1799; A.B. Union College; ordained 1821; professor at Trinity College, Hartford, Conn., 1824–1828; rector of Trinity Church, Boston, 1828–1832; bishop of New Jersey 1832; d. Burlington, N. J., April 27, 1859; published *Songs by the Way*, 1824; later and enlarged editions in 1859 and 1874.

use of English sources, was greatly enriched by these original contributions, some of which are today sung throughout the English-speaking world.

As has already been noted, the Unitarian hymn writers of New England alone equalled the Episcopalians in the number and quality of the hymns which they produced, although those hymns were scattered through several different volumes, instead of being collected in a single authorized hymnal. The earliest Unitarian hymnbooks, published before 1800, have been noted in the preceding chapter. In 1808 Rev. William Emerson (father of Ralph Waldo Emerson) issued a handsomely printed *Collection* of 150 hymns, from which he omitted "what savors of party spirit and sectarian notions," with the result that the book was attacked in the orthodox *Panoplist* for its exclusion of "most of the capital doctrines of the gospel." Two laymen, Ralph Eddowes and James Taylor, in Philadelphia edited a *Selection of Sacred Poetry*, 1812, for use in the church which Joseph Priestley had founded. A layman, Dr. Henry F. Sewall, in 1820, prepared a book containing 504 hymns for the First Congregational Society, now All Souls' Church in New York, commonly called *The New York Collection*, chiefly notable for its inclusion of five original hymns by William Cullen Bryant [14] who was a member of the congregation. The best-known of these hymns, still widely used, is the one which he had written in 1819 for the dedication of a church in Prince Street, New York.

> Thou, whose unmeasured temple stands,
> Built over earth and sea,
> Accept the walls that human hands
> Have raised, O God, to Thee.

[14] William Cullen Bryant, b. Cummington, Mass., Nov. 3, 1794; d. on Long Island, N. Y., July 12, 1878; studied at Williams College; a lawyer, later a journalist in New York; the earliest of the famous group of New England poets of the 19th century.

Bryant also wrote a lovely christening hymn, "Lord, who ordainest for mankind" — but he was not a great hymn writer. Rev. F. M. Bird rightly says of him that his "genius was cool, meditative, and not distinguished by lyric fire. His hymns are correct and solid, but none reach the highest rank." [15]

Neither of these collections had much use beyond the churches for which they were prepared, nor was Belknap's *Sacred Poetry* superseded in general use among the Unitarians until the publication, in 1830, of *A Collection of Psalms and Hymns for Sacred Worship*, edited by Rev. Francis W. P. Greenwood of King's Chapel, Boston. Greenwood's *Collection*, although still based on Watts, included hymns by James Montgomery, Harriet Auber, Sir John Bowring and Reginald Heber, and practically introduced those of Charles Wesley to American Unitarians. It was used in King's Chapel for more than sixty years, and long and widely elsewhere, running to fifty editions. Ralph Waldo Emerson in his journal for 1847 noted his opinion that it was "still the best."

Several other Unitarian writers of this period, whose hymns soon found their way into general use, must be mentioned. Rev. John Pierpont [16] was a powerful preacher and an ardent reformer whose aggressive antislavery and protemperance advocacy kept him in hot water during a good part of his Boston pastorate. But he was also a poet of considerable abilities whose verses were in demand for special occasions, such as the 200th anniversary of the founding of Boston and the centennial of Washington's birth. In 1824 he wrote for the opening of the Barton

---

[15] Julian, *Dictionary of Hymnology*, p. 1902.

[16] John Pierpont, b. April 6, 1785, at Litchfield, Conn.; d. Aug. 27, 1866, at Medford, Mass.; A.B. Yale, 1804; teacher and lawyer; graduated from Harvard Divinity School 1818; minister of the Hollis Street Church, Boston, 1819–1845; of the Unitarian Church at Troy, N. Y., 1845–1849; of the First Church in Medford, Mass., 1849–1859.

Square Church in Salem a hymn which Garrett Horder calls "The earliest really great hymn I have found by an American writer." [17] Omitting two stanzas appropriate to the special occasion for which it was written, the remaining four, beginning, "O Thou, to whom in ancient time," make a fine hymn of universal worship, which has, as it deserves, considerable use. Pierpont's morning and evening hymns "for a child," of two stanzas each, beginning,

> O God, I thank Thee that the night
> In peace and rest hath passed away, —

and

> Another day its course hath run,
> And still, O God, thy child is blest, —

are tender and loving little lyrics, though now seldom used.

Professor Andrews Norton was a Cambridge gentleman of the old school, formal in manner and conservative in thought, but he was a sound scholar for his time, and his four-volume work on *The Genuineness of the Gospels*, published after his retirement as professor of the New Testament in the Harvard Divinity School, was the first important American contribution to New Testament scholarship. He has the misfortune to be remembered today less for his solid accomplishments than for his unhappy reference to Ralph Waldo Emerson's *Divinity School Address* as "the latest form of infidelity." [18] He wrote a good deal of poetry in a rather formal, eighteenth-century style, with, like so much of the verse of the period, an oppressive em-

[17] W. Garrett Horder, *The Treasury of American Sacred Song*, New York, 1896, p. 337.

[18] Andrews Norton, b. Dec. 31, 1786, at Hingham, Mass.; d. Sept. 18, 1853, at Newport, R. I.; A.B. Harvard, 1804; professor in the Harvard Divinity School, 1819–1830; an eminent scholar and author.

phasis on sorrow and death. In 1809 he published in the *Monthly Anthology* a hymn beginning,

> My God, I thank thee! May no thought
> E'er deem thy chastisements severe, —

which was widely used and highly esteemed by a generation more given to "submission" than is the present one. And in 1833 he wrote for the dedication of a church a really fine hymn, still in use, which is equally available for the opening of worship,

> Where ancient forests widely spread,
> Where bends the cataract's ocean-fall,
> On the lone mountain's silent head,
> There are thy temples, God of all.

Nathaniel Langdon Frothingham belonged to the same school of early Unitarianism.[19] He was called upon to write hymns for various occasions, but only one, written in 1828 for the ordination of William P. Lunt, has survived in use, possibly, because, with the omission of one stanza, it is so well adapted for the opening of worship, but also because of its stately and coolly flawless beauty:

> O God, whose presence glows in all
> Within, around us, and above;
> Thy word we bless, thy name we call,
> Whose word is Truth, whose name is Love.

Another of this first group of Unitarian hymn writers was Rev. Henry Ware, Jr.[20] In 1817 he printed in *The*

---

[19] Nathaniel Langdon Frothingham, b. Boston, July 23, 1793; d. April 4, 1870, Boston; A.B. Harvard, 1811; minister of the First Church in Boston, 1815–1850; published *Metrical Pieces, Translated and Original*, 1855, and a second volume in 1870.

[20] Henry Ware, Jr., b. April 21, 1794, at Hingham, Mass.; d. Sept. 25, 1843, at Framingham, Mass.; A.B. Harvard, 1812; minister of the Second Church in Boston, 1817–1829; professor in the Harvard Divinity School, 1829–1842; author and poet.

Christian Disciple a hymn which Dr. Ninde says "holds a place among our noblest Easter lyrics," [21] although its mood is too otherworldly to make it acceptable to modern Unitarians:

> Lift your glad voices in triumph on high,
> For Jesus hath risen and man cannot die.

The most interesting of his hymns for its historical associations is the one which he wrote for the ordination of Jared Sparks at Baltimore, in 1819, the occasion on which Channing preached his "Baltimore Sermon" which was the battle cry of the Unitarians in their controversy with the orthodox wing of Congregationalism. This hymn, which has had considerable use, begins,

> Great God, the followers of thy Son,
> We bow before thy mercy-seat.

The one hymn by Ware which is still widely used was written in 1822 for the "Opening of an Organ." It is a good, though not a great hymn, and one of the very few available for the dedication of an organ, but it is also suitable for general praise:

> All nature's works his praise declare
> To whom all praise belongs.

The mere fact that a hymn for such an occasion could be written in New England at this period illustrates vividly the change of opinion about instrumental music which had taken place in the eleven decades since the Brattle Square Church had refused Thomas Brattle's organ. No less than eight pieces of Henry Ware's poetry were included in the English compilation *Lyra Sacra Americana*, published in 1868 by the Religious Tract Society.

[21] Ninde, *Story of the American Hymn*, p. 289.

The last of this group was Frederic Henry Hedge, whose earliest hymn was written for the ordination of a friend in December, 1829.[22] Like some of the hymns already considered, it was afterwards rewritten and adapted to the opening of worship. Few hymns in English make a grander invocation than the four stanzas now in common use, beginning,

> Sovereign and transforming Grace,
> We invoke thy quickening power;
> Reign the spirit of this place,
> Bless the purpose of this hour.

Undoubtedly the best-known of Hedge's later hymns is his great translation (1853), of Luther's "Ein' feste Burg," beginning "A mighty fortress is our God." It is the best version in English for singing, though Carlyle's rugged lines, "A safe stronghold our God is still," are more commonly used in England.

Carlyle, to whom Hedge was introduced by Emerson, wrote of him, "Hedge is one of the sturdiest little fellows I have come across for many a day. A face like a rock, a voice like a howitzer, only his honest gray eyes assure you a little."

In another hymn, written for a Good Friday service in 1843, Hedge reverted to the metrical form of the great Latin sequence, "Stabat Mater dolorosa." The last three stanzas of this hymn are found in a number of hymnbooks, beginning,

[22] Frederic Henry Hedge, b. Dec. 12, 1805, at Cambridge, Mass.; d. Aug. 21, 1890, at Cambridge; A.B. Harvard, 1825 (class poet); Harvard Divinity School, 1828; minister of churches in Arlington, Mass., 1829–1835; Bangor, Maine, 1835–1850; Providence, R. I., 1850–1856; Brookline, Mass., 1856–1872; professor of ecclesiastical history, 1857; professor of German literature, 1872–1882, at Harvard; editor, with F. D. Huntington, of *Hymns for the Church*, 1865; the learned author of numerous works.

It is finished. Man of sorrows!
From thy cross our frailty borrows
   Strength to bear and conquer thus.
While exalted there we view thee,
Mighty Sufferer, draw us to thee,
   Sufferer victorious!

The hymn is one of the best available for Good Friday, and deserves a wider use than it has had.

These early Unitarian hymn writers, significant as their work was, were but the forerunners in a long succession of singers belonging to the same denomination who have made some of the most precious contributions to American hymnody, as we shall see in the following chapters.

CHAPTER VII

The Mid-Century Flood Tide, 1831-1865

IN THE fourth decade of the nineteenth century the development of American hymnody continued at an accelerated pace. We have seen how Nettleton's *Village Hymns* met the demand for a more popular type of song than the church hymnbooks provided, especially for use at revival meetings. Even *Village Hymns*, however, set too high a standard for some tastes, and it was followed in 1831 by *The Christian Lyre*, prepared by Rev. Joshua Leavitt, a Congregational minister, to aid the evangelical revival conducted by Finney. Leavitt says in his preface,

Every person conversant with revivals must have observed that wherever meetings for prayer and conference assume a special interest, there is a desire to use hymns and music of a different character from those ordinarily used in church.

Therefore, he included lively hymns and melodies, sometimes with "chorusses," on a distinctly lower literary and musical level than that of *Village Hymns*. His disregard of musical standards reminds one of William Billings, for he admitted that he had "no musical skill beyond that of ordinary plain singers," and that his book was not designed "to please scientific musicians." But, though he introduced music of a rather cheap popular type, he did take another forward step by printing the music on the page opposite the words, instead of in a separate tune-book. *The Christian Lyre* was immensely popular in evangelical circles, running to a twenty-sixth edition in 1846.

The book, in spite of its generally low standards, did contain one notable contribution to American hymnody in J. W. Alexander's [1] famous hymn, "O Sacred Head! now wounded," the most beautiful and moving of all the English translations of Paul Gerhardt's hymn, "O Haupt voll Blut und Wunden," which, in turn, was translated from the "Salve caput cruentatum," commonly, though erroneously, attributed to St. Bernard of Clairvaux. Dr. Alexander, the first American Presbyterian, except the Indian Samson Occom, to follow Samuel Davies as a hymn writer, was a brilliant, devout and scholarly man, who made other translations from both German and Latin hymns, of which one from "Jesu dulcis memoria" beginning "Jesus, how sweet thy memory is" and another from "Stabat Mater dolorosa" beginning "Near the cross was Mary weeping" have had some use. Through these translations he helped to awaken some interest in Latin hymnody among Americans, to whom it had hitherto been a sealed book.

Leavitt's *Christian Lyre*, with its words and music of a type anticipatory of the "gospel songs" of a later period, soon produced a wholesome reaction in favor of better hymns and tunes. The leader in this movement was Lowell Mason, a Congregational layman.[2] While a young bank

[1] James Waddell Alexander, b. Hopewell, Va., March 13, 1804; d. Sweet Springs, Va., July 31, 1859; A.B. Princeton, 1820; Princeton Theological Seminary; pastor of Presbyterian churches in Virginia and New Jersey; professor of rhetoric, College of New Jersey, 1833–1844; pastor of the Duane St. Presbyterian Church, New York, 1844–1849; professor of church history, Princeton Seminary, 1849–1851; pastor Fifth Ave. Presbyterian Church, New York, 1851–1859.

[2] Lowell Mason, b. Jan. 8, 1792, at Medfield, Mass.; d. Aug. 11, 1872, at Orange, N. J. At sixteen years of age he was a choir leader and teacher of singing classes. At twenty-three he went to Savannah, Ga., as a bank clerk, and returned to Boston in 1827, soon becoming president and conductor of the Handel and Haydn Society, and a noted choir leader. In 1835 he received the first honorary degree of Doctor of Music conferred by an American college.

clerk in Savannah, Mason had compiled a book of church music, largely based on Samuel Gardiner's *Sacred Melodies*, published in England in 1812. Unable to find a publisher, he brought it to Boston, where it appeared, in 1822, as the Handel and Haydn Society's *Collection of Church Music*, without his name, though later editions contained an acknowledgment to him. It was widely successful and established his reputation as a musician. After his return to Boston to live he published, in collaboration with David Greene, another book entitled *Church Psalmody* (1831), which ran through fourteen editions, the latest in 1864. *Spiritual Songs*, in which he collaborated with Thomas Hastings, was his third venture, and other volumes followed periodically and set the standard of church music in most of the more progressive American churches down to the last decade of the nineteenth century.

Mason was the foremost American musician of the period. If his equipment and capacities seem small today, we must remember that in his youth this country afforded few opportunities for education in music except what was given in the singing schools, or by organists or fiddlers whose abilities as teachers seldom went beyond what would now be regarded as elementary instruction. It was not until he went to Europe, about 1830, for a year of travel and study, that he made the acquaintance of professional musicians of wide reputation. Nevertheless his enthusiasm and his skill in adapting what he knew to the needs of the time made him the leader in the third revival of music in New England, a movement which spread far and wide to other parts of the country.

A comparison of his accomplishment with the work of Tufts and Walter in the seventeen-twenties, and of Billings in the seventeen-seventies, vividly illustrates both the change in social conditions and the progress in music which had occurred in a little over a century. Mason did not have to fight the almost complete ignorance and the unreasoning prejudices which his predecessors had met, and his musical standards were far higher, but he used their methods, beginning with a revival of enthusiasm for the local singing schools which had been their sole instrument for the spread of education in music. From this starting point he organized (with George J. Webb [3]) the Boston Academy of Music (1832), to teach music to children, and eventually succeeded in introducing music into the public schools. In 1834 he organized the first of a series of very successful musical conventions for music teachers, which helped to spread better methods and standards to other parts of the country. And he edited, alone or with others, many collections of church music which had wide circulation. While his methods were fundamentally the same as those of his earlier predecessors, the immense change in social conditions which had taken place since the end of the Revolution gave them an effectiveness beyond the dreams of the eighteenth century.

Mason composed a large number of hymn tunes, most of which first appeared in one or another of his publications. Some were original with him, but many were adaptations which he made of music which he had brought back with him from Europe. Consequently, his tunes seldom have a distinctive style, for he lacked the background, the originality, or the self-confidence to work out an independent style for himself. Few of his tunes have been used in

[3] George James Webb, b. June 24, 1803, near Salisbury, England; d. Oct. 7, 1887, at Orange, N. J.; an English musician who emigrated to Boston in 1830, where he was organist in the Old South Church, taught in the Boston Academy of Music, and was associated with Mason in many activities. He is now chiefly remembered for his tune *Webb*, which he composed on the voyage from England as a secular tune for the words "'Tis dawn, the lark is singing." The music was published with those words in 1837; first used as a hymn-tune in *The Wesleyan Psalmist*, 1842; later set by Mason and Webb to S. F. Smith's missionary hymn, "The morning light is breaking."

England, and the great majority have disappeared from recent American hymnbooks.[4] Perhaps his best are *Missionary Hymn*, which he wrote in Savannah in 1823 for Heber's "From Greenland's icy mountains" — *Hamburg*, which he wrote the next year, based on suggestions of the first Gregorian tone, *Uxbridge* (1831), which approaches the style of the older psalm tunes, *Olivet*, written in the same year for Ray Palmer's hymn "My faith looks up to thee" — and the tune for "Nearer, my God, to thee" — which was curiously misnamed *Bethany*, when *Bethel* would have been far more appropriate. This last tune first appeared in the *Sabbath Day Hymn Book* of 1859. It appears to be based on a suggestion derived from the secular tune for "Oft in the stilly night." Modern musical taste frequently disparages *Olivet* as sentimental, and *Bethany* too easily lends itself to a tendency to drag it out into a dismal wail which destroys the vigor and lift attainable when it is sung with careful attention to timing. Nevertheless, the fact remains that no later composer has ever written a successful rival to either tune for the words with which each is associated. With all the limitations which his period imposed, Lowell Mason rendered an invaluable service to American hymnody.

For our purposes the most important book which Mason produced was that in which he had the collaboration of Thomas Hastings, a Presbyterian layman who, like Mason, had already been working to improve congregational singing.[5] To both Mason and Hastings it seemed as though the vogue for the cheaper melodies popularized by *The Chris-*

---

[4] *The Methodist Hymnal*, 1935, includes 22, including adaptations, with several repetitions; *The Hymnal* of the Presbyterian Church, 1933, includes 14, with fewer repetitions.

[5] Thomas Hastings, b. Oct. 15, 1784, at Washington, Conn.; d. May 15, 1872, at New York, N. Y.; a prolific composer of hymn tunes and author of hymns. He published some fifty books of music, some of them in collaboration with Lowell Mason and William Bradbury.

tion Lyre threatened to undo all that they were trying to accomplish. So, in 1832, they joined forces and published *Spiritual Songs for social worship; adapted to the use of families and private circles in seasons of revival, to missionary meetings, to the monthly concert,*[6] *and to other occasions of special interest. Words and music arranged by Thomas Hastings, of Utica, and Lowell Mason, of Boston.* Their aim is revealed in a sentence in the preface in which they state their opposition to the type of music which asks the public,

in these enlightened days of reform . . . to recognize in the current love songs, the vulgar melodies of the street, of the midnight reveller, of the circus and the ballroom, the very strains which of all others, we are told, are the best adapted to call forth pure and holy emotions, in special seasons of revival.[7]

The tunes in the *Spiritual Songs*, many of them by the editors, were simple but appealing, devout and well adapted to the needs of the times. But the book was equally notable for the original hymns which it included. Among them was the missionary hymn, "The morning light is breaking" — by Samuel F. Smith, who was destined to become the foremost American Baptist hymn writer of the century; many by Thomas Hastings, including his "Gently, Lord, O gently lead us" — "How calm and beautiful the morn" — and "Return, O wand'rer, to thy rest" — and his missionary hymn, "Hail to the brightness of Zion's glad morning" — set to the tune *Wesley*, still in use, which Mason wrote for his colleague's words.

Most notable of all was the inclusion in the book of Ray

---

[6] "The Monthly Concert" was the misleading name given to monthly prayer meetings on behalf of the new missionary movement which had aroused great enthusiasm in the evangelical churches. Many missionary hymns were written during this period to provide songs available for such gatherings.

[7] Quoted from Benson, *The English Hymn*, p. 379.

Palmer's [8] "My faith looks up to thee," — to Mason's tune *Olivet*. The hymn had been written soon after Palmer's graduation from Yale in 1830, but had remained unseen in his pocketbook until he chanced to meet Lowell Mason on a Boston street. Mason told him of the intended publication of *Spiritual Songs* and asked him if he had anything to contribute. Palmer produced his hymn, which Mason took home, and for which he promptly wrote the tune. Meeting again in the street a few days later, Mason said, "Mr. Palmer, you may live many years and do many good things, but I think you will be best known to posterity as the author of 'My faith looks up to thee.' "

Another notable contribution to the hymnody of the period made by *Spiritual Songs* was its inclusion of Augustus M. Toplady's famous hymn, "Rock of Ages, cleft for me," to the tune *Toplady* which Hastings had written for it, and which here appeared for the first time. The hymn had found little acceptance in England for forty-five years after its publication in 1776, but during the last century and a quarter it has had world-wide use, in a form considerably altered from the original, and has been rated by many authorities to be in the first rank among English hymns, although it has also been drastically criticized by others for its mixed metaphors and false rhymes. Today it still survives in most hymnals, but its mood is increasingly alien to modern religious thought and feeling. In England it has usually, if not always, been set to other tunes, but in America it has been universally sung to Hastings' music. Popular and easily sung though the tune is, its sentimentality

[8] Ray Palmer, b. Nov. 12, 1808, at Little Compton, R. I.; d. March 29, 1887, at Newark, N. J.; educated at Phillips Academy, Andover, Mass.; A.B. Yale, 1830; minister of the Central Congregational Church, Bath, Maine, 1835–1850; of the First Congregational Church of Albany, N. Y., 1850–1865; secretary of the American Congregational Union, New York, 1865–1878; author of several works in prose and verse, including thirty-eight hymns of high quality, some of which still have wide use.

and its rocking-chair rhythm prevent the well-educated musician from giving it high musical rank, though it is characteristic of the period from which it comes. Hastings was not, in truth, a great musician, and only three or four, out of the thousand tunes he is said to have composed, have survived in modern use. The same is true of his hymns. They had a widespread popularity but lacked the excellence necessary to give them survival value. Professor F. M. Bird wrote of him,[9]

Although not a great poet, he yet attained considerable success. If we take the aggregate of American hymnals published in the last fifty years [i.e. between 1835 and 1885], or any portion of that time, more hymns by him are found in common use than by any other native writer. Not one of his hymns is of the highest merit, but many of them have become popular and useful.

Today, out of the more than six hundred which he is said to have written, hardly any remain in use beyond those already noted.

Although Hastings and Mason's *Spiritual Songs* was an immediate success and was generally acceptable in evangelical circles, it had surprisingly little influence in the Presbyterian churches when we remember that Hastings was the leading Presbyterian church musician of the day, and the first popular hymn writer whom the denomination had produced. The fact is that the Presbyterians were still divided into "New School" and "Old School" groups and adhered, if not to the old psalmody, at least to Watts. The General Assembly had authorized no book since its approval of *Dwight's Watts*, in 1802. In 1831, however, it accepted and published *Psalms and Hymns adapted to public worship, and approved by the General Assembly of the Presbyterian Church in the United States of America* — a col-

---

[9] Julian, *Dictionary*, p. 494.

lection of 531 hymns, those by Watts comprising two-fifths of the whole number. This book was not very successful and failed of general adoption.

Both the "Old School" and the "New School" assemblies followed *Psalms and Hymns* with other books, of which the most important were the *Church Psalmist* (1843), and *Parish Psalmody* (1844). The latter book included hymns by Mrs. Lydia Sigourney, Ray Palmer, and George W. Bethune, but made no notable contributions to American hymnody. The result of this series of publications was an unfortunate diversity of usage in the Presbyterian churches, so that at the New School Assembly of 1863 it was reported that at least fifteen different books were in use among them. Most of these, however, were variants of the *Watts and Select* type, and the same Assembly of 1863 put itself on record as totally disapproving "those books of Psalmody which, in their arrangement, blot out the distinction between those songs of devotion which are God-inspired and those which are man-inspired." [10]

Perhaps this attitude was responsible for the paucity of hymn writing among the Presbyterians at this period. Aside from the hymns by Alexander and by Hastings, almost the only ones which have had any general use, or which have survived today, are the two written by Elizabeth Payson Prentiss [11] in 1856 and by George Duffield, Jr., [12] in 1858. Mrs. Prentiss' hymn is, in verse form and sentiment, an echo of "Nearer, my God, to thee" — for which the writer

---

[10] See Benson, *The English Hymn*, pp. 380–388, 478–480, for further details about the Presbyterian hymnody of this period.

[11] Elizabeth Payson, b. Portland, Me., Oct. 26, 1818; d. Dorset, Vt., Aug. 13, 1878. Married Rev. George L. Prentiss, 1845. Published *Religious Poems*, 1873, containing a number of hymns, and two other books.

[12] George Duffield, Jr. b. Carlisle, Pa., Sept. 12, 1818; d. Bloomfield, N. J., July 6, 1888; educated at Yale and Union Theological Seminary; pastorates in Brooklyn, Philadelphia, Galesburg, Ill., Adrian, Saginaw and Lansing, Michigan. His son, Samuel Willoughby Duffield, was the author of *English Hymns; their Authors and their History.*

sought to provide a substitute more explicitly Christian in
tone:

> More love to thee, O Christ,
> More love to thee!
> Hear thou the prayer I make,
> On bended knee;
> This is my earnest plea,
> More love, O Christ, to thee,
> More love to thee!

George Duffield's hymn is the militant,

> Stand up, stand up for Jesus,
> Ye soldiers of the cross;
> Lift high his royal banner,
> It must not suffer loss:
> From vict'ry unto vict'ry
> His army he shall lead,
> Till every foe is vanquished,
> And Christ is Lord indeed.

This hymn was written under circumstances which gave it
a strong emotional appeal. Duffield had been very active
in the great revival of 1858 which was known as "the Work
of God in Philadelphia," in which a young Episcopal
minister, Rev. Dudley Atkins Tyng, an effective evangelistic preacher, had been his associate. Tyng had been rector
of the Church of the Epiphany, Philadelphia, but had been
forced out because of his pronounced antislavery views.
While the revival was in progress he was shockingly in-
jured by a piece of farm machinery, dying a few hours
later. His last words were a message, "Tell them, Let us
all stand up for Jesus: now let us sing a hymn." After
Tyng's funeral Duffield wrote the hymn, and incorporated
it into his sermon the following Sunday. It was soon printed
in a Baptist periodical, and quickly spread far and wide.

Its stirring quality and excellence as a hymn of the Christian warfare made it popular among the soldiers of the Union army during the Civil War. Duffield wrote several other hymns, but none which approached this one, and none which survive in use today.

Although the majority of the Presbyterians were still largely dominated by the tradition of psalmody and the prestige of Watts, one minister, Rev. Charles S. Robinson, broke away and in 1862 published the first of his series of hymn collections which ran over a period of thirty years, his *Songs of the Church; or, Hymns and Tunes for Christian Worship*. It was influenced by Beecher's *Plymouth Collection*, and by Park and Phelps' *Sabbath Day Hymn Book*, which we shall consider presently, and printed the hymns "for the congregation" under the tunes, adding, however, a large collection of hymns "for the choir," without tunes. It was followed in 1865 by his *Songs for the Sanctuary*, the wide vogue of which was largely due to its musical editor, J. P. Holbrook, who resorted to popular melodies of an inferior type. While Robinson's books did much to wean both Presbyterians and the more conservative Congregationalists from their dependence on psalmody, they did not contribute anything to the higher standards of American hymnody.

In the eighteen-thirties the Congregationalists were for the most part still using *Dwight's Watts* or Worcester's *Watts and Select*, both of which survived in local use until some thirty years later. As late as 1863 Charles Beecher complained that the latter book "still weighs down the psalmody of some antediluvian districts like a nightmare." [13]

In 1845, however, an important book appeared, the true successor of *Dwight's Watts*, in Leonard Bacon's [14]

[13] Benson, *The English Hymn*, p. 389.
[14] Leonard Bacon, b. Feb. 19, 1802, at Detroit, Mich.; d. Dec. 23, 1881, at New Haven, Conn.; A.B. Yale; Andover Theological Seminary; min-

Psalms and Hymns, for Christian Use and Worship: prepared and set forth by the General Association of Connecticut. Dr. Bacon was chairman of the editorial committee and himself contributed five hymns. He was the son of a Congregational missionary to the Indians at Detroit when it was still a frontier village, and, while he was a student at Andover in 1823, he had brought out a little collection of *Hymns and Sacred Songs for the Monthly Concert,* to which he had contributed three hymns, and which was the earliest American attempt to provide hymns giving utterance to the fervor for missions which was sweeping the evangelical bodies. In 1825 he had written a hymn for his own installation as pastor of the Centre Church in New Haven, beginning

Here, Lord of life and light, to thee, —

and in 1833 he had written a hymn for the two-hundredth anniversary of the founding of New Haven, several stanzas of which form the great hymn by which he is best remembered,

O God, beneath thy guiding hand
Our exiled fathers crossed the sea;
And when they trod the wintry strand,
With prayer and psalm they worshipped thee.

Bacon's *Psalms and Hymns* was a very large collection, containing 1203 items, of which the hymns, following the psalms, numbered 705. While conservative on the side of psalmody, it was progressive in its hymnody, including some seventy new to this country drawn from English sources.[15]

---

ister of the Centre (Congregational) Church, New Haven, Conn., 1825–1866; professor and lecturer, Yale Divinity School, 1866–1881.
 [15] Benson, *The English Hymn,* p. 389.

Psalms and Hymns was followed, in a few years, by two other books which were even more influential. In 1847 Henry Ward Beecher had come to the newly organized Plymouth church in Brooklyn.[16] There he found a condition which was widely prevalent in those Congregational churches which had gone in for paid choirs, generally quartets. The *Psalms and Hymns* in the hands of the congregation "were without music, and the singing was wholly in the hands of the choir." Although himself neither a musician nor a hymn writer, "one of Mr. Beecher's oddities" was a belief in congregational singing. At his instigation the church's director of music, Darius E. Jones, prepared a small book, published in 1851; and four years later a larger, better, and much more famous successor appeared, *The Plymouth Collection*, the music edited by Charles Beecher and John Zundel, organist of Plymouth Church. In addition to the assistance of his brother Charles, Mr. Beecher had that of his sister, Harriet Beecher Stowe, who contributed to the book her three best-known hymns:

Still, still with thee, when purple morning breaketh, —
and
That mystic work of thine, O sovereign Lord, —
and
When winds are raging o'er the upper ocean.[17]

The music, printed above the words for the first time in an American hymnbook, was of fair quality but of popular appeal. The congregational singing at Plymouth Church

[16] Henry Ward Beecher, b. Litchfield, Conn., June 24, 1813; d. Brooklyn, N. Y., March 8, 1887; A.B. Amherst College, 1834; Lane Theological Seminary; pastor at Lawrenceburg, Ind., 1837–1839; of a Presbyterian church in Indianapolis, 1839–1847; and of Plymouth Congregational Church, Brooklyn, 1847–1887; famous as a preacher, lecturer, and author.

[17] Harriet Beecher, daughter of Lyman Beecher, b. June 14, 1811, at Litchfield, Conn.; d. July 1, 1896 at Hartford, Conn.; married Calvin E. Stowe; author of *Uncle Tom's Cabin*, and of other books.

soon became famous and carried the book, which had been published by private subscription because no publisher would take the risk of printing a book with its novel make-up, into many Baptist and Presbyterian as well as Congregational churches. There were no less than 1374 hymns in the book, selected not for literary excellence but for "power to excite religious emotions," and the note is strongly evangelical. Aside from Mrs. Stowe's contribution, the book contained few, if any, original hymns, Beecher contenting himself with those already in current use.

The second of the two books was of a different and less popular type. It was *The Sabbath Day Hymn Book: for the service of song in the House of the Lord* (New York, 1858), prepared by Professors Edwards A. Park and Austin Phelps of Andover Theological Seminary. This was a scholarly work with good literary standards, carefully edited. Park and Phelps were like Beecher in being strongly evangelical in their views, and, like him, they made a large book, 1290 hymns, arranged for homiletical rather than liturgical use, with an extraordinarily elaborate Analytical Index of Subjects, so that the preacher could find hymns to fit almost anything about which he might preach. But they differed from Beecher in having better taste, and in their introduction of a good many new hymns by living authors, among them those of the Scotch hymn writer, Horatius Bonar, and a number by Ray Palmer.

Palmer had written but few hymns since his

My faith looks up to thee, —

and none which have survived in common use. But for *The Sabbath Day Hymn Book* he produced the remarkable group of lyrics which established his reputation as one of the foremost hymn writers of his time and which remain today as his chief contribution to American hymnody. Four of them are free translations from the Latin.

> Jesus, thou joy of loving hearts, —

is the translation of a cento from

> Jesu, dulcis memoria, —

his communion hymn,

> O Bread to pilgrims given, —

is from

> O Esca viatorum; —

his

> O Christ our King, Creator Lord, —

is from

> Rex Christe, factor omnium; —

and his

> Come, Holy Ghost, in love, —

is from the "Golden Sequence," one of the greatest hymns of the medieval church,

> Veni, Sancte Spiritus.

In these translations Palmer carried forward the work of introducing the old Latin hymnody to Americans to whom it had been hitherto unknown.

Three other hymns by Palmer in *The Sabbath Day Hymn Book* were originals. One is his very beautiful,

> Jesus, these eyes have never seen
> That radiant form of thine.

Another is,

> Lord, my weak thought in vain would climb.

The third has dropped out of use, as have almost all of Palmer's later hymns. These half-dozen hymns by him, which are still found in modern hymnbooks, are among the choicest products of the American hymnody of this period, alike for their spiritual insight, their tenderness of feeling, and their literary excellence.

The publication of *The Plymouth Collection* and *The Sabbath Day Hymn Book* marks the transition from the older type of hymnbook to the modern, for thereafter fewer books appeared without music, and singing passed increasingly from the paid choir to the congregation. Park and Phelps followed *The Sabbath Day Hymn Book* with what Benson calls "the first and still the only American treatise on hymnody," [18] entitled *Hymns and Choirs* (1860). It is a capital, but apparently almost unknown book, which, perhaps because it appeared on the eve of the Civil War when men's minds were engrossed with other matters, has never had the attention it deserves.

Another Congregationalist of the period whose name is associated with the translation of an ancient hymn was Dr. Henry M. Dexter, who in 1848 wrote, in connection with one of his sermons, his hymn,

> Shepherd of tender youth.[19]

He based it on a Greek poem which is found in one of the books of Clement of Alexandria, about the end of the second century, and which is the earliest known Christian hymn, outside of fragments of hymns embedded in the later books of the New Testament. The original does not appear to have been intended for liturgical use, and Dexter's version is not so much a translation as a free paraphrase, his method of treating it being similar to that of John Mason

---

[18] Benson, *The English Hymn*, p. 475.
[19] Henry Martyn Dexter, b. Plympton, Mass., Aug. 13, 1821; d. Boston, Nov. 13, 1890; A.B. Yale, 1840; Andover Theological Seminary, 1844; Congregational minister at Manchester, N. H., and Boston; editor and author.

Neale in his translations from the Greek hymnody, the first
of which appeared only a few years after Dexter's. The
fact is that Greek hymnody differs so much from English
in form and content that close metrical translations are almost impossible. Dexter's hymn, though found in many
books, is not very serviceable, but it is interesting as an
interpretation of early Christian piety and as the earliest
American translation of a Greek hymn.

During the second third of the nineteenth century the
Episcopal churches were using the *Prayer Book Collection*,
described in the previous chapter, supplemented in a few
places by selections of "Additional Hymns" for occasions
for which the rather inadequate hymnal did not provide.
American Episcopalians, however, at an early date began
to feel the influence of the romantic movement in hymnody
initiated in England by the publication of Heber's *Hymns*
(1827), and of the Oxford Movement, of which Keble's
The Christian Year (also 1827) was one of the first fruits.
In 1834 George Washington Doane edited the first American reprint of Keble's book. The Church of England was
also profoundly affected at this time by the rediscovery of
the Latin hymnody embedded in the Breviary offices.
Chandler, Newman, Bishop Mant, Neale and others brought
out English versions of many of these office hymns, though
at first they made their translations from the *Paris Breviary*,
quite unaware that the hymns it contained were in but
few instances really ancient hymns of the church at all,
and were mostly the pseudo-classical effusions of French
Catholics of the seventeenth and eighteenth centuries. Half
of them, in fact, were not so old as the metrical psalms of
Sternhold and Hopkins, and at least one which Chandler
translated for his *Hymns of the Primitive Church* was not
written until forty years after Isaac Watts had written his
first hymns.[20] Nevertheless, the new interest in the re-

[20] Percy Dearmer, *Songs of Praise Discussed*, London, 1933, pp. 44–45.

discovered liturgical Latin hymns strongly influenced all later Anglican hymnals, as did Heber's arrangement of his book to follow the order of the Christian year.

The result in England was the development of the liturgical type of church hymnal, with the great bulk of the hymns arranged for the church year, more or less on the Breviary model, followed by a collection of "General Hymns," topically arranged, as in the earlier collections of the dissenting churches. A great many hymnals for Anglican use were published during this period because the Church of England, unlike the daughter church in this country, has never had an official hymnbook, so that individual parishes were free to use whatever book they chose, subject only to the approval of their bishop. From this situation there emerged, in 1861, the greatest Anglican hymnal of the nineteenth century, *Hymns Ancient and Modern.* Although an attempt to have it adopted as the official hymnal of the church came to naught, it was so widely used that many Anglican laymen were hardly aware of the existence of other collections, and its supremacy in the Church of England was not challenged until the opening years of the twentieth century.[21] It was one of the chief agents for the introduction of the great body of fine hymns produced in this period by Anglican writers, and also for the tunes written by the leading church musicians of the day, — Goss, Elvey, Monk, Stainer, S. S. Wesley, Dykes, Barnby, Sullivan and others.

It was natural that the Episcopal Church in this country

[21] J. R. Fleming in *The Highway of Praise*, Oxford University Press, London, 1937, states that during the first sixty years of the nineteenth century at least 150 hymnals were brought out for use in the Church of England alone (p. 42), but that by 1894 *Hymns Ancient and Modern* was in use in 10,340 Anglican churches, and only 3,319 churches used some other book. Probably an even greater number of hymnbooks were published during the same period for use by Nonconformists, almost all of them, like the great majority of the Anglican books, of inferior literary and musical quality.

should be the first to be affected by these developments, although, as we have seen, *The Sabbath Day Hymn Book* had included four of Palmer's translations from the Latin, and, as we shall see, the Unitarians made, or included, some translations of Breviary hymns at an earlier date. An English clergyman who had come to America brought out, in 1859, *Sacred Hymns; Chiefly from ancient sources. Arranged according to the seasons of the Church, By Frederick Wilson, Rector of St. James the Less* (Philadelphia), and a committee, which included Dr. Mühlenberg and Bishop Coxe, published in 1860 *Hymns for Church and Home*, which was less definitely liturgical in type, but both were private ventures and served only to call attention to the new resources of Anglican hymnody. In 1866 there was an American reprint of *Hymns Ancient and Modern*, the use of which was permitted in several dioceses, but it was not until 1872 that a new *Hymnal* was issued for the Protestant Episcopal Church in the United States. In other words, although the leaven of the English example had long been at work, it worked very slowly.[22]

It is both surprising and regrettable that the impulse for hymn writing which gave the *Prayer-Book Collection* its notable new hymns by American authors should not have flowered more richly than was the case as the century wore on. It is surprising because the Episcopal Church included in both its clergy and its laity a high proportion of persons of literary culture, and because the Church of England, to which the Episcopalians in this country naturally turned, was at this period producing a large number of fine hymns. Whatever the cause, in the middle third of the century the early promise of the *Prayer-Book Collection* was fulfilled in a far smaller measure than might have been anticipated.

[22] For further details of these developments in the Church of England and in the Protestant Episcopal Church in the United States, see Benson, *The English Hymn*, pp. 493–522, 544–548.

The harvest, however, though small,[23] was fine. In 1848
Bishop G. W. Doane, always keenly interested in the great
missionary movement of the period, contributed his fine
missionary hymn,

> Fling out the banner! let it float
>   Skyward and seaward, high and wide;
> The sun that lights its shining folds,
>   The cross, on which the Saviour died.

It was written for a flag-raising at the request of the girls in
St. Mary's School at Burlington, New Jersey, which he had
founded, but he gave the occasion a far wider significance
than the girls had foreseen. Calkin's tune, for which the
most appropriate name is *Camden*, although it is also called
Waltham or *Doane*, was written for the words in 1872,
and has made no small contribution to their widespread use.

   Three other less-known writers each produced a single
hymn which has had wide use. In 1833 Rev. Charles W.
Everest,[24] at the age of nineteen, published a little volume
of verse entitled *Visions of Death and other Poems*, which
included the hymn,

> 'Take up thy cross,' the Saviour said,
>   'If thou wouldst my disciple be;
> Take up thy cross with willing heart,
>   And humbly follow me.'

This was one of the few American hymns admitted to
Hymns Ancient and Modern. In 1839 Miss Catherine H.

[23] In addition to the hymn writers belonging to the Episcopal Church
named in the next three pages, Julian's *Dictionary*, under American
Hymnody, Protestant Episcopal Church, p. 60, also lists Harriet Beecher
Stowe, F. D. Huntington, and Eliza Scudder. But Mrs. Stowe was a
Congregationalist, and Dr. Huntington and Miss Scudder were Unitarians
throughout their productive period of hymn writing.
[24] Charles W. Everest, b. East Windsor, Conn., 1814; d. 1877; A.B.
Trinity College, Hartford; rector of an Episcopal Church near New
Haven for thirty years.

Watterman wrote the one hymn by which she is remembered,

> Come unto me, when shadows darkly gather,
> When the sad heart is weary and distressed,
> Seeking for comfort from your heavenly Father,
> Come unto me, and I will give you rest.[25]

Both of these hymns express the rather somber and depressed mood which characterized so much of the hymn writing of the period. Very different in tone was the lovely carol

We three kings of Orient are, —

published in 1859 by John H. Hopkins, to whose name "Jr." is frequently added to distinguish him from his father, who was Bishop of Vermont. He also composed the tune to which it is sung. Although the words and music soon became popular it was a long time before they were admitted to the hymnbooks. Other hymns by Hopkins had some use, but none survive today.[26]

Much the most important contribution made in this period to American hymnody by an Episcopalian was that of Bishop Coxe. He really belongs, in temperament and outlook, with the earlier group of hymn writers, though born later. In early life, between 1837 and 1845, he published several volumes of verse, in which most of his hymns first appeared. Nearly twenty of them have been included in various hymnbooks, and two or three have come into use throughout the English-speaking world. It was a misfortune for the Episcopal Church that none of them were

[25] Catherine H. Watterman, b. Philadelphia, 1812; m. George H. Esling, 1840; d. Philadelphia, 1897.

[26] John H. Hopkins, b. Oct. 28, 1820, Pittsburgh, Pa.; d. Troy, N. Y., Aug. 13, 1891; studied at the University of Vermont; ordained 1850; rector of Christ Church, Williamsport, Pa.; published *Carols, Hymns and Songs*, 1862; *Poems by the Wayside*, 1883.

admitted to the church *Hymnal* of 1872, but he was a member of the editorial committee, and a mistaken sense of modesty on his part led him to refuse their use. His earliest hymn is part of a ballad, printed in *The Churchman*, in 1839,

> O where are kings and empires now,
> Of old that went and came?
> But, Lord, thy church is praying yet,
> A thousand years the same.

In 1840 he published in *Christian Ballads* the hymn beginning,

> How beauteous were the marks divine,
> That in thy meekness used to shine,
> That lit thy lonely pathway, trod
> In wondrous love, O Lamb of God, —

and in 1842 he wrote,

> We are living, we are dwelling,
> In a grand and awful time;
> In an age, on ages telling,
> To be living is sublime.

But his finest and most widely used hymn is one for missions, written in 1851;

> Saviour, sprinkle many nations;
> Fruitful let thy sorrows be;
> By thy pains and consolations
> Draw the Gentiles unto thee:
> Of thy cross, the wondrous story,
> Be it to the nations told;
> Let them see in thee thy glory,
> And thy mercy manifold.[27]

[27] Arthur Cleveland Coxe, b. May 10, 1818, at Mendham, N. J.; d. July 20, 1896, at Clifton Springs, New York; graduated from the University of New York, 1838; General Theological Seminary, 1841; rector

Perhaps with this group should also be included Miss Anna Warner Bartlett, although her only church affiliation seems to have been with the Chapel of the United States Military Academy at West Point, where she taught a Bible Class for many years, and near which she lived on Constitution Island. She was the author of a number of hymns, as well as of many stories for children and of Sunday school literature. In 1851 she wrote a hymn which she included in her novel, *Dollars and Cents*, published in 1852 over the pseudonym "Amy Lothrop." It was included in Hastings' *Church Melodies*, 1858, and in many later books:

> We would see Jesus, for the shadows lengthen
> Across this little landscape of our life;
> We would see Jesus, our weak faith to strengthen,
> For the last weariness, the final strife.

More widely used, however, have been her verses for children from the collection of poems by her sister Susan and herself, entitled *Say and Seal*;

> Jesus loves me, this I know,
> For the Bible tells me so.

Both hymns still have occasional use.[28]

The Baptists were fortunate, during this period, in having as a hymnbook editor Rev. Samuel F. Smith. He was a New Englander of good stock, a graduate of both Harvard College and Andover Theological Seminary, with an intellectual and cultural background less common then among

St. John's Church, Hartford, Conn., 1842–1851; of Grace Church, Baltimore, 1854–1863; of Calvary Church, New York, 1863–1865; bishop of western New York, 1865.

[28] Anna Warner Bartlett, b. New York, Aug. 31, 1827; d. Highland Falls, N. Y., Jan. 22, 1915; besides her novels and children's stories she published *Hymns of the Church Militant*, 1858; *Say and Seal*, 1860; *Wayfaring Hymns*, 1869. Her sister Susan, a more successful novelist, collaborated in much of her work.

American Baptists than it is today. At Harvard he was a fellow member with Oliver Wendell Holmes in the famous class of 1829 which contained an extraordinary group of distinguished men, and the lines with which Holmes saluted him in a poem written for the class reunion on the 30th anniversary of its graduation are well-known:

> And there's a nice youngster of excellent pith —
> Fate tried to conceal him by naming him Smith:
> But he shouted a song for the brave and the free —
> Just read on his medal, "My Country," "of thee."

This, of course, is a reference to Smith's authorship of the national hymn,

> My country, 'tis of thee,
> Sweet land of liberty,
> Of thee I sing, —

written in 1832 while he was still a student at Andover.[29] Lowell Mason, not knowing German, had sent to Smith some German chorale books which he had received from Europe, in the hope that Smith would find therein something suitable for translation. Smith glanced through a volume, his eye was caught by a tune set to patriotic verses, and in a half-hour he had written his own words for the same tune. He did not know until later that the music was that to which the English hymn "God save the king" is sung.[30] He sent his words to Mason and they were first

---

[29] Samuel Francis Smith, b. Oct. 31, 1808, at Boston; d. Nov. 16, 1895, at Newton Centre, Mass.; A.B. Harvard, 1829; Andover Theological Seminary, 1832; minister of a Baptist Church, Waterville, Maine, 1834–1842; and of the First Baptist Church, Newton Centre, Mass., 1842–1854; Secretary, Baptist Missionary Union, 1854–1869; editor, with Rev. Baron Stow, of *The Psalmist.*

[30] The origin of the tune, known in this country as "America," in England as "The National Anthem," is still a matter of dispute. It was first published in *Harmonia Anglicana*, about 1743, and is perhaps based on an "Ayre" by the 17th century English composer, Dr. John Bull. The English words, often attributed to Henry Carey (d. 1743), are

sung at a children's festival in the Park Street Church, Boston, on July 4, 1832. Thereafter the hymn spread quickly to all parts of the country and found its way into most subsequent American hymnbooks. The hymn originally had five stanzas, but the third was removed at an early date by the author, because of its rather belligerent references to British tyranny, which reflected the Revolutionary animosities still smouldering in the North End of Boston where Smith was brought up under the shadow of Copp's Hill and of the church in which Paul Revere's lanterns had been hung. Dr. Smith earnestly desired that that stanza should be forgotten, so we will not print it here, but the reader may rest assured that the hymn loses nothing by its omission.

While the hymn has no official standing as a national anthem, such as was granted to "The Star-Spangled Banner," it is commonly regarded as America's national hymn. It is sometimes criticized by citizens of other parts of the country because of its New England coloring, and it is quite true that its author had the outlook of a New Englander of the early nineteenth century rather than that of a dweller in the deep South, or on the great plains, or in California. It was natural that he should have pictured the only section of America with which he was personally acquainted, and he had, of course, no idea that what he was writing would be widely adopted. Many other patriotic hymns have since been written which make reference to wider ranges of the American landscape and life, but none of them, except Katharine Lee Bates' hymn,

O beautiful for spacious skies,

---

apparently based upon a Jacobite song of the end of the 17th century. The tune was used towards the end of the 18th century for a national hymn in Denmark, with the words, "Heil dir dem liebenden," and in Germany for an adaptation of those words beginning "Heil Dir, im Siegerkrantz," widely used in Prussia and other North German states. See Julian, *Dictionary of Hymnology*, pp. 437–440; also Grove, *Dictionary of Music*.

is as yet in any sense a real rival of Smith's lyric in popular estimation.

In 1843 Smith, in coöperation with Rev. Baron Stow of Boston, edited for the Baptists a far better hymnbook than any they had hitherto possessed, entitled *The Psalmist*. It was a large book, with 1180 hymns, generally well selected from standard evangelical sources though strangely negligent of the Wesleyan hymnody, but the editors adopted the mistaken policy of cutting the hymns to four stanzas or less, either to save space or perhaps to allow more time for the sermon. The book passed into general use among the northern Baptists, but in the South books of a lower standard were preferred.[31]

Eleven American Baptist hymn writers were represented in *The Psalmist*, but of these the only important contribution is that of Smith himself, with twenty-six out of the thirty-two hymns which he wrote. His great missionary hymn,

> The morning light is breaking,

has been already referred to. It was written in 1832, while Smith was still a student at Andover, after he had read an inspiring report by the great missionary Adoniram Judson about his work in Burmah. Smith wanted to be a missionary too, but it was his son instead who later carried on Judson's work. His great hymn, however, has been translated into several languages and has been sung round the world. Only a little later he wrote "The Missionary's Farewell," which was long sung on appropriate occasions:

> Yes, my native land, I love thee;
>   All thy scenes, I love them well;
> Friends, connections, happy country,
>   Can I bid you all farewell?
>   Can I leave you,
>   Far in heathen lands to dwell?

---

[31] Benson, *The English Hymn*, pp. 361–365.

In 1833 he wrote a funeral hymn, better than most for such occasions:

> Sister, thou wast mild and lovely,
>   Gentle as the summer breeze,
> Pleasant as the air of evening,
>   When it floats among the trees.

Eleven of his hymns found their way into the English *Lyra Sacra Americana* (1868), including one for evening:

> Softly fades the twilight ray,
> On the holy Sabbath day;
> Gently as life's setting sun,
> When the Christian's course is run; —

his morning hymn,

> How calmly wakes the hallowed morn, —

and his,

> Planted in Christ, the living Vine.

Dr. Smith's last hymn, written when he was eighty-six, is one for the Church:

> Founded on thee, our only Lord,
>   On thee, the everlasting Rock,
> Thy church shall stand as stands thy word,
>   Nor fear the storm, nor dread the shock.

While we can hardly accept Dr. Ninde's statement that Ray Palmer and S. F. Smith "are recognized today as probably the two greatest hymnists that America has produced," [32] it is true that both made great contributions to American hymnody, and that Palmer is the foremost Congregationalist, as Smith is foremost Baptist hymn writer of the nineteenth century.

[32] Ninde, *Story of the American Hymn*, p. 268.

Two other Baptists made lesser contributions to the hymnody of this period. Rev. Sylvanus D. Phelps [33] wrote,

> Saviour! thy dying love
>   Thou gavest me;
> Nor should I aught withhold,
>   Dear Lord, from thee.
> In love my soul would bow,
> My heart fulfil its vow,
> Some off'ring bring thee now,
>   Something for thee.

Far more widely used, however, has been Rev. Joseph Henry Gilmore's, [34]

> He leadeth me! O blessed thought!
> O words with heavenly comfort fraught!
> Whate'er I do, where'er I be,
> Still 'tis God's hand that leadeth me.

It was first published in *The Watchman and Examiner* in 1862, and has owed much of its popularity to W. B. Bradbury's swinging but musically inferior tune.

The Methodists, during the second third of the century used *A Collection of Hymns for the use of the Methodist Episcopal Church, principally from the Collection of the Rev. John Wesley (1836)*, which appears to have been the first official hymnbook of the Methodists in this country. [35] It did not contain a single hymn of American origin nor so much as recognize the existence of the camp-meeting songs

[33] Sylvanus Dryden Phelps, b. Suffield, Conn., May 15, 1816; d. 1895; A.B. Brown University, 1844; pastor of the First Baptist Church, New Haven, Conn., 1854–1882.

[34] Joseph Henry Gilmore, b. Boston, April 29, 1834; d. Rochester, N. Y., July 23, 1918; A.B. Brown University; Newton Theological Institution; teacher, preacher, editor, professor of English literature at Rochester University.

[35] Benjamin Franklin Crawford, *Religious Trends in a Century of Hymns*, Carnegie, Pa., 1937, p. 33.

which were sweeping the country and which were especially popular in the newer settlements and among the Methodists.

After the separation of the Methodist Episcopal Church, South, from the main body in the north, over the issue of slavery, both branches issued new books. Of these the most important was *Hymns for the use of the Methodist Episcopal Church*, published in New York in 1849. It was practically a revised edition of the *Collection* of 1836 and has been described as "the fullest and most correct presentation of Wesleyan Poetry" which American Methodists have ever had.[36] The book was a large one, containing 1148 hymns, of which about fifty were attributed to American authors. It was too good to be popular, though it remained the authorized book for thirty years, and in many places it was supplemented, if not supplanted, by books of the camp-meeting, or, presently, of the gospel-song type.

Rev. William Hunter, the editor of several collections of hymns in which he included 125 of his own authorship, wrote in 1838 a hymn of heaven of the conventional type, but of no outstanding excellence:

> My heavenly home is bright and fair,
> Nor pain nor death shall enter there:
> Its glitt'ring towers the sun outshine;
> That heavenly mansion shall be mine.

A number of others by him had some use, although this was the most popular, but all have disappeared from view, with those of the forgotten Methodist hymn writers of his generation.[37]

The Universalists at this period were little more prolific.

---

[36] Benson, *The English Hymn*, pp. 299–300.

[37] William Hunter, b. near Ballymoney, Antrim, Ireland, May 26, 1811; d. 1877. He was brought to this country as a child, studied at Madison College, and entered the Methodist ministry.

In 1846 Rev. John Greenleaf Adams contributed to *Hymns of Christian Devotion*, which he edited with Dr. E. H. Chapin, his hymn, still in use, beginning:

> Heaven is here: its hymns of gladness
> Cheer the true believer's way,
> In this world where sin and sadness
> Often change to night our day.

> Heaven is here: where misery lightened
> Of its heavy load is seen,
> Where the face of sorrow brightened
> By the deed of love hath been.[38]

In the next decade the two sisters Alice and Phoebe Cary produced two hymns which have had some vogue. Shortly before her death Alice Cary wrote,

> Earth, with its dark and dreadful ills,
> Recedes and fades away;
> Lift up your heads, ye heavenly hills;
> Ye gates of death give way! [39]

Phoebe Cary's hymn was written in 1852 and was revised for publication in a hymnbook which her pastor was preparing for The Church of the Strangers in New York. Like her sister's, it is a contemplation of heaven, less admirable as verse, but more popular because of its sentimentality. The first three stanzas run,

> One sweetly solemn thought
> Comes to me o'er and o'er, —
> I am nearer my home today
> Than I ever have been before;

[38] John Greenleaf Adams, b. Portsmouth, N. H., July 30, 1810; d. Melrose Highlands, Mass., May 4, 1887; he edited two hymnbooks, much Sunday School material, and published a number of books.

[39] Alice Cary, b. 1820, on a farm near Cincinnati, Ohio; d. New York, Feb. 12, 1871; Phoebe Cary, b. 1824; d. Newport, R. I., July 31, 1871. They published together a small volume of verse in 1849. Their friendship with Whittier was a noted factor in their lives.

> Nearer my Father's house,
>   Where the many mansions be;
> Nearer the great white throne;
>   Nearer the crystal sea;
>
> Nearer the bound of life,
>   Where we lay our burdens down;
> Nearer leaving the cross;
>   Nearer gaining the crown.

Meantime the Congregationalists of the liberal wing, now definitely Unitarian, were pursuing their own way with characteristic independence. Between 1830 and 1865 they brought out no less than fifteen separate hymnbooks, in addition to the widely used *Collection* by Greenwood, discussed in the preceding chapter. All of these books represented a higher literary standard than most of the books we have been considering, with the exception, perhaps, of the *Sabbath-Day Hymn Book*, but most of them were prepared by individual ministers and had only local use. Only the *Springfield Collection* of 1835, edited by Rev. William B. O. Peabody, and the *Cheshire Collection* of 1846, edited by a committee of which Rev. A. A. Livermore was chairman, had any extended use as rivals to Greenwood's *Collection*.

Several of these books, however, were notable for their contributions to American hymnody, for the Unitarians of this period were now definitely embarked upon the hymn writing which, with their intellectual liberalism and their leadership in social reform, was to be their most significant contribution to the religious life of America. The first of these books was Rev. W. P. Lunt's *Christian Psalter* (1841). Lunt was minister of the First Church in Quincy, Mass., and ex-President John Quincy Adams [40] was one of his

[40] John Quincy Adams, b. July 11, 1767, at Braintree (now Quincy), Mass.; d. Feb. 21, 1848, at Washington; son of President John Adams;

parishioners. We remember Adams as a high-minded and aggressive political fighter, rather than as a hymn writer, but the old statesman, in the midst of a still busy political life, had made a complete metrical version of the psalms, besides writing several hymns, one of which, beginning,

Alas! how swift the moments fly, —

had been written for the two hundredth anniversary of the Quincy church in 1839. Adams' wife entrusted his manuscripts to his pastor, who included seventeen of the psalms and five hymns in his book — the only hymns by an American president which have ever been published. It cannot be said of them that any rise above the level of respectable verse, but one,

Hark! 'tis the holy temple bell,

found its way into the English publication, *Lyra Sacra Americana*, and his version of Psalm 43 still appears occasionally in a modern hymnbook.

Although Adams made no contribution of permanent importance to American hymnody, he is entitled, by virtue of his personal distinction, to a niche among the hymn writers. And in his diary he made an entry which is a touching revelation of the heart behind his austere, determined exterior:

June 29, 1845. Mr. Lunt preached this morning from Ecclesiastes iii. I, "To everything there is a season and a time for every purpose under the heaven." He had given out as the first hymn to be sung the 138th of the Christian Psalter — his compilation, and the hymn-book now used in our church. It was my version of the 65th Psalm; and no words can express the

A.B. Harvard; President of the United States, 1825–1829; member of Congress, 1831–1848; his Poems of *Religion and Society* were published in 1848, after his death.

sensations with which I heard it sung. Were it possible to compress into one pulsation of the heart the pleasure which, in the whole period of my life, I have enjoyed in praise from the lips of mortal man, it would not weigh a straw to balance the ecstasy of delight which streamed from my eyes as the organ pealed and the choir of voices sung the praise of Almighty God from the soul of David, adapted to my native tongue by me.

Three years later, at Adams' funeral in the same church, Lunt said of him, "He who had occupied the throne of the people was, like the Hebrew monarch, also a Psalmist in our Israel."

In 1843 Chandler Robbins [41] of Boston brought out his *Social Hymn Book* which introduced twenty translations by Bishop Mant from the Roman Breviary. His book reappeared in revised and enlarged form in 1854 as *Hymn Book for Christian Worship*, and included his hymn for Sunday evening,

Lo! the day of rest declineth.

In 1844 James Freeman Clarke [42] published *The Disciples' Hymn Book* for the Church of the Disciples, Boston, of which he was minister. It was a small but fine collection, in which Sarah Flower Adams' hymn,

Nearer, my God, to thee, —

which had appeared four years earlier in England, was for the first time included in an American book.[43] Clarke was

[41] Chandler Robbins, b. Lynn, Mass., Feb. 14, 1810; d. Weston, Mass., Sept. 11, 1882; A.B. Harvard, 1829; Harvard Divinity School, 1833; minister of the Second Church in Boston, 1833–1874.

[42] James Freeman Clarke, b. Hanover, N. H., April 4, 1810; d. Jamaica Plain, Mass., June 8, 1888; A.B. Harvard, 1829; Harvard Divinity School, 1833; minister at Louisville, Kentucky, 1833–1840; of the Church of the Disciples, Boston, 1841–1888.

[43] Lowell Mason's tune, *Bethany*, was written for this hymn in 1856, and was first published in the *Sabbath Day Hymn Book*, 1859.

distinguished both as a preacher and a scholar. He wrote a good deal of poetry of considerable merit. His occasional hymns have disappeared, but one hymn,

> Father, to us thy children, humbly kneeling,
> Conscious of weakness, ignorance, sin and shame,
> Give such a force of holy thought and feeling,
> That we may live to glorify thy name, —

remains in use. It is a rewritten portion of one of his poems.

Much the most important Unitarian publications of this period, however, were those of Samuel Longfellow [44] and Samuel Johnson,[45] who brought out their *Book of Hymns* in 1846, and its successor, *Hymns of the Spirit*, in 1864. Longfellow and Johnson were lifelong friends; both were associated with the Transcendentalist movement in New England which had so important an influence in liberalizing religious thought; and both made notable contributions to American hymnody. Denominational ties sat lightly on both. Indeed, Johnson would not acknowledge them at all and his only pastorate was in the Independent Church at Lynn, which he organized and which ceased to exist when he resigned. Nevertheless he belongs by temperament, outlook, and associations with the Unitarian hymn writers.

In 1846 Longfellow and Johnson were young men and fellow students in the Harvard Divinity School. For a friend who, like themselves, found even the latest Uni-

[44] Samuel Longfellow (younger brother of Henry Wadsworth Longfellow), b. Portland, Me., June 18, 1819; A.B. Harvard, 1839; Harvard Divinity School, 1846; minister of the Second Unitarian Church, Brooklyn, N. Y., 1853–1860; Unitarian Church, Germantown, Pa., 1878–1883; besides these two pastorates he did much occasional preaching and literary work; died at Cambridge, Mass., Oct. 31, 1892.

[45] Samuel Johnson, b. Salem, Mass., Oct. 10, 1822; d. North Andover, Mass., Feb. 10, 1882; A.B. Harvard, 1842; Harvard Divinity School, 1846; minister of the Independent Church, Lynn, Mass., 1853–1870; author of *Oriental Religions*, one of the first competent American studies in the field of Comparative Religion.

tarian hymnbooks too traditional in tone, they compiled their first book, *A Book of Hymns*, to give utterance to the more radical religious outlook of the day. It was published in the year of their graduation, and was reissued in larger form in 1848. It was first used by the church in Worcester of which Edward Everett Hale was minister, and by Theodore Parker's congregation in the Music Hall in Boston. Parker, on receiving a copy, is said to have remarked, "I see we have a new book of Sams!" It ran to twelve editions and marked a new epoch in American hymnody because of the freshness and originality of its viewpoint, and even more because of the new materials which it introduced and upon which later editors drew heavily. The young editors were the first to see and make use of the hymnic possibilities of Whittier's poems. And they were the first to introduce into an American hymnbook Newman's "Lead, kindly Light," which they found printed anonymously in a newspaper, though they changed the first line to read,

Send, kindly light.[46]

This is but one instance among a great many in which they allowed themselves a very free hand in altering the work of other writers to suit their taste or to adapt them to their own views. A sister of their schoolmate Thomas Wentworth Higginson promptly poked fun at this practice in the following limerick:

There once were two Sams of Amerique
Who belonged to profession called cleric;

---

[46] Newman's hymn was reprinted in this form in Beecher's *Plymouth Collection* of 1855. In *Hymns for Church and Home, Compiled by Members of the Protestant Episcopal Church*, Phila., 1860, it read,

"Send, Lord, Thy light amid the encircling gloom,"

and, in the second stanza,

"I loved day's dazzling light."

They hunted up hymns
And cut off their limbs
These truculent Sams of Amerique.

They did, indeed, lay themselves open to a good deal more
drastic criticism than this, yet it must be admitted that in
most cases their alterations were improvements on the
originals, and that every editor of a hymnbook finds himself under the necessity of adapting the work of many hymn
writers, or of accepting the adaptations made by others.

Longfellow was the more prolific of these two friends.
Some two dozen of his hymns are still in use, besides one
or two which he never claimed as his because in part based
upon the work of other persons.[47] At least ten or twelve
of those which survive are of excellent quality, and three
or four are of the first rank. Some are tender confessions
of personal religion; others are noble outpourings of a
prophetic faith. The literature of devotion contains few
songs of trust which surpass his,

I look to thee in every need,
And never look in vain;
I feel thy strong and tender love
And all is well again.
The thought of thee is mightier far
Than sin and pain and sorrow are.

For the vesper services which he instituted in his church
in Brooklyn he wrote two of the most beautiful evening
hymns in the language:

Now on land and sea descending
Brings the night its peace profound,
Let our vesper hymn be blending
With the holy calm around, —

[47] See H. W. Foote, "The Anonymous Hymns of Samuel Longfellow,"
Harvard Theological Review, x (October 1917).

and,

> Again as evening's shadow falls,
> We gather in these hallowed walls;
> And vesper hymn and vesper prayer
> Rise mingling on the holy air.

Those of his hymns, however, which mark most distinctively his great contribution are lyrical outpourings of the free spirit, akin to other expressions of the Transcendentalist movement, and characteristic of the new religious idealism of the period. We find this in hymns like that well-nigh perfect one which beings,

> God of the earth, the sky, the sea,
> Maker of all above, below,
> Creation lives and moves in thee;
> Thy present life through all doth flow, —

and which ends,

> But higher far, and far more clear,
> Thee in man's spirit we behold,
> Thine image and thyself are there, —
> The indwelling God, proclaimed of old.

The same mood is expressed in the beautiful hymn beginning,

> O Life that maketh all things new, —
> The blooming earth, the thoughts of men;
> Our pilgrim feet, wet with thy dew,
> In gladness hither turn again.

These and others of Longfellow's are among the purest and loftiest of all the lyrics arising out of that epoch of religious development which brought forth so much of the best thought in New England three-quarters of a century ago.

A third group of his hymns, hardly less distinctive and

no less valuable, includes those of which the theme is the Church Universal, the great company of faithful souls of every age and land; the life of God in the race, rather than in the individual soul, or in an ecclesiastical organization. Here is his hymn:

> Light of ages and of nations,
>   Every race and every time
> Hath received thine inspirations,
>   Glimpses of thy truth sublime, —

that other beginning,

> Eternal One, thou living God,
>   Whom changing years unchanged reveal,
> With thee their way our fathers trod;
>   The hand they held, in ours we feel, —

and finally that great hymn,

> One holy Church of God appears,
>   In every age and race,
> Unwasted by the lapse of years,
>   Unchanged by changing place.

It is a noble affirmation, in warm, simple, vigorous phraseology, of the all-inclusive character of what is truly "the holy catholic church."

Samuel Johnson wrote a parallel hymn on the same theme, so like Longfellow's, yet so individual. It is less happy in the accent of its opening line, possibly not quite so stirring in its climax, but it goes forward with equal vigor, and surpasses Longfellow's hymn in the perfection of its imagery as it develops the symbolism of the "City of God":

> City of God, how broad and far,
>   Outspread thy walls sublime,

The true thy chartered freemen are,
Of every age and clime.

. . . .

One holy church, one army strong,
One steadfast, high intent,
One working band, one harvest song,
One King omnipotent!

When, in 1924, the splendid new Anglican cathedral at Liverpool was consecrated with imposing ceremony, at the climax of the service, after the words of consecration had been spoken, the massed choirs burst forth with this hymn, which could not have been more appropriate had it been written for the occasion. But probably most of the congregation attributed the authorship to Samuel Johnson, the eighteenth-century lexicographer, and not to an obscure minister in Lynn, Massachusetts. The hymn was again sung, and broadcast, at the great service for the League of Nations in Westminster Abbey in 1935, and at the jubilee service for the twenty-fifth anniversary of the coronation of George V; and it was one of seven hymns included in the special service prepared by the Archbishops of Canterbury and York for use throughout England at the time of the coronation of George VI. Probably no other American hymn is so widely known or used in the British Empire.

Samuel Johnson wrote fewer hymns than Longfellow, only half-a-dozen besides the one just quoted, but those few are amongst the choicest contributions of this school of hymnody. The parallelism of thought between these close friends is notable. Only three years apart in age, of similar training and experience in life, both writing in familiar hymnic meters, it was inevitable that there should be a marked similarity between their hymns. The remarkable thing is that when they wrote upon the same theme, as in the case of the hymns on the Church Universal, just quoted, the production of each should be so distinctive and original. Longfellow's hymn,

> I look to thee in every need,

is paralleled by Johnson's intimate and tender lyric written for a collection made by Dorothea L. Dix for use in an asylum for the insane:

> I bless thee, Lord, for sorrows sent
> To break my dream of human power,
> For now, my shallow cisterns spent,
> I find thy founts and thirst no more.

Longfellow's,

> O Life that maketh all things new,

may be compared with Johnson's greater hymn, entitled "Inspiration," one of our most stirring lyrics of a prophetic faith:

> Life of Ages, richly poured,
> Love of God, unspent and free,
> Flowing in the prophet's word,
> And the people's liberty!

There remains one more poem by Johnson which must be mentioned, the beautiful hymn of contrition which begins,

> Father, in thy mysterious presence kneeling,
> Fain would our souls feel all thy kindling love;
> For we are weak, and need some deep revealing
> Of trust and strength and calmness from above.

Most of the hymns by Longfellow and Johnson are included in one or the other of their two collections. Their second book, *Hymns of the Spirit*, is the finer collection of the two, but it represents their more radical tendencies, being theistic rather than explicitly Christian in its emphasis. Samuel Longfellow's brother, Henry Wadsworth Longfellow, was far more famous as a poet, but far less successful as a hymn writer. He wrote one for Samuel's ordination in 1848 beginning,

> Christ to the young man said, —

of which John White Chadwick said that it "must have troubled Samuel's sense of what a hymn should be." A few verses have been quarried out of his poems to make one or two other hymns, without much success. He did, however, write one for Christmas which has real merit and is to be found in several hymnbooks:

> I heard the bells on Christmas day
> Their old familiar carols play,
> And wild and sweet the words repeat
> Of 'Peace on earth, good will to men.' [47a]

One other Unitarian hymnbook, published in 1853, should be mentioned; *Hymns for the Church of Christ*, edited by Frederic H. Hedge and Frederic D. Huntington.[48] The work of Hedge as a hymn writer has already been noted, and it was in this volume that his translation of "Ein' feste Burg" first appeared. Huntington also contributed three hymns to the book, but they had little use outside it. Like earlier books in this series it included translations of some of the Breviary hymns. By contrast with the collections of Longfellow and Johnson the book was conserva-

[47a] *Christmas Bells.* Copyright by Houghton Mifflin Co. Quoted by permission.
[48] Frederic Dan Huntington, b. Hadley, Mass., May 28, 1819; d. Hadley, July 11, 1904; A.B. Amherst College, 1839; Harvard Divinity School, 1842; a Unitarian minister in Boston, 1842–1855; Professor of Christian Morals, Harvard University, 1855–1859; he joined the Episcopal Church in 1859, and became Bishop of Central New York in 1869.

tive in tone, but it set a high standard of literary excellence which led to its being hailed as "much the best book of hymns yet published." With its publication we reach the end of the series of Unitarian hymnbooks for the period covered by this chapter.

There remain, however, a number of individual writers who, during this time, each produced one or more hymns which require notice. Since there have been something like fifty authors among the Unitarians whose hymns have found their way into one or another hymnbook, we can touch only upon the best known and most significant.

The most famous was Ralph Waldo Emerson, who, after his brief experience in the ministry of the Second Church in Boston, wrote for the ordination of his successor, Rev. Chandler Robbins, the single hymn which he produced. It was rather curiously unsuited to the occasion, for it is not an ordination hymn at all, though it is a beautiful expression of feeling for a beloved house of worship, as applicable to a cathedral as to a New England meetinghouse:

> We love the venerable house
> Our fathers built to God;
> In heaven are kept their grateful vows,
> Their dust endears the sod.

Contemporary with Emerson was Rev. William H. Furness,[49] whose pastorate in the First Unitarian Church of Philadelphia has seldom been equalled for length, or, indeed, for distinction. He served the church for a full half-century, and was minister emeritus for twenty years more before his death. His hymn,

> Feeble, helpless, how shall I
> Learn to live and learn to die?

[49] William Henry Furness, b. Boston, April 20, 1802; d. Philadelphia, Jan. 30, 1896; A.B. Harvard, 1820, Harvard Divinity School, 1823; First Unitarian Church, Philadelphia, 1825–1875; pastor emeritus, 1875–1896.

though in sentiment not very characteristic of the Unitarianism of the period, was long popular. Better known today are his two hymns for morning and evening, which have something of the charm of Bishop Ken's famous pair. Furness wrote,

> In the morning I will raise
> To my God the voice of praise,
> With his kind protection blest,
> Sweet and deep has been my rest,—

and, for evening,

> Slowly by thy hand unfurled,
> Down around the weary world,
> Falls the darkness: O how still
> Is the working of thy will.

Rev. James Flint [50] really belonged to the earlier generation, but his hymns did not appear in use until their publication in his *Collection of Hymns for the Christian Church and Home*, 1840. The single one which survives today is a fine memorial hymn:

> In pleasant lands have fallen the lines
> That bound our goodly heritage;
> And safe beneath our sheltering vines
> Our youth is blest, and soothed our age.

> What thanks, O God, to thee are due,
> That thou didst plant our fathers here;
> And watch and guard them as they grew
> A vineyard, to the Planter dear.

Oliver Wendell Holmes [51] was the son of the soundly orthodox minister of the First Parish in Cambridge, but

---

[50] James Flint, b. Reading, Mass., Dec. 10, 1779; A.B. Harvard, 1802; minister at East Bridgewater, Mass., 1806–1821; East Church, Salem, Mass., 1821–1855; d. Salem, March 4, 1855.

[51] Oliver Wendell Holmes, b. Cambridge, Aug. 29, 1809; d. Boston,

when he established himself as a physician in Boston he joined the Unitarian congregation worshipping in King's Chapel, and his poem "The One-Hoss Shay," is said to have been written as a humorous allegory of the collapse of the old New England Calvinism. Of all his writings nothing is now so widely known as are the two hymns which he included in "The Autocrat of the Breakfast Table," first published in the *Atlantic Monthly* in 1859. In November of that year appeared his tender "Hymn of Trust,"

> O Love divine, that stooped to share
> Our sharpest pang, our bitterest tear,
> On thee we cast each earth-born care;
> We smile at pain while thou art near.

A month later came the poem which Julian calls "a hymn of great merit." Holmes could not resist the temptation to give it a punning title, "A Sun-day Hymn,"

> Lord of all being, throned afar,
> Thy glory flames from sun and star;
> Center and soul of every sphere,
> Yet to each loving heart how near.

His hymn,

> Thou gracious Power, whose mercy lends
> The light of home, the smile of friends, —

is a loving expression of gratitude "for all the blessings life has wrought." His "'Army Hymn," written for a meeting in Boston to celebrate the Emancipation Proclamation,

> O Lord of Hosts! Almighty King!

Oct. 7, 1894; A.B. Harvard, 1829; Harvard Medical School; a distinguished physician and professor of anatomy at the Harvard Medical School, but better known today as an essayist, poet, and wit. His hymns are quoted by permission of Houghton Mifflin Co., publishers.

is still an appropriate expression of the militant national spirit in time of war. His last hymn was written when he was eighty-two years old, only a year before his death:

> Our Father! while our hearts unlearn
> The creeds that wrong thy name,
> Still let our hallowed altars burn
> With faith's undying flame.

Possibly the two opening lines are reminiscent of the Calvinism of his boyhood's home, but today we can all join in a prayer to be delivered from any beliefs which are unworthy in our thought of God, and the stanzas which follow express an interpretation of Christianity in which all can unite.

Theodore Parker,[52] famous preacher and reformer, was the author of a number of pieces of poetry, none of them intended for use as hymns. But from one of his sonnets a fine hymn, which has increasing use today, was taken by Longfellow and Johnson for their *Book of Hymns*, 1846:

> O thou great Friend to all the sons of men,
> Who once appeared in humblest guise below,
> Sin to rebuke, to break the captive's chain,
> And call thy brethren forth from want and woe.

Perhaps no one would have been more surprised than Parker himself to find this hymn written by him included in the recent Presbyterian *Hymnal*, or to read the injunction of the editors of the *Handbook to the Hymnal* that "it should be sung with full faith in Christ as the divine Saviour"!

[52] Theodore Parker, b. Lexington, Mass., Aug. 24, 1810; d. Florence, Italy, May 10, 1860; Harvard Divinity School, 1836; minister at West Roxbury, Mass., 1837–1846; 28th Congregational Society, worshipping in the Music Hall, Boston, 1846–1860; author of numerous discourses on social and religious topics and one of the earliest translators of German theological literature.

Born in the same year as Parker, but completely different in temperament, was Edmund Hamilton Sears.[53] He was content to be a country minister, but he was a writer of rare beauty in both prose and poetry and his two Christmas hymns have gone far and wide. His first was written in 1834 while he was a student in the Harvard Divinity School:

> Calm on the listening ear of night
> Come heaven's melodious strains,
> Where wild Judea stretches far
> Her silver-mantled plains.

His second was written in 1849 while he was minister at Wayland. It is more mature in thought, a prayer of aspiration, a noble song of courage, cheer, and hope:

> It came upon the midnight clear,
> That glorious song of old,
> From angels bending near the earth
> To touch their harps of gold:
> 'Peace on the earth, good will to men,
> From heaven's all-gracious King.'
> The world in solemn stillness lay
> To hear the angels sing.
>
> . . . .
>
> But with the woes of sin and strife
> The world has suffered long;
> Beneath the angel-strains have rolled
> Two thousand years of wrong;
> And man, at war with man, hears not
> The love song which they bring:
> O hush the noise, ye men of strife,
> And hear the angels sing.

[53] Edmund Hamilton Sears, b. Sandisfield, Mass., April 10, 1810; d. Weston, Mass., Jan. 16, 1876; Union College, 1834; Harvard Divinity School, 1837; he had pastorates at Wayland, Lancaster, and Weston, Mass.; author of several volumes, notably *The Fourth Gospel the Heart*

Of these two songs by Sears Dr. Ninde says, "His two Christmas hymns, the finest of American origin, [are] poems that worthily take a place with the choicest nativity lyrics in English hymnody,"[54] and he quotes O. W. Holmes as saying of the first, in a Lowell Lecture, that it is "one of the finest and most beautiful hymns ever written."

Better known to the world of letters was James Russell Lowell.[55] Strictly speaking, he was hardly a hymn writer at all, although as early as 1842 he wrote an unpublished hymn for the dedication of the new edifice of the First Parish in Watertown, and in 1866 he wrote a lovely Christmas carol for the children of the Church of the Disciples in Boston,

> 'What means this glory round our feet,'
>   The magi mused, 'more bright than morn?'
> And voices chanted clear and sweet,
>   'Today the Prince of Peace is born.'

But from his poems two or three passages have been adapted for use as hymns, of which the most successful is:

> Once to every man and nation
>   Comes the moment to decide,
> In the strife of truth with falsehood,
>   For the good or evil side;
> Some great cause, God's new Messiah,
>   Offering each the bloom or blight,
> And the choice goes by forever
>   'Twixt that darkness and that light.

---

of Christ. He included a number of original hymns in his books, but only his two for Christmas have come into general use.

[54] Ninde, Story of the American Hymns, p. 154.

[55] James Russell Lowell, b. Cambridge, Mass., Feb. 22, 1819; d. Cambridge, Aug. 12, 1891; succeeded H. W. Longfellow as Professor of Belles Lettres at Harvard; U. S. Minister to Spain, 1877-1880; to Great Britain, 1880-1885; poet, essayist, scholar, and author of many books. Quotations from his poems are made by permission of Houghton Mifflin Co., publishers.

The words, rearranged from his poem "The Present Crisis," set to the stirring Welsh tune *Ton-y-Botel*, make a powerful hymn of national righteousness.

William Henry Burleigh [56] was another layman, whose hymns have been more widely used in Great Britain than in this country. He wrote of himself "You must remember that I do not claim to be a poet." Nevertheless his hymns have considerable merit. Perhaps the two best known are the following:

> Lead us, O Father, in the paths of peace;
> Without thy guiding hand we go astray,
> And doubts appall, and sorrows still increase:
> Lead us through Christ, the true and living way, —

and one which first appeared in *Lyra Sacra Americana*,

> Still will we trust, though earth seems dark and dreary,
> And the heart faint beneath his chastening rod;
> Though rough and steep the pathway, worn and weary,
> Still will we trust our God.

More inspiring, however, than these rather despondent hymns, and more characteristic of the author's own vigorous activities for social reform, is the hymn beginning:

> Abide not in the realm of dreams,
> O man, however fair it seems:
> But with clear eye the present scan,
> And hear the call of God and man.

The Class of 1846 at the Harvard Divinity School included not only Longfellow and Johnson, but one other hymn writer who must be mentioned, Octavius Brooks

[56] William Henry Burleigh, b. Woodstock, Conn., Feb. 12, 1812; d. Brooklyn, N. Y., March 18, 1871; printer and editor; agent of the New York Temperance Society, 1849–1855; Harbor Master, New York, 1855–1870; published *Poems*, 1841; enlarged edition, 1871.

Frothingham,[57] who wrote his only hymn for the class graduation. It is a lyrical and stirring trumpet call to service:

> Thou Lord of Hosts, whose guiding hand
> Has brought us here before thy face,
> Our spirits wait for thy command,
> Our silent hearts implore thy peace.

A year later came Thomas Wentworth Higginson,[58] who remained in the ministry only a short time and had a varied career as an Abolitionist, an officer in the Union Army in the Civil War, and a man of letters. While still a student he contributed four hymns to the *Book of Hymns* which his friends Longfellow and Johnson were preparing. Two of them have had considerable use. Both express the pessimism with which the young man looked at the evils of his time, but the mood may well be shared by our own day. One begins,

> The past is dark with sin and shame,
> The future dim with doubt and fear,
> But, Father, yet we praise thy name,
> Whose guardian love is ever near.

The other, suitable for Lent, runs,

> To thine eternal arms, O God,
> Take us, thine erring children in,
> From dangerous paths too boldly trod,
> From wandering thoughts and dreams of sin.

[57] Octavius Brooks Frothingham, b. Boston, Nov. 26, 1822; d. Nov. 17, 1895; A.B. Harvard, 1843; Harvard Divinity School, 1846; minister of the North Church, Salem, Mass., 1847–1855; of the Independent Liberal Church, Jersey City, N. J., 1855–1859; of the Third Congregational Unitarian Society, New York, 1859–1879.

[58] Thomas Wentworth Higginson, b. Cambridge, Mass., Dec. 22, 1823; d. Cambridge, May 9, 1911; A.B. Harvard, 1841; Harvard Divinity School, 1847; minister at Newburyport, Mass., 1847–1850, and at Worcester, 1852–1858.

One of his later poems of social justice has also been used as a hymn,

> From street and square, from hill and glen,
> Of this vast world beyond my door,
> I hear the tread of marching men,
> The patient armies of the poor.

Three women hymn writers belong with the Unitarians of this period. The earliest was Julia Ward Howe,[59] who made herself famous almost as quickly by her "Battle Hymn of the Republic" as Samuel F. Smith had done with his "My country, 'tis of thee." The "Battle Hymn" was written in Washington in 1861 soon after the opening of the Civil War. She had been with a party to visit some army camps, and heard the soldiers singing the ballad,

> John Brown's body lies a-mouldering in the grave, —

to the familiar, stirring, camp-meeting tune. The tune ran in her head and she wished it could be set to better words. That night she wrote,

> Mine eyes have seen the glory of the coming of the Lord;
> He is trampling out the vintage where his grapes of wrath are
>   stored;
> He has loosed the fateful lightning of his terrible swift sword;
>   His truth is marching on.

The hymn was published in the *Atlantic Monthly* for February, 1862, at once became popular, and, since it rose above the passions of the immediate conflict, remains as a battle hymn of militant Christianity in the cause of humanity and freedom. It came into renewed use during the

[59] Julia Ward, b. New York, May 27, 1819; d. Newport, R. I., Oct. 17, 1910; married Samuel Gridley Howe, one of the most enlightened and progressive American philanthropists and educators of the nineteenth century; she published two volumes of verse, as well as other writings.

Great War, and was sung by the American and Australian troops when they broke the Hindenburg line. It was a characteristic utterance of Mrs. Howe's own intense convictions, for she and her husband had been parishioners of Theodore Parker, and shared his Abolitionist views.

The second woman writer of this group was as different as possible from Mrs. Howe, both in temperament and in her experience of life. She was Miss Eliza Scudder,[60] a quiet, retiring person of deep spiritual insight. She published a slender little volume,[61] rich in mystical verse. Three of her hymns remain in use, and are comparable with those of Harriet Beecher Stowe:

> I cannot find thee. Still on restless pinion
>   My spirit beats the void where thou dost dwell,
> I wander lost in all thy vast dominion,
>   And shrink beneath thy light ineffable.
>
> .   .   .   .
>
> Yet high above the limits of my seeing,
>   And folded far within the inmost heart,
> And deep below the depths of conscious being,
>   Thy splendor shineth; there, O God, thou art,

and,

> Thou Life within my life, than self more near,
>   Thou veilèd presence infinitely clear,
> From all illusive shows of sense I flee,
>   To find my center and my rest in thee.
>
> Below all depths thy saving mercy lies,
>   Through thickest glooms I see thy light arise;

[60] Eliza Scudder, b. Boston, Nov. 14, 1821; d. Weston, Mass., Sept. 27, 1896. She was a niece of Edmund Hamilton Sears, whom she resembled in spirit and outlook. Towards the end of her life she joined the Episcopal Church, but all of her hymns which have come into use were written earlier.

[61] *Hymns and Sonnets*, Boston, 1880.

Above the highest heavens thou art not found
More surely than within this earthly round.

More widely used, though not more moving, is her hymn,

Thou Grace Divine, encircling all,
A shoreless, soundless sea,
Wherein at last our souls must fall,
O love of God most free!

. . . .

And though we turn us from thy face,
And wander wide and long,
Thou hold'st us still in thine embrace,
O love of God most strong!

The third of these writers was Caroline A. Mason.[62] She wrote a good deal of occasional verse of a high order and the last four stanzas of a poem called "Matin Hymn" have had wide use, beginning:

O God! I thank thee for each sight
Of beauty that thy hand doth give, —
For sunny skies and air and light,
O God, I thank thee that I live.

John Greenleaf Whittier [63] was closely akin in temper and outlook to these writers whom we have been considering. Although he was a lifelong member of the Society of Friends, and when in Philadelphia was associated with the orthodox rather than with the "Hicksite" branch of

---

[62] Caroline Atherton Briggs, b. Marblehead, Mass., 1823; d. 1890; married Charles Mason of Fitchburg, Mass.
[63] John Greenleaf Whittier, b. Haverhill, Mass., Dec. 17, 1807; d. Hampton Falls, N. H., Sept. 7, 1892; largely self-educated, he was a prolific writer of poetry and of prose, especially during the Abolitionist controversy. Quotations from his poems are made by permission of Houghton Mifflin Co., publishers.

their body,[64] he was not far removed in spirit from the liberal religious movement in New England. Both in temperament and thought he was certainly much nearer to the Channing Unitarians than he was to the orthodox evangelicals of his day. His attitude may be deduced from his admiration for Channing; his coöperation with the Unitarian Abolitionists; and from many of his poems, notably "Worship," and "The Brewing of Soma." As we have seen, Longfellow and Johnson were the first to make use of Whittier's poems for the purposes of hymnody, and the later Unitarian hymnbooks have included them more extensively than have the books of most other denominations.

Although with the passing years his hymns have become more widely used and dearly loved than those of any other American hymn writer, Whittier represents some curious anomalies. In the first place the Quakers, both in England and in this country, had no place for singing in their meetings for worship, until, in the Middle West half a century ago, some groups among them abandoned the traditional position in favor of singing and other practices adopted from other bodies. For this reason there have been very few Quaker hymn writers. Whittier always associated himself with the "silent meetings" of the Friends, in which hymns were never used.

In the second place, although he wrote a number of hymns by request for special occasions in other churches, they are never his best work, and in some instances are very far from meeting the tests of a good hymn. A striking case is the "hymn" which he wrote for "the opening of Thomas Starr King's House of Worship" (the First Unitarian Church of San Francisco), late in 1863, beginning,

---

[64] The split which divided the Society of Friends in Pennsylvania did not extend to the New England Meetings. It was contemporaneous with, and in many respects parallel to, the split between the orthodox and the Unitarian branches of New England Congregationalism.

Amid these glorious works of thine.

This is really a poem in fifteen stanzas, with references to Mt. Shasta and the Golden Gate. Only the last four have survived in use in altered form, beginning,

Thy grace impart; in time to be.

Yet Whittier wrote in a letter to his publisher, James T. Fields, "I have just sent what I think *is* a hymn to T. S. King for the opening of his new 'steeple-house.' "[65] And on another occasion he wrote, "I am not really a hymn-writer, for the very good reason that I know nothing of music. Only a few of my pieces were written for singing. A good hymn is the best use to which poetry can be devoted, but I do not claim that I have succeeded in composing one."[66] His failure, however, to produce a good hymn when he set himself to the task was due less to his ignorance of music, a deficiency which he shared with some other excellent hymn writers, than to his unfamiliarity with the limitations of form imposed by the actual use of hymns. His earliest hymn appears to have been one written for a Sabbath School celebration at Haverhill in 1833, but it has not survived. Indeed, almost the only one written by request which has had any general use is that written in 1873 for the opening of Plymouth Church, St. Paul, Minnesota, beginning,

All things are thine; no gift have we.

If, therefore, Whittier's fame as a hymn writer depended upon the hymns which he wrote as such, his place in American hymnody would be a very small one indeed.

Nevertheless, he stands in the front rank among American hymn writers of the nineteenth century by virtue of what

[65] T. F. Currier, *A Bibliography of John Greeleaf Whittier*, Cambridge, 1937, p. 96.
[66] Julian, *Dictionary of Hymnology*, p. 1278.

may be called his unintended hymns, made up of stanzas quarried from his poems like jewels cut out of their matrix, in many cases with some adaptation to fit them for use. It is impossible to state with any exactitude the number of hymns which have thus been extracted from his writings. A list [67] of nearly one hundred, taken from sixty different poems, has been compiled, but it includes a great number of variant forms of what are essentially the same hymns. Those of his hymns which have come into common use, with many variant readings and arrangements, are about thirty.

The hymns taken from his earlier poems, written during the antislavery struggle in which he took so prominent a part, are those which most emphasize the note of reform. His hymn beginning,

> O pure reformers, not in vain
> Your faith in human kind,
> The good which bloodshed could not gain
> Your peaceful zeal shall find, —

is made up of selected and rewritten stanzas from the poem "To the Reformers of England" at the time of the Anti-Corn-Law agitation. Not infrequently much of the deeper significance of the hymns is lost for those who do not know the context from which they are taken. Thus one of his most widely used hymns today is made up of stanzas selected from "Worship," written in 1848 at the close of the Mexican War. The poem begins with an almost satirical account of crude pagan worship, merging into that of paganized Christianity:

> As if the pomp of rituals, and the savor
> Of gums and spices could the Unseen One please;
> As if His ear could bend, with childish favor,
> To the poor flattery of organ keys!

[67] Currier, *Bibliography of John Greenleaf Whittier*, pp. 597-600.

Feet red from war-fields trod the church aisles holy,
With trembling reverence: and the oppressor there,
Kneeling before his priest, abased and lowly,
Crushed human hearts beneath his knee of prayer.

Not such the service the benignant Father
Requireth at His earthly children's hands,

. . . .

For he whom Jesus loved hath truly spoken;
The holier worship which he deigns to bless
Restores the lost, and binds the spirit broken,
And feeds the widow and the fatherless.

. . . .

O brother man! fold to thy heart thy brother;
Where pity dwells, the peace of God is there;
To worship rightly is to love each other,
Each smile a hymn, each kindly deed a prayer.

. . . .

Then shall all shackles fall; the stormy clangor
Of wild war music o'er the earth shall cease;
Love shall tread out the baleful fire of anger,
And in its ashes plant the tree of peace.

In similar fashion the first part of "The Brewing of
Soma" gives the key to the concluding six stanzas which
have been taken from it to form the hymn. The poem is
said to have been written after a particularly noisy and dis-
tasteful revival in Whittier's neighborhood. It begins with
an account of the brewing of the intoxicating drink Soma,
to promote supposedly religious exhilaration, and continues:

And yet the past comes round again,
And new doth old fulfil;
In sensual transports wild as vain
We brew in many a Christian fane
The heathen Soma still.

> Dear Lord and Father of mankind,
> Forgive our foolish ways!
> Reclothe us in our rightful mind,
> In purer lives thy service find,
> In deeper reverence, praise.

The second stanza just quoted, and the five which follow it, seem to have been first taken from the poem for use as a hymn by Garrett Horder in his (English) *Congregational Hymns* (1884). Probably no hymn by Whittier is now more widely used and dearly loved.

Several of his tenderest and most beautiful hymns are the various centos taken from "My Psalm" (1859), "The Eternal Goodness" (1865), and "Our Master" (1866). These poems are written in common metre with the stanzas loosely strung like pearls on a thread, with hardly more logical sequence or climactic development than in Fitzgerald's translation of the *Rubaiyat*. This is a weakness in the poems, though it is very convenient for the hymnbook editor, who can easily detach and rearrange the stanzas to suit his taste, but the result is that hardly any two editors have made the same selection and arrangement.

From "My Psalm" comes,

> All as God wills, who wisely heeds
> To give or to withhold,

(or

> No longer forward nor behind
> I look in hope or fear).

"The Eternal Goodness" was written after a theological argument with friends who had urged upon him "the scheme of salvation":

> But still my human hands are weak
> To hold your iron creeds;
> Against the words ye bid me speak
> My heart within me pleads, —

and he goes on with the stanzas from which are selected the hymns beginning,

> Who fathoms the Eternal Thought?
> Who talks of scheme and plan?
> The Lord is God! He needeth not
> The poor device of man, —

and,

> I see the wrong which round me lies,
> I feel the guilt within;
> I hear, with groan and travail-cries,
> The world confess its sin.
>
> Yet, in the maddening maze of things,
> And tossed by storm and flood,
> To one fixed stake my spirit clings;
> I know that God is good!

From "Our Master" come,

> Immortal Love, forever full,
> Forever flowing free,
> Forever shared, forever whole,
> A never-ebbing sea! —

and,

> We may not climb the heavenly steeps,
> To bring the Lord Christ down;
> In vain we search the lowest deeps,
> For him no depth can drown, —

and,

> O Love! O Life! our faith and sight
> Thy presence maketh one,
> As through transfigured clouds of white
> We trace the noon-day sun, —

and other hymns made up of various selections of the exquisitely tender stanzas of this, perhaps Whittier's most precious religious poem.

It is impracticable to list or comment upon the many hymns of less importance which have been drawn from Whittier's other poems, but one complete poem should be mentioned which has found its way in its entirety into some hymnbooks. It is his "At Last," written in 1882, in contemplation of death. It begins:

> When on my day of life the night is falling,
> And, in the winds from unsunned spaces blown
> I hear far voices out of darkness calling
>   My feet to paths unknown,
>
> Thou who hast made my home of life so pleasant,
> Leave not its tenant when its walls decay;
> O Love Divine, O Helper ever present,
>   Be Thou my strength and stay.

Obviously this is not a hymn for frequent congregational use, nor is the noble French melody *Christe Fons Jugis*, which fits it beautifully, to be lightly undertaken, but for a funeral or memorial service it is of great beauty. It is our American equivalent of Tennyson's "Crossing the Bar," and its contrast with the appalling hymns about death, "calculated to strike terror in the heart of the sinner," so popular in some circles at the beginning of the century, marks the progress which had been made in religious thought.

Whittier's reputation as a poet has suffered a decline with the eclipse of all the Victorian writers, but his fame as a hymn writer has stood the test of time better than that of almost any other. Indeed, if widespread and continued use of an author's hymns be the test, he would doubtless be ranked, both in this country and in England, as the foremost American hymnist of the nineteenth century. In the collection prepared for use at the Parliament of Religions at Chicago in 1893, nine of his hymns were included, a larger number than from any other writer. His hymns have been eagerly accepted by many religious groups, though to a smaller degree among the Presbyterians than with most others, and least of all with the Episcopalians.[68] The 1904 edition of *Hymns Ancient and Modern* contains none by him, and the American Episcopal *Hymnal* (1916), has only four. This is no doubt due to the fact that his views about the church and its forms of worship are at the opposite pole from those of strict churchmen. Even with them, however, the old prejudices are dissolving, and *Songs of Praise*, which, though edited by Canon Dearmer of the Church of England, is undenominational and inclusive in spirit, contains eleven of Whittier's choicest hymns. It is safe to say that they are likely to last in use as long as those of any writer whom we have been considering.

[68] *The Pilgrim Hymnal* (1904), included 19; The Unitarian *New Hymn and Tune Book* (1914), had 17; The Episcopal *New Hymnal* (1916), 4; *The Presbyterian Hymnal* (1933), 7; *The Methodist Hymnal* (1935), 8; The Unitarian *Hymns of the Spirit* (1937), 18. English hymnals, other than Unitarian and Congregational, were slow to adopt them.

CHAPTER VIII

Hymns of the Last Third of the Nineteenth Century, 1866-1900

THE CLOSE OF THE CIVIL WAR marked the end of an era in many aspects of American thought and life, and from it may be dated a new period in hymn writing. Such a division of what is, in reality, an uninterrupted stream of human thought and life is, of course, an arbitrary, though convenient, procedure, yet the flowing stream does continually change its character with the varying type of terrain through which it passes.

During the last third of the century many of the hymns written a generation earlier were slowly coming into use, for it often takes at least twenty-five years for even an admirable hymn to become widely known and accepted. And some of the hymns which have already been mentioned, because their writers began their activities before the middle of the century, were not written until after the Civil War. This was notably the case with some of the finest work of Whittier, Samuel Longfellow, and Samuel Johnson. But other and younger hymn writers soon followed in the steps of the mid-century group, and produced hymns of distinctive types, especially in the field of evangelism, and in the more advanced interpretations of religion. The great wave of enthusiasm for missions which marked the period from about 1820 to about 1870 had passed its crest, and with it ebbed the impulse to write missionary hymns. In their place came the gospel songs which swept the country as a concomitant of the revival movement in which Moody and Sankey were the leaders. And finally, hymns of the social gospel began to appear, and with them a few which sought to give a religious interpretation to the doctrine of evolution, so that we hear the beginning of new notes in worship song.

The gospel songs represent a nineteenth-century phase of that search for an utterance, "more to the popular liking" than the staid hymnody of the churches, which is to be traced in the religious life of America as early as the seventeen-sixties and seventies, and which then took the form of folk hymns. The folk hymns merged into the camp-meeting hymns, of which there were many collections. On a somewhat higher level were books like the *Village Hymns* and the *Christian Lyre*, which were expressly intended for revivals, rather than for use in the regular services of the church.

In 1863 W. B. Bradbury published his *Pilgrim's Songs; a musical Pocket Companion, or Hymn and Tune Book for Prayer and Social Meetings;* "intended only as supplementary to any hymn-book in use. . . . Put forth as a response to the repeated question 'Can not something be done to awaken new life in our social religious meetings?'" This was followed in 1867 by a collection of popular words and melodies, suited to what is nowadays called "community singing," published for use in the Young Men's Christian Association, which had been founded a few years earlier. This collection included Joseph H. Gilmore's, "He leadeth me! O blessed thought," — and W. W. Walford's "Sweet hour of prayer," — both set to music by W. B. Bradbury.

Rev. Robert Lowry [1] also did much to promote the gospel-song movement. Beginning in the eighteen-sixties he edited for the publishing house of Biglow and Main,

---

[1] Robert Lowry, b. Philadelphia, March 12, 1826; A.B. Bucknell University; d. Plainfield, N. J., Nov. 25, 1899; pastor of the Hanson Place Baptist Church, Brooklyn, N. Y., and also held a college professorship.

New York, a series of eight books with such titles as *Bright Jewels*, and *Pure Gold*, to which he contributed a large number of sentimental and catchy tunes. He had no serious training in music and did not take up composition until middle life, and, like William Billings, he was concerned only to produce music which would be popularly effective. He also wrote a number of songs, of which the best known are,

> Where is my wandering boy tonight?

and,

> Shall we gather by the river?

One of his parishioners, Annie Sherwood Hawks [2] wrote,

> I need Thee every hour,

which Lowry set to music.

Philip P. Bliss,[3] whose *Gospel Songs* in 1874 followed his less-known earlier works, had a fine voice and a handsome presence which helped to give popularity to his songs. The best known of them were, "Pull for the shore, boys; pull for the shore," — "Hold the fort, for I am coming," — "Let the lower lights be burning," — "I know not the hour when my Lord will come," — and, "Almost persuaded." Two of his hymns and tunes are included in *The Methodist Hymnal* of 1935, but most of them are obviously suited for evangelistic revivals rather than for use in church.

While these song writers were beginning their work Dwight L. Moody, who may fairly be described as the most famous evangelistic preacher in this country since

[2] Mrs. Annie Sherwood Hawks, b. Hoosick, N. Y., May 28, 1835; d. Bennington, Vt., Jan. 3, 1918.

[3] Philip Paul Bliss, b. Rome, Pa., July 9, 1838; killed in a railroad accident near Ashtabula, Ohio, Dec. 29, 1876; music teacher, composer, and publisher, he joined Major Whipple as a singing evangelist in 1874.

Whitefield visited it, had started his work in Chicago. In 1871 Ira D. Sankey joined him as his singing partner.[4] In 1873 they ventured to visit Great Britain, with such popular success that they remained there for two years. At first they used *Hallowed Songs*, one of the books brought out by Philip Phillips, but in 1875 Sankey combined with P. P. Bliss in the publication of *Gospel Hymns*, a name which was retained for a numbered series of evangelistic song-books issued at frequent intervals for the next sixteen years. Dr. Theodore L. Cuyler, in his introduction to Sankey's *Story of the Gospel Hymns* (1906), claims that they, "introduced a peculiar style of popular hymns which are calculated to awaken the careless, to melt the hardened, and to guide inquiring souls to the Lord Jesus Christ." This claim to originality cannot be sustained, since the use of words and music of a similar type goes back at least to the folk hymns of the latter part of the eighteenth century. Dr. Robert Guy McCutchan more correctly says of *Gospel Hymns* that

neither the name nor the type was new. They had been appearing since early in the century, both in England and the United States, and had had wide use at religious gatherings other than the regular services of public worship, such as prayer-meetings, revivals, etc. Essentially folklike, in that they consisted of easily remembered words with a simple melody and harmonization, the hold they took on the public mind was extraordinary. . . . Each had its "chorus," probably borrowed from the camp-meeting, and this feature in time came to be an abomination.[5]

The long-continued success of Moody and Sankey's revival meetings was due in no small part to the vogue of

[4] Ira David Sankey, b. Edinburgh, Pa., Aug. 28, 1840; d. Brooklyn, N. Y., Aug. 13, 1908; Y. M. C. A. Secretary before he joined Mr. Moody.

[5] R. G. McCutchan, *Our Hymnody*, Methodist Book Concern, 1937, pp. 277–278. Quoted by permission.

Gospel Hymns, and of Sankey's earlier book, *Sacred Songs and Solos*. It is said that fifty million copies of Sankey's books were sold. The publisher's profits were enormous and led to an unedifying scramble to occupy the field, though the evangelists themselves kept honorably clean of commercialism. Many hundred rival publications were issued, cheap in form and ephemeral in content.

Mr. Moody contributed neither words nor music to this phase of his revival work, but Mr. Sankey composed many tunes, although he said of himself, "I am no musician," as he was not, in the sense of being educated in music. Most of his tunes have dropped out of sight but his music for "There were ninety and nine," — which he improvised as he sang it on the platform of a meeting in Edinburgh, Scotland, is to be found in some hymnbooks. It is one of the best known and most popular of all the *Gospel Hymns*, but it is surely something of an exaggeration to call it a "melody which will never die so long as English songs are sung." [6]

Of the great number of other writers and composers who contributed to this popular hymnody which swept the country between the Civil War and the end of the century it is necessary to discuss only Fanny Crosby,[7] as she was familiarly called. She was blind from infancy, but began to write verse when she was eight, and continued to do so for eighty years. As she published verses signed by between two and three hundred pennames besides her own name, the exact number of her productions is not known, but it has been computed to be at least eight thousand. For many years she was under contract to furnish three songs a week to Biglow and Main, the publishers of many books of the gospel-song type, and such was her extraordinary facility

[6] From *Our Hymnody*, by Robert Guy McCutchan. Copyright 1937. Used by permission of The Methodist Book Concern.

[7] Fanny Jane Crosby, b. South East, Putnam Co., N. Y., March 24, 1820; d. Bridgeport, Conn., Feb. 12, 1915; married Alexander van Alstyne.

for emotional versification that she was able to meet the requirement. Indeed, she herself said, "I have often composed as many as six or seven hymns in one day."

Some of her songs attained wide popularity because of the tunes to which they were set, and her intensely evangelical temperament, naïve simplicity, and cheerfulness, combined with public sympathy for her blindness, made her a figure beloved by multitudes. Nevertheless her songs have very little real merit, being superficial in thought and weak in form. They are, in fact, an evangelical counterpart to the ephemeral products of certain secular song writers of today, who in similar fashion turn out under contract an unceasing stream of trivial ditties which sell for a few weeks and are forgotten. Only a profound ignorance of the accepted standards of hymnody could have led Will Carleton to write,

All over this country, and, one might say, the world, Fanny Crosby's hymns are singing themselves into the hearts and souls of the people. They have been doing this for many years, and will continue to do so as long as civilization lasts. There are today used in religious meetings, more of her inspired lines, than of any other poet, living or dead. . . . She is easily the greatest living writer of hymns.[8]

Out of the thousands of songs which she wrote only a very few remain in use, and those almost entirely outside the range of the standard hymnbooks. Perhaps the following are the best and most widely known: "Blessed assurance, Jesus is mine," — "Jesus, keep me near the cross," — "Saviour, more than life to me," — "Rescue the perishing, care for the dying," — and "Safe in the arms of Jesus." This last is said to have been written in fifteen minutes at the request of W. H. Doane, composer of the tune, while he

[8] Introduction to *Fanny Crosby's Life Story, by Herself*, Everywhere Publ. Co., N. Y., 1905.

waited to go to a train. *The Methodist Hymnal* (1935), in its section headed Songs of Salvation includes seven by Fanny Crosby, but few other books of similar grade admit as many, if any at all.

It is frequently assumed that the gospel songs were a peculiarly American product, and it is true that the great bulk of them were produced in this country and had here their widest use. But they were produced and used also in England and Canon Dearmer cites one example from *Salvation Solos* (c. 1890), presumably an English publication, which is quite as banal as anything ever written here:

> Good Elijah went to heaven
>   In a chariot of fire;
> Bright and warm to glory driven,
>   Fiery horses drew him higher.
>
> Up God's deathless way of glory,
>   Where God's holy seraphs burn,
> Enoch traveled by translation,
>   With no ticket to return.

And there is that jingling rhyme which the Salvation Army is, perhaps falsely, said to have used:

> The bells of hell go ting-a-ling-a-ling,
>   For you but not for me;
> The blessed angels sing-a-ling-a-ling,
>   Through all eternity.
>
> O death where is thy sting-a-ling-a-ling
>   O grave thy victory?
> No sting-a-ling-a-ling, no ting-a-ling-a-ling,
>   But sing-a-ling for me!

To such depths is religious song in danger of sinking when it leaves sound standards and seeks unreservedly to cater to the popular taste.

It is difficult to pass an unbiased judgment on the value of the gospel hymns. On the one hand they were enthusiastically received as an invaluable aid to soul-saving. The *Handbook to the Hymnal* [Presbyterian], p. 353, speaks of the period during which they flourished as "the notable era of informal church music to which the work of Dwight L. Moody and Ira D. Sankey gave great prominence." There was no question of their popularity, which was so great as to lead to the temporary abandonment of the standard hymnody in some churches. This was especially true among the Methodists and Baptists. The Presbyterians and Congregationalists were less affected by them: the Episcopalians and Unitarians practically not at all.

On the other hand, they were severely criticised alike by trained musicians for their musical illiteracy, and by the better educated clergy and laity for the overwrought sentimentality and the often downright vapidity of their words. If they helped to draw the ignorant and untrained to Christianity, they also served to repel the more intelligent and experienced. It is not unfair, perhaps, to regard their emotionalism as a Protestant form of that sentimental aspect of Christianity which in Catholicism finds expression in the cult of the Sacred Heart. Phillips Barry, recognizing their kinship with earlier forms of folk song calls "the gospel-hymn type, a lower form of folk-hymnody." [9] Perhaps the following quotation gives as lenient a judgment of them as can be expected from the serious historian:

Forms of song which, to the musician, lie outside the pale of art may have a legitimate place in seasons of special religious quickening. No one who is acquainted with the history of religious propagation in America will despise the revival hymn, or deny the necessity of the part it has played. But these seasons of spiritual upheaval are temporary and exceptional; they are

[9] Phillips Barry, "American Folk Music," in *Southern Folklore Quarterly*, June, 1937.

properly the beginning and not the end of the church's effort. The revival hymn may be effective in soul-winning, it is inadequate when treated as an element in the larger task of spiritual development.[10]

Set beside the great hymns of the Christian Church the gospel songs are slight and ephemeral in value. But considered in their own right, not as church hymns but as religious songs for revivals and for social use, they express one of the more dramatic phases of the religious life of the later nineteenth century.

Another variant from the normal type of American hymnody which first came to public attention after the Civil War, although much older in its origins, is to be found in the "spirituals" developed by the Negroes in this country, for the most part during the days of slavery. They are an expression of the religious hopes and longings of the oppressed Negroes after they came under the influence of Christianity, and are pure folk song, since they sprang out of the hearts of the people and the names of the composers are quite unknown. In this respect they are comparable to the old English ballads and to the folk hymns of the whites which have already been discussed. They seem to have originated in the native musical talent of song leaders, or bards, at Negro gatherings on plantations before the Civil War, or in Negro churches since. These leaders paraphrased some scripture passage, often in quaint phrasing, and created a melody to carry it which the group harmonized by ear, at least for the refrain, with the natural gift for harmony which the Negro possesses.

Before the Civil War very few Negroes were sufficiently educated to write down the words, much less the music, and the "spirituals," like other Negro songs, were orally

[10] E. Dickinson, *Music in the History of the Western Church*, N. Y., 1902, p. 404. Quoted by permission of Charles Scribner's Sons, publishers.

transmitted. Hence many of them appear in variant forms in different localities. After emancipation a good many Negroes who acquired education turned away from this body of folk song, which savored of slavery and seemed uncouth and illiterate, and sought to introduce into the worship of the Negro churches the hymns which white people sang, and, later, the gospel songs. But the "spirituals" survived on the lips of the older, uneducated Negroes and in more backward districts, very much as the ballads had survived in remote corners of England and of this country during the long period of their neglect. Before the Civil War probably none were written down by the whites who heard them sung by their slaves. During the war the words of a few were recorded by white officers of Negro regiments in the Union Army, like General Armstrong and Col. Thomas Wentworth Higginson. The first definite step towards their preservation was taken when a collection, *Slave Songs of the United States*, was published in 1867. They were first introduced to the American public and the European world by the Jubilee Singers of Fisk University in the eighteen-seventies. Other schools like Hampton, Tuskegee, Penn, Calhoun, and many more, followed the example of Fisk University and encouraged their students not only to sing these beautiful songs of their race, but to search out and to record hitherto unknown ones. In the last thirty years much has been done in this field by appreciative trained musicians, both white and Negro, and there is now a considerable body of reliable information on the subject. Several hundred "spirituals" have been published, but unrecorded ones still reward the searcher.

Many of the "spirituals" are undoubtedly old, perhaps very old, but their age is impossible to determine. Probably with the spread of education the spontaneous creation of new ones has very nearly ceased, and many, no doubt, have utterly perished from the memory of man. Those that remain, however, constitute a body of folk song unique in

America; indeed, they have been described by a competent authority as

a body of folk music . . . unsurpassed among the folk songs of the world, and, in the poignancy of their beauty, unequalled. . . . America's only folk music, and, up to this time, the finest distinctive artistic contribution she has to offer the world.[11]

And Anton Dvořák, writing about his *New World Symphony*, said, "These beautiful and varied themes are the product of the soil. They are American. They are the folk-songs of America."

In earlier days the naïveté of these "spirituals" often provoked sophisticated but unsympathetic audiences to laughter or to parody. At that time and to such people the cheap imitations by "Nigger Minstrels," in grotesque costume and with faces blackened by burnt cork, seemed amusing. That time is happily forgotten, and even when the words are simple-minded or quaint paraphrases of Biblical language, or ungrammatical in structure, we perceive the depth of feeling beneath the surface, generated by centuries of suffering. And often the words attain great beauty and power by their direct simplicity. Few hymns on the crucifixion have greater power to move the heart than,

> Were you there when they crucified my Lord?
> Were you there?
> Were you there when they nailed him to a tree?
> Were you there?

or,

> They crucified my Lord, an' he never said a mumblin' word,
> Not a word, not a word.
> He bowed his head and died, an' he never said a mumblin' word,
> Not a word, not a word.

[11] From *The Book of American Negro Spirituals*, by James Weldon Johnson and J. Rosamond Johnson. Copyright 1925, 1926. By permission of The Viking Press, Inc., New York.

Or they sing of the depths of personal need, in words of universal application:

> Somebody's knocking at yo' do',
> Somebody's knocking at yo' do',
> O sinner, why don't you answer?
> Somebody's knocking at yo' do'.

That, of course, springs directly from the text, "Behold I stand at the door and knock."

Or again,

I couldn't hear nobody pray, O Lord,
Way down yonder by myself an' I couldn't hear nobody pray:
In the valley, I couldn't hear nobody pray,
On my knees, I couldn't hear nobody pray,
Wid my burden, I couldn't hear nobody pray; —

or,

Everytime I feels the spirit, movin' in my heart, I will pray.
Up on the mountain my Lord spoke,
Out o' his mouth came fire and smoke; —

an obvious reference to Mt. Sinai. Or there were songs expressive of the longing for freedom, like the famous

> Go down Moses, way down in Egypt land,
> Tell ole Pharaoh, let my people go, —

or like the poignantly touching,

> No more auction block for me,
> No more.

Deeply moving as the words of many of the "spirituals" are, as utterances of the depths of human suffering and sorrow, their great power lies in their music.[12] Almost with-

---

[12] There are differences of opinion as to whether the Negro melodies are of remote African origin, or whether, as George Pullen Jackson holds,

out exception the melodies possess dignity in their simplicity and breathe the spirit of a deep religious experience. It is in this respect that they stand out in most marked contrast to the gospel songs, which too often represent a deliberate cheapening of literary and musical standards in an effort to cater to a popular taste. It is the difference which we feel between the unsophisticated but beautiful old English or Irish folk songs, which are genuine musical expressions of untrained but aspiring souls, and the cheap, meretricious effusions of the professional writer of popular songs today, whose only art consists in the ability to strike off quickly a catchy melody which tickles the musically illiterate for a moment and is gone.

With all their beauty, however, the "spirituals" are not adapted for use in the churches of white Americans, though a few of them have been introduced into one or two hymn-books. They belong to the Negro people; they are not a natural expression of the thought and feeling of white people, who can seldom sing them well. But they do represent a rich contribution to one aspect of sacred song in this country. The humble, unheeded, and long-forgotten singers out of whose hearts they sprang well deserve the tribute paid them by James Weldon Johnson:

> O black and unknown bards of long ago,
> How came your lips to touch the sacred fire?
> How, in your darkness, did you come to know
> The power and beauty of the minstrel's lyre?
>
> .   .   .   .
>
> You sang far better than you knew; the songs,
> That for your listeners' hungry hearts sufficed,

---

they have been adapted from the music which the Negroes learned from the whites. Probably there is a measure of truth in each contention, but at least it may be said that the Negro has richly colored and transmuted whatever he has borrowed from the music of his white neighbors.

Still live — but more than this to you belongs,
You sang a race from wood and stone to Christ.[13]

Turning now from these specialized forms of worship song, let us take up the story of American hymnody of the standard type through the last third of the century.

Until the eighteen-seventies the Episcopalians continued to use the inadequate *Prayer Book Collection*, with supplements, except in a few dioceses where the use of the 1866 American edition of *Hymns Ancient and Modern* was permitted. By 1872, however, the desire for uniformity and the demand for an improved book resulted in the publication of a new *Hymnal*, which reappeared in a slightly revised and enlarged form in 1874. This book was "a compromise between Metrical Psalmody, the Liturgical and the Evangelical Hymnodies." [14] Sixty psalms from the *New Version* were retained, and a large proportion of the hymns were still those of the eighteenth century. Some use, however, was made of the new school of Anglican hymn writers. Dr. J. Ireland Tucker prepared a musical edition of both issues (1872 and 1874), the tunes set above the words, the first stanzas interlined. For the first time in an American compilation this musical edition made use of a considerable number of the tunes by the English composers of the "cathedral school," — Dykes, Hopkins, Elvey, Goss, Monk, Smart, Redhead, and others, — whose compositions had, in such large measure, been introduced by *Hymns Ancient and Modern*.

In 1892 another *Hymnal* appeared which conformed rather more closely to the pattern of the Anglican hymnals, though it was still inferior to the best of them, following the timid and compromising policy which has been characteristic of all the hymnals of the Protestant Episcopal

[13] From *Saint Peter relates an Incident*, by James Weldon Johnson. Copyright 1917, 1921, 1935 by James Weldon Johnson. By permission of the Viking Press, Inc., New York.
[14] Benson, *The English Hymn*, p. 546.

Church in America. *The Church Hymnal* of 1892, like its predecessors, was issued without music, leaving the way open for musical editions published by private enterprise. There were half-a-dozen such musical editions, representing somewhat diverse standards of church music. The collection of tunes edited by Rev. Charles L. Hutchins, commonly called *Hutchins' Hymnal* (1894), was the one most generally used, although those by Horatio Parker (1903), and by J. M. Helfenstein, *The Grace Church Hymnal* (1909), set higher standards. These musical editions were, generally speaking, much superior as collections of tunes to those in other American churches, since they drew heavily upon the great English group of church musicians of the nineteenth century who were then at the height of their popularity. This musical superiority, and the popularity of the boy choirs which were introduced by the Episcopal churches, gave the *Hymnal* a distinction which it hardly deserved as a collection of hymns.

The improvement in musical standards thus brought about was, indeed, the chief contribution made to American hymnody by the Episcopalians in the last third of the century, for during this period they produced but few hymn writers. The hymns by Bishop Coxe, though written much earlier, did not get into the *Hymnal* until 1892. Phillips Brooks [15] wrote in 1868, for the children of his church in Philadelphia to sing at their Christmas service, his lovely and beloved carol,

> O little town of Bethlehem,
> How still we see thee lie!
> Above thy deep and dreamless sleep
> The silent stars go by.

[15] Phillips Brooks, b. Boston, Dec. 13, 1835; d. Boston, Jan. 23, 1893; A.B. Harvard, 1855; Episc. Theological Seminary, Alexandria, Va., 1859; Rector of the Church of the Advent, and later of Holy Trinity Church, Philadelphia, 1859–1869; and of Trinity Church, Boston, 1869–1891; Bishop of Massachusetts, 1891–1893; one of the greatest American preachers of the nineteenth century.

It was the fruit of his own experience on a visit to Palestine in 1865, when, on the day before Christmas, he rode from Jerusalem to Bethlehem where he attended the Christmas Eve service in the Church of the Nativity. Describing the trip he wrote, "Before dark we rode out of town to the field where they say the shepherds saw the star. . . . As we passed, the shepherds were still 'keeping watch over their flocks' or 'leading them home to fold.'"

The tune to which the carol is commonly sung in this country is rather inappropriately named *St. Louis*, and was written by Lewis H. Redner, organist of Holy Trinity Church, for the original occasion on which the carol was sung. The words and tune are inseparably associated in American minds, but in England the tunes generally used are the traditional melody *Forest Green*, or Barnby's *Bethlehem*. Bishop Brooks wrote a number of other hymns and carols, one or two of which have had some use, more because they were his than because of any outstanding excellence.

In the same year in which "O little town of Bethlehem" was written, a woman, Mrs. Mary Ann Thomson,[16] produced one of the latest of the many fine missionary hymns so frequent in American hymnody between 1820 and 1870:

> O Sion haste, thy mission high fulfilling,
>   To tell to all the world that God is light,
> That he who made all nations is not willing
>   One soul should perish, lost in shades of night;
>   Publish glad tidings, tidings of peace,
>   Tidings of Jesus, redemption and release.

Mrs. Thomson contributed more than forty hymns and poems to various church papers, and four of her hymns

[16] Mary Ann (Faulkner) Thomson, b. London, Eng., Dec. 5, 1834; d. Philadelphia, Mar. 11, 1923; author of many hymns. She came to this country as a girl and married John Thomson.

appeared in *The Hymnal* of 1892. In addition to the one quoted they include,

Now the blessèd Day-spring
Cometh from on high; —

an admirable "hymn of heaven" for All Saints' Day,

O King of saints, we give thee praise and glory,
For the bright cloud of witnesses unseen,
Whose names shine forth like stars, in sacred story,
Guiding our steps to realms of light unseen, —

and a good hymn for the burial of a child.

In 1876 Rev. Daniel C. Roberts,[17] then rector of the Church of St. Thomas in Brandon, Vermont, wrote, for a local celebration of the one hundredth anniversary of the Declaration of Independence, a hymn of a very different type, and the only one by which he is remembered:

God of our fathers, whose almighty hand.

It is a fine hymn of broad-minded patriotism, set in 1892 by George C. Warren to the tune called *National Hymn*, which, though stirring, goes to the verge of melodramatic militancy.

In 1886 Bishop William C. Doane [18] wrote for the bicentenary of the city of Albany the only hymn from his pen which has come into general use:

Ancient of Days, who sittest throned in glory.

[17] Daniel Crane Roberts, b. Bridgehampton, Long Island, N. Y., Nov. 5, 1841; d. Concord, N. H., Oct. 31, 1907; A.B. Kenyon College, 1857; a soldier in the Civil War; ordained 1866; rector of St. Thomas Church, Brandon, Vt., and of St. Paul's Church, Concord, N. H.

[18] William Croswell Doane (son of G. W. Doane), b. Boston, March 2, 1832; d. Albany, N. Y., May 17, 1913; educated at Burlington College, Burlington, N. J.; rector of churches at Burlington, Hartford, Conn., and Albany, N. Y.; Bishop of Albany, 1869–1913; author of a volume of poems, a biography of his father, and other works.

The tune *Ancient of Days* was written for the same occasion by John A. Jeffery, organist of the cathedral. Both tune and hymn have been widely popular, but neither has that degree of excellence required for long survival.

Among the Methodists there were only two conspicuous hymn writers at this time, aside from Fanny Crosby of gospel-song fame. Mary Artemesia Lathbury [19] was associated with the Chautauqua Assembly on Lake Chautauqua, New York, from the time of its inception by Bishop John H. Vincent on the site of what had been a Methodist camp meeting. She did writing and editorial work for the Methodist Sunday School Union, but her fame rests upon the two beautiful and moving hymns which she produced in 1877 for use at Chautauqua. The first has become one of the most widely known and used evening hymns of American origin:

Day is dying in the west.

Garrett Horder wrote that,

it is one of the finest and most distinctive hymns of modern time. It deserves to rank with 'Lead, kindly Light,' of Cardinal Newman, for its picturesqueness and allusionness, and above all else for this, that devout souls, no matter what their distinctive beliefs, can through it voice their deepest feelings and emotions.[20]

Miss Lathbury's second hymn, which is nearly as fine, is her,

Break thou the bread of life
Dear Lord, to me,
As thou didst break the loaves
Beside the sea.

Although often used as a communion hymn, it was not intended for that purpose. As the text indicates, the "breaking

[19] Mary Artemesia Lathbury, b. Manchester, N. Y., Aug. 10, 1841; d. East Orange, N. J., Oct. 20, 1918.
[20] Ninde, *Story of the American Hymn*, p. 312.

of the bread" refers not to the Last Supper but to the miracle of the loaves and fishes by the Sea of Galilee, and the "bread of life" is the teaching of Jesus.

The tunes with which both of these hymns are indissolubly associated were composed by William Fiske Sherwin, a teacher at the New England Conservatory of Music in Boston, who was also closely associated with the Chautauqua Assembly. Both have greatly endeared themselves to multitudes. The tune *Chautauqua* for "Day is dying in the west," is probably the best known American hymn tune written since Hastings' *Toplady*. Ninde calls it a "matchless melody." That is not, however, the judgment of the trained musician, or of any others who judge a tune by any other standard than its power to sway the emotions of a throng, for its swinging waltz rhythm seems peculiarly inappropriate to the solemnity of the words.

Among her other productions Miss Lathbury wrote a fine hymn for the centenary of American independence, the first stanza of which, though limiting the hymn to the special occasion, indicates her skill:

> Arise and shine in youth immortal,
> Thy light is come, thy King appears,
> Beyond the century's swinging portal,
> Breaks the new dawn, the thousand years,

and in 1881 she wrote a hymn of the Church Universal which has been strangely omitted from the present Methodist *Hymnal*:

> O Shepherd of the Nameless Fold,
> The blessed church to be, —
> Our hearts with love and longing turn
> To find their rest in Thee.

'Thy Kingdom come,' — its heavenly walls
Unseen around us rise,
And deep in loving human hearts
Its broad foundation lies.

The second Methodist writer of this period was Rev. Frank Mason North,[21] although his best known hymn was not written until the opening years of the twentieth century. But as early as 1884 he wrote some tender lines, evidently suggested by the "Jesu dulcis memoria," which has been so often translated:

Jesus, the calm that fills my breast,
No other heart but thine can give;
This peace unstirred, this joy of rest,
None but thy loved ones can receive.

His one great hymn,

Where cross the crowded ways of life, —

was written in 1903, when he was Secretary of the New York City Missionary Society, on request for a hymn for the *Methodist Hymnal* of 1905 which was then in preparation. It was based on a sermon which Dr. North had preached, and was first printed in 1903 in *The Christian City* of which he was editor. It is one of the finest hymns written in the twentieth century and is a noble utterance of the modern missionary spirit which finds expression in the service of mankind. Few hymns have been more quickly, more widely, or more gratefully adopted.

The Presbyterians during the last third of the century were badly divided and poorly led in the matter of hymn-

[21] Frank Mason North, b. New York, N. Y., Dec. 3, 1850; d. Madison, N. J., Dec. 17, 1935; A.B. Wesleyan University, 1872; he had pastorates in New York and Connecticut; Secretary, New York City Missionary Society, 1892–1912; and of the Methodist Board of Foreign Missions, 1912–1935.

books until the appearance in 1895 of *The Hymnal published by authority of the General Assembly of the Presbyterian Church in the United States of America*, provided a standard which they rather slowly accepted. A *Hymnal of the Presbyterian Church* had appeared in 1866, without success. After the reunion in 1870 of the "Old School" and "New School" groups, *The Presbyterian Hymnal* came out in 1874. It was strongly influenced by *Hymns Ancient and Modern*, introducing to the Presbyterians not only the hymns of the current Anglican hymn writers and many translations from the Latin, but also the then unfamiliar tunes of the Anglican composers. In these respects it had an important influence, but it had to compete with several publications brought out by individuals, and by publishing houses not unaffected by commercial motives. The most important of these rivals were the books edited by that indefatigable compiler of hymnbooks, Rev. Charles S. Robinson, the best known of his later collections being *Laudes Domini* (1885), and *In Excelsis* (1897).

Rev. Samuel A. W. Duffield [22] (son of George Duffield, Jr.) rendered valuable service during this period as the author of two books which were very useful in promoting acquaintance with the history of hymns; *English Hymns: the Authors and their History* (1886), and *Latin Hymnwriters*, published in 1889 after his death. These books were, at the time of their publication, the best sources of information in a field which had, up to that time, received very inadequate attention. They are discursively written with wide knowledge and great enthusiasm, and are still useful, though they have more to say about the writers than about the hymns which they wrote. Five hymns by

[22] Samuel Augustus Willoughby Duffield, b. Brooklyn, N. Y., Sept. 24, 1843; d. Bloomfield, N. J., May 12, 1887; A.B. Yale, 1863; ordained, 1867; pastor of Westminster Church, Bloomfield, N. J.; author of *Warp and Woof: a Book of Verse*, 1868, and of other works.

Samuel Duffield were included in *Laudes Domini*, four
of which were taken from his many translations from the
Latin, but all have dropped out of use.

By contrast with these earlier publications the Presbyterian *Hymnal* of 1895 was a book of a new type,
edited with great knowledge and skill by Dr. Louis F.
Benson,[23] who, in the twentieth century, became the greatest hymnologist whom this country has produced. It was
the first official hymnbook of the Presbyterian Church to
stand in the front rank with other hymnbooks of its day.
Most of Benson's own hymns were written in the twentieth century, but one for students,

O Thou whose feet have climbed life's hill, —

written in 1894, first appeared in this book,

In the last third of the nineteenth century very few
Presbyterians were writing hymns. Rev. Daniel March[24]
in 1868 wrote a missionary hymn, now little remembered:

Hark, the voice of Jesus calling,
'Who will go and work today?
Fields are white, and harvest waiting,
Who will bear the sheaves away?'
Loud and long the Master calleth,
Rich reward he offers free,
Who will answer, gladly saying,
'Here am I, send me, send me'?

[23] Louis Fitzgerald Benson, b. Philadelphia, July 22, 1855; d. Philadelphia, Oct. 10, 1930; graduated in law from the University of Pennsylvania; later attended Princeton Theological Seminary, and was ordained
a Presbyterian minister. After a pastorate at the Church of the Redeemer, Philadelphia, 1888–1894, he retired from the active ministry and
devoted himself to the study of hymnology. He edited several hymnals,
and was author of books and pamphlets on the subject, his great work
being the monumental and authoritative volume entitled *The English
Hymn.*

[24] Daniel March, b. Millbury, Mass., 1816; d. 1909; pastor of Presbyterian and Congregational churches.

In 1871 Rev. Edward Hopper [25] published anonymously in *The Sailors' Magazine* a hymn of the gospel-song type,

Jesus, Saviour, pilot me.

It has found its way into some of the standard hymnbooks. President Melancthon W. Stryker [26] of Hamilton College was the editor of a number of hymnbooks, including *The College Hymnal* (1896), and the author of several hymns, only one of which has survived in use. It was written for students and is often used at Commencements:

Almighty Lord, with one accord,
We offer thee our youth.

These few hymns constituted the very slender contribution of the Presbyterians to the American hymnody of the end of the century, but it was followed in the next period by a much richer harvest.

The Congregationalists during the last third of the nineteenth century had no single hymn writer as outstanding as Ray Palmer had been in the middle of the century, but several individuals produced a few hymns of fine quality. Rev. Samuel Wolcott [27] provides an exception to the rule that most successful hymn writers begin writing when

[25] Edward Hopper, b. New York, N. Y., Feb. 17, 1816; d. New York, April 23, 1888; educated at New York University and Union Theological Seminary; pastor of churches at Greenville and Sag Harbor, N. Y., and of the Church of the Sea and Land (Sailors' Mission), New York.

[26] Melancthon Woolsey Stryker, b. Mt. Vernon, N. Y., Jan. 7, 1851; d. Clinton, N. Y., Dec. 6, 1929; educated at Hamilton College and Auburn Theological Seminary; pastor of Presbyterian churches at Auburn and Ithaca, N. Y., Holyoke, Mass., and Chicago, Ill.; President of Hamilton College, 1892–1917.

[27] Samuel Wolcott, b. South Windsor, Conn., July 2, 1813; d. Longmeadow, Mass., Feb. 24, 1886; A.B. Yale, 1833; Andover Theological Seminary. He went to Syria as a missionary, but after two years returned on account of ill health, and held pastorates at Providence, R. I., Chicago, Ill., and Cleveland, Ohio.

young men. He wrote no hymn until he was fifty-six, but between then and his death he wrote two hundred. Only one, however, has come into general use. It was inspired by a convention of the Young Men's Christian Association at Cleveland in 1869, which had for its motto, "Christ for the world, and the world for Christ." Wolcott wrote:

> Christ for the world we sing;
> The world to Christ we bring
>   With loving zeal:
> The poor and them that mourn,
> The faint and overborne,
> Sin-sick and sorrow-worn,
>   Whom Christ doth heal.

An even better known hymn, and one more modern in its thought, is Dr. Washington Gladden's [28] great social service hymn,

> O Master, let me walk with thee,
> In lowly paths of service free.

It was written in 1879 and was published in a magazine, *The Sunday Afternoon*, of which Dr. Gladden was then editor, without any intention that it should be used as a hymn. The next year, however, it was included, with the omission of one stanza, in *Songs of Christian Praise* and thence passed into many hymnbooks. Few modern hymns are more widely used. Dr. Gladden always desired to have it sung to Canon H. P. Smith's tune, *Maryton*, with which it is generally associated, but the choice is not a very happy one, for the tune does not rise above mediocrity. It is a curious fact that not many hymn writers are also good

---

[28] Washington Gladden, b. Pottsgrove, Pa., Feb. 11, 1836; d. Columbus, Ohio, July 2, 1918; A.B. Williams College, 1859. After pastorates in Massachusetts and New York he went in 1882 to the First Congregational Church, Columbus, Ohio, which he served till his death, as one of the outstanding preachers of his day.

musicians, and their hymns generally fare better when the choice of tunes is left to competent musical editors. Dr. Gladden's second hymn,

> Behold a Sower! From afar
>   He goeth forth with might;
> The rolling years his furrows are,
>   His seed the growing light, —

is less well known, but it is a noble utterance. It first appeared in *The Pilgrim Hymnal* of 1904, and therefore properly belongs in the twentieth-century period.

Rev. Ernest W. Shurtleff [29] published several volumes of poetry, but is remembered for the noble hymn of consecration to service which he wrote in 1887 for the graduation of his class at Andover Theological Seminary:

> Lead on, O King Eternal,
>   The day of march has come;
> Henceforth in fields of conquest
>   Thy tents shall be our home.
> Through days of preparation
>   Thy grace has made us strong,
> And now, O King Eternal,
>   We lift our battle song.

Few better hymns have been written for such an occasion, and it has been widely popular for baccalaureate services.

Rev. Edwin Pond Parker [30] was the author of a number of hymns of which the most popular has been one written

[29] Ernest Warburton Shurtleff, b. Boston, April 4, 1862; d. Paris, France, Aug. 29, 1917; A.B. Harvard; Andover Theological Seminary, 1887; he held pastorates in Ventura, Cal., 1887–1891; Plymouth, Mass., 1891–1898; Minneapolis, Minn., 1898–1905; organized the American Church at Frankfort, Germany, 1905; later worked among American students in Paris.

[30] Edwin Pond Parker, b. Castine, Maine, Jan. 13, 1836; d. Hartford, Conn., May 28, 1925; educated at Bowdoin College and Bangor Theological Seminary; minister of Center Church, Hartford, for fifty years.

in 1888, for which he also composed the music with which it is associated:

> Master, no offering
> Costly and sweet,
> May we, like Magdalene,
> Lay at thy feet;
> Yet may love's incense rise,
> Sweeter than sacrifice,
> Dear Lord, to thee,
> Dear Lord, to thee.

Neither words nor music, however, have any great merit, and are more akin to the gospel-song type than those of the other Congregationalists whom we have been considering.

The Unitarian stream of hymnody, which was so strong during the middle of the century, continued without slackening until its end, though there were somewhat fewer hymnbooks issued. In 1867 the American Unitarian Association brought out a *Hymn and Tune Book* which had no marked excellence to distinguish it from the compilations made by individual ministers but which had two marked advantages over its rivals: it had a certain prestige as a denominational publication though there was no authority to require its use, and it was the first Unitarian hymnbook to be completely furnished with tunes printed above the words. It was revised and improved in 1877, and in this revised form had considerable use until the publication of *The New Hymn and Tune Book* in 1914. It shared the field, however, with several other publications, of which the most important were *Hymns of the Church Universal* (1890), which superseded Greenwood's *Collection* in King's Chapel, Boston; *Amore Dei* (1890, revised 1897), edited by Mrs. Theodore C. Williams; and *Hymns for Church and Home* (1895), which was practically an enlarged edition of *Hymns of the Church Universal*. These three books introduced to the Unitarian churches many of the English hymns and tunes which had first appeared in *Hymns Ancient and Modern*, and which had been largely overlooked by the editor of the *Hymn and Tune Book* of 1877. And they also included for the first time many of the hymns written by the new school of Unitarian hymn writers.

The first of these writers to be considered is John White Chadwick,[31] who wrote in 1864, for his class "Visitation Day" (graduation) at the Harvard Divinity School, what is probably his best-known hymn:

> Eternal Ruler of the ceaseless round
> Of circling planets singing on their way,
> Guide of the nations from the night profound,
> Into the glory of the perfect day,
> Rule in our hearts, that we may ever be
> Guided and strengthened and upheld by thee.
>
> . . . .
>
> We would be one in hatred of all wrong,
> One in our love of all things sweet and fair,
> One with the joy that breaketh into song,
> One with the grief that trembles into prayer,
> One in the power that makes thy children free
> To follow truth, and thus to follow thee.

This exceptionally fine hymn of brotherhood is better known and more generally used in England than here. Its full significance is understood when we recall that it was written during the dark days of the Civil War.

Another of Chadwick's hymns which has, perhaps, wider

[31] John White Chadwick, b. Marblehead, Mass., Oct. 19, 1840; d. Brooklyn, N. Y., Dec. 11, 1904; Harvard Divinity School, 1864; minister of the Second Unitarian Church, Brooklyn, 1864–1904; author of biographies of Channing and Parker, and of considerable poetry.

use in this country, is his memorial hymn, written for an anniversary service in the church of which he was minister. He had in mind the old Scotch melody *Auld Lang Syne*, of which he was fond, and sought to write for it better words than the traditional ones. *The Methodist Hymnal* (1935) includes it set to that air, but it is difficult for a congregation to overcome the convivial associations of the melody which are so incongruous with Chadwick's words. Croft's stately tune *St. Matthew* makes a much more appropriate setting. Few memorial hymns are more tender or more universal in their appeal:

> It singeth low in every heart,
> We hear it each and all,
> A song of those who answer not,
> However we may call:
> They throng the silence of the breast,
> We see them as of yore,
> The kind, the brave, the true, the sweet,
> Who walk with us no more.
>
> . . . .
>
> More homelike seems the vast unknown,
> Since they have entered there;
> To follow them were not so hard,
> Wherever they may fare;
> They cannot be where God is not,
> On any sea or shore;
> Whate'er betides, thy love abides,
> Our God, forevermore.

Another anniversary hymn in a similar vein begins:

> O Thou whose perfect goodness crowns
> With peace and joy this sacred day,
> Our hearts are glad for all the years
> Thy love has kept us in thy way, —

and a New Year's hymn beginning,

> Another year of setting suns, —

ends,

> Another year to follow hard
>   Where better souls have trod,
> Another year of life's delight,
>   Another year of God.

More than one of his hymns are so akin in spirit to Whittier's that they might easily pass for his, for example:

> O Love Divine, of all that is
>   The sweetest still and best,
> Fain would I come and rest my heart
>   Upon thy faithful breast.
>
> . . . .
>
> I do not pray because I would:
>   I pray because I must:
> There is no meaning in my prayer
>   But thankfulness and trust.

One of his hymns, written in 1890,

> Thou whose Spirit dwells in all,
>   Primal source of life and mind, —

is one of the earliest attempts to express the evolutionary concept in lyrical form. It is not his best verse, but it was characteristic of the man and of his spiritual inheritance that he should have seen the religious significance of the new doctrine and should have sought to give expression to it. Several other hymns have been quarried from Chadwick's poems, of excellent quality though less widely used.

In 1866 the admirable custom of asking the students at the Harvard Divinity School to try their hand at hymn writing for Visitation Day resulted in the production of a hymn by Seth Curtis Beach [32] which has passed into general use as a noble invocation for the beginning of worship:

> Mysterious Presence, source of all,
> The world without, the soul within,
> Fountain of life, O hear our call,
> And pour thy living waters in.

Dr. Beach later wrote a number of other hymns, only one of which, of the Divine Immanence, has had any wide use:

> Thou One in all, thou All in One,
> Source of the grace that crowns our days,
> For all thy gifts, 'neath cloud or sun
> We lift to thee our grateful praise.

In 1867 the Harvard Visitation Day hymn was written by Edward Rowland Sill.[33] It was his single contribution to American hymnody, written in the year that he spent in the Divinity School before turning to the path of literature:

> Send down thy truth, O God!
> Too long the shadows frown;
> Too long the darkened way we've trod:
> Thy truth, O Lord, send down!

Two other hymns of this period should be here noted. A layman, Hiram O. Wiley,[34] in 1865 wrote and published in

[32] Seth Curtis Beach, b. Marion, N. Y., Aug. 8, 1837; d. Watertown, Mass., Jan. 30, 1932; educated at Antioch and Union Colleges; Harvard Divinity School, 1866; minister of churches at Dedham, Mass., Bangor, Me., and Wayland, Mass.

[33] Edward Rowland Sill, b. Windsor, Conn., April 29, 1841; d. Cleveland, O., Feb. 27, 1887; educated at Yale; Professor of English Literature at the University of California, 1874–1882; author of several volumes of poems. His hymn was included in *The Hermitage*, 1867.

[34] Hiram Ozias Wiley, b. Middlebury, Vt., May 20, 1831; d. Peabody, Mass., Jan. 28, 1873; a lawyer in Peabody, Mass. A small collection of his poems was printed as a memorial after his death.

the *South Danvers* (Mass.) *Wizard* a poem which might be called an American counterpart of Newman's "Lead, kindly Light." It begins:

> He leads us on by paths we did not know:
> Upward he leads us, though our steps be slow;
> Though oft we faint and falter on the way,
> Though clouds and darkness oft obscure the day,
>   Yet when the clouds are gone,
>   We know he leads us on.

It somehow crossed the ocean and was included without the author's name in an English collection, whence it passed into other hymnals, sometimes falsely described as a translation from Zinzendorf by Jane Borthwick. Later it came into use in this country but its true authorship did not come to light until 1911. The second, which has been described as "a rhapsody of gratitude for the love of God," [35] was written by Rev. Oscar Clute: [36]

> O Love of God, most full,
>   O Love of God most free,
> Thou warm'st my heart, thou fill'st my soul,
>   With might thou strengthenest me.

Neither of these has had as extensive use as its merits deserve.

More important than any of these writers, however, were two men who, in the last third of the nineteenth century, took very much the place that Longfellow and Johnson had held in the middle period. Like that earlier pair, Frederic Lucian Hosmer [37] and William Channing Gan-

---

[35] *Handbook to the Hymnal*, Presbyterian, p. 99.

[36] Oscar Clute, b. Bethlehem, N. Y., Mar. 11, 1837; d. Los Angeles, Cal., Jan. 27, 1902; he held pastorates at Vineland, N. J., Keokuk, Iowa, Iowa City, and Pomona, Cal.; was later president of the Agricultural College of Michigan.

[37] Frederic Lucian Hosmer, b. Framingham, Mass., Oct. 16, 1840; d. Berkeley, Cal., June 7, 1929; A.B. Harvard, 1862; Harvard Divinity

nett [38] were in the Divinity School together (though not in the same class), were lifelong friends, and were both hymn writers and joint editors of a hymnbook.

Like Johnson, Gannett was the less prolific of the two. In 1873 he wrote a hymn interpreting the idea of evolution which preceded Chadwick's by seventeen years and is certainly one of the earliest, if not the very first to make use of the religious possibilities of the new scientific thought. It is the Immanent God who is addressed in his lyric,

> He hides within the lily,
>   A strong and tender Care,
> That wins the earth-born atoms
>   To glory of the air;
> He weaves the shining garments
>   Unceasingly and still,
> Along the quiet waters,
>   In niches of the hill.
>
> . . . .
>
> O Toiler of the lily,
>   Thy touch is in the man!
> No leaf that dawns to petal
>   But hints the angel-plan.

The thought is perhaps too abstract for the average congregation, but there are few if any other poems adapted for singing which express the thought so well. Dr. Gannett wrote a half-dozen other hymns of fine quality. In 1893, for the Parliament of Religions at Chicago, he returned

School, 1869; minister of churches at Northboro, Mass., Quincy, Ill., Cleveland, Ohio, St. Louis, Mo., and Berkeley, Cal.; published jointly with W. C. Gannett *The Thought of God in Hymns and Poems*, 1885; Second Series, 1894; *Unity Hymns and Chorals* (with W. C. Gannett and J. V. Blake), 1880; revised edition, 1911.

[38] William Channing Gannett, b. Boston, March 13, 1840; d. Rochester, N. Y., Dec. 23, 1923; A.B. Harvard, 1860; Harvard Divinity School, 1868; minister of churches at St. Paul, Minn., 1877–1883; Hinsdale, Ill., 1887–1889; Rochester, N. Y., 1889–1908.

to the theme of the immanent God who is working out his
will through the great evolutionary processes. In the background is a suggestion of the first chapter of Genesis, but
the whole thought is recast in modern terms:

Bring, O morn, thy music! Night, thy starlit silence!
Oceans, laugh the rapture to the storm-winds coursing free!
Suns and planets chorus, Thou art our Creator,
Who were, and art, and evermore shalt be.

In lovely quiet lines he wrote of the continuity of the life
of the spirit down the centuries,

> From heart to heart, from creed to creed,
>   The hidden river runs;
> It quickens all the ages down,
>   It binds the sires to sons; —

and he produced a noble hymn of thanksgiving for the end
of the year,

> Praise to God and thanks we bring, —
> Hearts, bow down, and voices, sing!
> Praises to the Glorious One,
> All his year of wonder done!

In 1875 he wrote for the dedication of a church in Chicago
what Canon Dearmer calls an "admirable hymn," beginning:

> The Lord is in his Holy Place,
>   In all things near and far:
> Shekinah of the snowflake, he,
>   And Glory of the star.

> Our art may build its house of God,
>   Our feet on Sinai stand,
> But Holiest of Holies knows
>   No tread, no touch of hand.

.   .   .   .

> O everywhere his Holy Place,
>   If love unseal the eyes,
> And everywhere the waiting Face
>   To welcome and surprise!

Several other of his hymns, hardly less excellent, have had some use.

The hymns of Dr. Hosmer, however, were not only more numerous, but more generally usable, and of such excellence as to warrant calling him the foremost American hymn writer of the end of the nineteenth and beginning of the twentieth century. He wrote more hymns than Samuel Longfellow, and of as fine a quality. At least thirty-five have come into more or less use, the best of them being included in many hymnbooks both in this country and in England. He studied carefully the technique of his art, each hymn expresses a definite mood or thought, wrought out with care, and finished with the artist's love of perfection. Each one is a lyrical phrasing of some religious emotion, of some universal and eternal theme, but the speech is vernacular, not anachronistic; simple and not theological; natural and not pietistic.

Several of his hymns express his "thought of God." One of the finest begins:

> O Thou, who art of all that is
>   Beginning both and end,
> We follow thee through unknown paths,
>   Since all to thee must tend;
> Thy judgments are a mighty deep,
>   Beyond all fathom line;
> Our wisdom is the childlike heart,
>   Our strength to trust in thine.

Another, which Canon Dearmer calls "this flawless poem, one of the completest expressions of religious faith," begins,

> O Thou, in all thy might so far, —

and puts into two lines in its second stanza what is perhaps as perfect an example of the mystic's definition of God as can be found in modern verse:

> What heart can comprehend thy name,
> Or searching, find thee out,
> *Who art, within, a quickening Flame,*
> *A Presence round about.*

The same note is struck in his hymn,

> O Name, all other names above,
> What art thou not to me, —

and in,

> One thought I have, my ample creed.

Hosmer resembles Longfellow in his hymns on "the goodly fellowship of the prophets," for his religion was essentially of the prophetic type, the religion of the spirit rather than of authority, of humanity rather than of an ecclesiastical organization. Few writers have more perfectly expressed the thought of the essential unity of the spirit in the prophets of all ages:

> From age to age how grandly rise
> The prophet souls in line!
> Above the passing centuries
> Like beacon lights they shine.
>
> Through differing accents of the lip
> One message they proclaim,
> One growing bond of fellowship,
> Above all names one Name.
> .   .   .   .
> Through every race, in every clime,
> One song shall yet be heard;
> Move onward in thy course sublime
> O everlasting Word!

Other hymns on the same theme are,

> Forward through the ages,
> In unbroken line,
> Move the faithful spirits
> At the call divine, —

written to be sung to *St. Gertrude*, and,

> O prophet souls of all the years, —

written for the Parliament of Religions in 1893, the purpose
of which is finely expressed in the second and third stanzas:

> From tropic clime and zones of frost,
> They come, of every name, —
> This, this our day of Pentecost,
> The Spirit's tongue of flame.

> One Life together we confess,
> One all-indwelling Word,
> One holy Call to righteousness,
> Within the silence heard.

Dr. Hosmer's hymn written for the commencement at
Meadville Theological School in 1891, beginning,

> Thy kingdom come! On bended knee,
> The passing ages pray,

has been called by Canon Dearmer "one of the noblest
hymns in the language." Canon Dearmer goes on to say
that it is one of the two hymns written in the whole of the
nineteenth century on the petition "Thy kingdom come,"
in the Lord's Prayer, the other being Lewis Hensley's,

> Thy Kingdom come, O God!

Canon Dearmer is correct in his estimate of Hosmer's hymn,
but inexact as to the number of hymns written on this text.

Hosmer himself had written an earlier one (1891), beginning,

> Thy kingdom come, O Lord, —

as had the English Unitarian Henry Warburton Hawkes,

> Thy kingdom come! O Lord, we daily cry.

Two other of Hosmer's hymns are beautiful expressions of his thought of the eternal life. They seem centuries away from the old hymns about death and heaven and hell. He indulges in no rapturous descriptions of "Jerusalem the golden," but his song is no less filled with trust and faith. The earlier one, written in 1876 after the death by drowning of a young parishioner, suggests Whittier,

> I cannot think of them as dead
> Who walk with me no more;
> Along the path of life I tread
> They have but gone before.

The second is the great hymn which he wrote for the music of Palestrina's *Victory*, a hymn which ends on a note of exultation:

> O Lord of life, where'er they be,
> Safe in thine own eternity,
> Our dead are living unto thee,
>   Alleluia.

His hymn written in 1890 for the fiftieth anniversary of the church in Quincy, Illinois, of which he was minister,

> O Light, from age to age the same,
> Forever living Word,
> Here have we felt thy kindling flame,
> Thy voice within have heard, —

is a beautiful one for a memorial service. His,

> Father, to thee we look in all our sorrow,
> Thou art the fountain whence our healing flows, —

written in 1881, is quite equal to Samuel Johnson's,

> Father, in thy mysterious presence kneeling,

and ends with the striking lines:

> Yet shalt thou praise him when these darkened furrows,
> Where now he ploweth, wave with golden grain.

While these are perhaps the best of Dr. Hosmer's hymns there are as many more on various themes and for varied occasions which fall little below them for excellence. No other hymn writer of the nineteenth century, not even Whittier and Longfellow, has made a larger contribution to our American hymnody, nor one of more permanent value. His hymns are coming into increasing use, not only in this country but in England. Canon Dearmer included seven in *Songs of Praise.*

Two other writers who, though of differing temperament and quality, both belonged to the Unitarian group, did most of their work before the end of the century. Rev. Minot J. Savage [39] was an effective popular preacher, a pioneer in the interpretation of religion in terms which would reconcile it with the then novel and suspected doctrine of evolution. For his church in Boston he brought out in 1883 a book of *Sacred Songs for Public Worship,* which included 195 hymns and songs of a popular type,

[39] Minot Judson Savage, b. Norridgewock, Me., June 10, 1841; d. May 22, 1918; Bangor Theological Seminary, 1864; Congregational home missionary in California, 1864–1867; Congregational pastorates Framingham, Mass., and Hannibal, Mo.; Unitarian pastorates, Third Unitarian Church, Chicago, 1873–1874; Church of the Unity, Boston, 1874–1896; Church of the Messiah, New York, 1896–1906.

forty-two items being from his own pen, the music being arranged by Howard M. Dow. It was more of a "one-man book," and was musically nearer akin to the typical gospel-song book than any other collection issued from Unitarian sources. Most of his hymns do not rise above the level of respectable verse, but a few of them survive in use. Perhaps the best is his lovely hymn of God in nature, —

> Seek not afar for beauty. Lo! it glows
> In dew-wet grasses all about thy feet.

Others are,

> O star of truth, down shining
> Through clouds of doubt and fear,
> I ask but 'neath thy guidance
> My pathway may appear, —

and,

> How shall come the kingdom holy,
> In which all the earth is blest,
> That shall lift on high the lowly,
> And to weary souls give rest?

The other of these two writers was Rev. Theodore C. Williams.[40] He was a classical scholar, the author of a considerable amount of carefully studied poetry, and of a fine metrical translation of Virgil's *Aeneid*. His most widely used hymn is his appealing song of brotherhood,

> When thy heart with joy o'erflowing,
> Sings a thankful prayer,
> In thy joy, O let thy brother
> With thee share.

[40] Theodore Chickering Williams, b. Brookline, Mass., July 2, 1855; d. Boston, May 6, 1915; A.B. Harvard, 1876; Harvard Divinity School, 1882; minister of All Souls' Church, New York, 1883–1896; headmaster of Hackley School, 1899–1905.

An earlier hymn,

> Lord, who dost the voices bless, —

was written in 1881 while Mr. Williams was still a student in the Divinity School, for the ordination of a friend. It is one of the best ordination hymns in the language and would be as appropriate for a young man entering the Roman priesthood as for one in any Protestant communion. Williams' hymn,

> God be with thee! Gently o'er thee
> May his wings of mercy spread, —

is a beautiful parting hymn of benediction; his

> When the world around us throws
> All its proud deceiving shows,
> And the heart no danger knows;
> Help us, Lord most holy, —

set to the Hungarian traditional *Regi Litania*, is a very effective hymn for a Lenten service; his

> In the lonely midnight, —

is a tender and loving Christmas hymn; and his

> Hast thou heard it, O my brother,
> Hast thou heard the trumpet sound?

is a stirring call to youth to enlist in the warfare of good against evil.

Less known, but hardly less excellent, is his hymn of nature,

> Thou rulest, Lord, the lights on high, —

a fine hymn for the Sabbath, beginning,

> By law from Sinai's clouded steep
> A toiling world was blest;
> And still the listening nations keep
> The day of sacred rest, —

and his hymn of mystical meditation,

> As the storm retreating
> Leaves the vales in peace
> Let the world's vain noises
> O'er our spirits cease.

All of these hymns by Mr. Williams are religious poetry of a high order.

A number of other writers of this period, who were not associated with any of the denominational groups which we have been considering, should be mentioned. Rev. Denis Wortman [41] was a minister of the Reformed Church who, in 1884, wrote for the centennial of the New Brunswick Theological Seminary, of which he was a graduate, a fine hymn on the ministry, well adapted for use in theological schools and for the ordination or installation of a minister. From the appropriate Old Testament reference with which it begins it goes on to summon the ministers of our day to go forth to the work of the world as prophets, priests, and apostles:

> God of the prophets, bless the prophets' sons;
> Elijah's mantle o'er Elisha cast;
> Each age its solemn task may claim but once;
> Make each one nobler, stronger than the last.

[41] Denis Wortman, b. Hopewell, N. Y., April 30, 1835; d. 1922; A.B. Amherst College, 1857; New Brunswick Theological Seminary, 1860; pastorates in Brooklyn, Philadelphia, and Schenectady, N. Y.; secretary of Ministerial Relief; president of the General Synod of the Reformed Church in 1901.

There have been many hymns of the heavenly Jerusalem since an unknown author of the sixth or seventh century wrote the great,

Urbs Jerusalem beata,

and almost all of them have been contemplations of the bliss of heaven. A quite new note has been struck in our modern "hymns of the city," in which the theme is the application of religion to human life in cities upon this earth. One of the first of these modern hymns was written in 1878 by Dr. Felix Adler [42] in his fine verses,

Hail the glorious golden city,
　Pictured by the seers of old;
Everlasting light shines o'er it,
　Wondrous things of it are told.
Only righteous men and women
　Dwell within its gleaming wall;
Wrong is banished from its borders,
　Justice reigns supreme o'er all.

We are builders of that city,
　All our joys and all our groans
Help to rear its shining ramparts;
　All our lives are building-stones.[43]

　．　．　．　．　．　．　．　．　．　．　．

Dr. Adler was of Jewish origin and was long the distinguished leader of the Ethical Culture movement in New York. His hymn contains no reference to God, but its ethical content is so fine that it has been included in a number of hymnbooks and it was the forerunner of a considerable group of hymns on the same general theme.

[42] Felix Adler, b. Germany, 1851; d. New York, 1933.
[43] From *Hymns of the Kingdom of God*, copyright 1910 by A. S. Barnes and Company. Quoted by permission.

Mrs. Mary Baker Eddy,[44] "discoverer and founder of Christian Science," wrote seven hymns which are included in the *Christian Science Hymnal* of 1922, the earliest of which were copyrighted as early as 1887. Three others were not copyrighted until the opening years of this century. Her hymns have, naturally, had wide use among her followers, but none of them appears to have found a place in other hymnbooks. This is due, not so much to any peculiarities of belief which they express (for most if not all of them would, in that respect, be usable by other Christian bodies), as to their lack of originality in thought and their mediocrity as verse. The same criticism must be made of the other original hymns in the *Christian Science Hymnal*, of which there are a considerable number. While they fill a place within the Christian Science church their adoption outside its ranks is unlikely. The book which contains them, being an official hymnal, is universally used by Christian Scientists, to whom it is no doubt acceptable, but it is a very one-sided collection, and the freedom with which standard hymns have been "adapted" to meet the views of its users has seldom been exceeded.

At the very end of the century a great hymn of love for America was published by Miss Katharine Lee Bates,[45] of Wellesley College, who cannot be classified with any denominational group since she appears to have had no formal church affiliation. The hymn was written in 1893, after a visit to the World's Fair at Chicago — which inspired the line, "Thine alabaster cities gleam" — followed by a journey across the plains to Colorado. She wrote of the trip, "My New England eyes delighted in the wind-waved gold of

[44] Mary Baker Glover Eddy, b. Bow, N. H., July 16, 1821; d. Chestnut Hill, Mass., Dec. 3, 1910.
[45] Katharine Lee Bates, b. Falmouth, Mass., Aug. 12, 1859; d. Wellesley, Mass., Mar. 29, 1929; educated at Wellesley College and later professor of English there; editor and author of many books.

the vast wheatfields," and from Pike's Peak "gazed in word-less rapture over the expanse of mountain ranges and sealike sweep of the plains. . . . It was then and there that the opening lines of 'America the Beautiful' were born":

> O beautiful for spacious skies,
>   For amber waves of grain,
>   For purple mountain majesties
>   Above the fruited plain!
>   America, America!
>   God shed his grace on thee
>   And crown thy good with brotherhood
>   From sea to shining sea! [46]

Miss Bates' hymn was not published until 1899. Several tunes were written for it, but popular preference has in-separably associated it with *Materna*, written by the Ameri-can composer Samuel A. Ward, in 1882, as a setting for "O Mother dear, Jerusalem," — and published with those words in the Episcopal *Hymnal* of 1892. Miss Bates' hymn has become the most popular national hymn today, over-shadowing even S. F. Smith's "My country, 'tis of thee," — because it so successfully envisages the whole country, rather than the limited New England landscape of Smith's hymn. Two other hymns of Miss Bates have had some use, but they were written much later and will be considered in the next chapter.

[46] Acknowledgement is made to Mrs. George S. Burgess, owner of the copyright, for permission to quote this hymn.

CHAPTER IX

Hymns of the Twentieth Century

A MERICAN HYMNODY in the twentieth century has continued to move along the paths which had been already marked out in the last decades of the nineteenth. It has almost wholly lost its denominational characteristics, so that the grouping of authors by denominations no longer has much significance save as the several communions take pride in their contributions to the common treasury of devotion, and the use of hymns in the churches tends towards a common practice. The gospel hymns linger in the less progressive churches, but the literary and musical standards are rising, and the religious outlook is broadening.

The new hymns have been increasingly songs of human brotherhood; of the redemption of the social order rather than of the salvation of the individual soul; and of the higher patriotism which looks beyond the nation to mankind. Peace hymns have taken the place of the older anti-slavery and temperance songs. Some of them are little more than a sentimental, unrealistic "wishful thinking" in doggerel. But, as a whole, these modern hymns of the social gospel have, with substantial success, filled a great gap in Christian hymnody, which, down to the last third of the nineteenth century, almost totally lacked such songs. It is true that the Latin hymnody, and still more the Anglo-American hymnody of the early nineteenth century, did inculcate certain humanitarian virtues, especially charity, but it was an individualistic virtue rather than the idealism of a regenerate social order.

Attention was drawn to this new hymnody of the social gospel when, in 1914, *The Survey* published a collection of *Social Hymns of Brotherhood and Aspiration, Collected by Mabel Hays Barrows Mussey*. The collection was without tunes and was not intended for church use, but it contained a hundred hymns, enough of which were of really fine quality to have a marked influence on later hymnbooks, most of which now have a respectable section of hymns expressive of modern humanitarian idealism.

Another helpful factor, in more general ways, has been the work of the interdenominational Hymn Society of America, founded in New York in 1922, which is steadily and effectively spreading its influence to other parts of the country. Its mission is to promote good congregational singing, and the knowledge, use, and production of hymns and tunes of the finest type, through its publications, and by means of hymn festivals. Perhaps we may view it as a far more effective twentieth-century counterpart of "The Society for Promoting Regular and Good Singing, and for reforming the Depravations and Debasements our Psalmody labours under," before which Rev. Thomas Walter preached his discourse on the *Sweet Psalmist of Israel*, in Boston in 1722.

The editorial standards of American hymnbooks have steadily risen since the turn of the century, and the collections which have been published have been, for the most part, greatly superior in catholicity, as well as in the quality of both words and tunes, to those of the nineteenth century. Almost every denomination has published one or more hymnals, and there have been others, far too numerous to list, issued either by individuals or by commercial publishers, though generally these last have been upon a lower level of excellence. Only the most influential or superior of these collections can be discussed. It should be said, however, that during this period there have been half-a-dozen hymnbooks issued for use in Great Britain or Canada, which, from almost every point of view, are superior to most American publications.

Of the outstanding American hymnbooks of the present period the first to be noticed is *The Pilgrim Hymnal*, issued in 1904 by The Pilgrim Press, the publication agency of the Congregationalists. Dr. Charles L. Noyes was editor, and Dr. Washington Gladden was associate editor. This was a very progressive book which sought to meet the demand for a hymnody to match the current "New Theology" of the day. It was markedly undogmatic, non-ecclesiastical, and humanitarian in tone, and more nearly approached the type of hymnbook in use among the Unitarians than had any book previously published by an evangelical body. In its index of authors it included information as to both their nationality and their church affiliations, which facilitated the discovery that out of 547 hymns 115 were ascribed to Unitarians, and that of 69 American authors, 32 were Unitarians who contributed considerably more than half the hymns of American authorship.[1] This high proportion of hymns from Unitarian sources opened the door to considerable criticism, to which Dr. Gladden replied that it was due to the simple fact that the Unitarians had, within recent years, written the largest number of the best hymns.[2] After the book passed out of the control of the editors the index of authors was re-set and information as to denominational affiliations was omitted.

Either because of this minor controversy, or because it was too far in advance of the sentiment of many Congregational churches, *The Pilgrim Hymnal* was not as widely

---

[1] Benson, *The English Hymn*, p. 582. Other estimates have varied slightly, as the classification of a few names may be a matter of doubt, but the general result is the same.

[2] *The Congregationalist*, July 30, 1904, p. 147.

accepted as might have been expected for a book issued with the denominational imprint. It was revised in 1913, and again in 1931, to conform more to the general taste, and ranks high among the books now in use. It has had to compete in the open market with other hymnbooks, edited either by Congregationalists or others, the best of which was the more conservative and churchly *Hymns of the Church, New and Old* (1913), edited by W. V. W. Davis and Raymond Calkins.

Since this century came in the Congregationalists have produced a considerable number of hymn writers, several of whom have written one or more hymns of excellent quality. One of the best is the loving and tender communion meditation written by Mrs. Alice Freeman Palmer [3] in 1901, the year before her death. It is not as well known as it should be:

> How sweet and silent is the place,
>   Alone, my God, with thee!
> Awaiting here thy touch of grace,
>   Thy heavenly mystery.

> So many ways thou hast, dear Lord,
>   My longing heart to fill,
> Thy lovely world, thy spoken word,
>   The doing thy sweet will,

> Giving thy children daily bread,
>   Leading thy weak ones on,
> The touch of dear hands on my head,
>   The thought of loved ones gone.

> Lead me by many paths, dear Lord,
>   But always in thy way;
> And let me make my earth a heaven
>   Till next communion day.

[3] Alice Elvira Freeman, b. Colesville, N. Y., Feb. 21, 1855; d. Dec. 6,

In 1903 President William DeWitt Hyde [4] of Bowdoin College wrote a hymn which has been curiously over-looked by most hymnbook editors. It is a stirring summons to the spiritual warfare for "the Kingdom of the Right," beginning,

> Creation's Lord, we give thee thanks
> That this thy world is incomplete;
> That battle calls our marshalled ranks,
> That work awaits our hands and feet;
>
> That thou hast not yet finished man,
> That we are in the making still, —
> As friends who share the Maker's plan,
> As sons who know the Father's will.

The great number of hymns which have been written for anniversary occasions, and the relative infrequency of opportunities for their use is perhaps the reason why Professor John Wright Buckham's [5] hymn, written in 1916 for the fiftieth anniversary at the Pacific School of Religion, has been similarly neglected. Yet, though it lacks originality of form or thought, it is far above the average of such occasional hymns:

> O God, above the drifting years,
> The shrines our fathers founded stand,
> And where the higher gain appears,
> We trace the working of thy hand.

. . . .

1902; president of Wellesley College, 1882–1888; married Professor George Herbert Palmer, Dec. 23, 1887.

[4] William DeWitt Hyde, b. Winchendon, Mass., Sept. 23, 1858; d. Brunswick, Me., June 29, 1917; A.B. Harvard, 1879; Andover Theological Seminary, 1882; president of Bowdoin College, 1885–1917.

[5] John Wright Buckham, b. Burlington, Vt., Nov. 5, 1864; A.B. University of Vermont, 1885; Andover Theological Seminary, 1888; pastorates at Conway, N. H., 1888–1890; Salem, Mass., 1890–1903; professor of theology, Pacific School of Religion, Berkeley, Cal., 1903–1939.

Fill thou our hearts with faith like theirs,
Who served the days they could not see;
And give us grace, through ampler years,
To build the Kingdom yet to be.

Two hymns of brotherhood were written in 1909 by
Dr. Ozora S. Davis,[6] of a type unknown to earlier American hymnody but now familiar:

At length there dawns the glorious day,
By prophets long foretold:
At length the chorus clearer grows
That shepherds heard of old.
The day of dawning brotherhood
Breaks on our eager eyes,
And human hatreds flee before
The radiant eastern skies, —

and,

We bear the strain of earthly care
But bear it not alone;
Beside us walks our Brother Christ,
And makes our task his own.

. . . .

Our brotherhood still rests in him,
The Brother of us all,
And o'er the centuries still we hear
The Master's winsome call.

Rev. Allen Eastman Cross [7] has written a half-dozen
hymns which have had some use. Perhaps the best are his
hymns for youth:

[6] Ozora Stearns Davis, b. Wheelock, Vt., July 30, 1866; d. Chicago,
Ill., March 15, 1931; educated at Dartmouth College, Hartford Theological Seminary, and the University of Leipzig; minister of Congregational
churches at Springfield, Vt., Newtonville, Mass., New Britain, Conn.;
president of Chicago Theological Seminary, 1909–1920.
[7] Allen Eastman Cross, b. Manchester, N. H., Dec. 30, 1864; Amherst
College; Andover Theological Seminary; pastorates at Cliftondale, Mass.,

The hidden years at Nazareth!
How beautiful they seem,
Like fountains flowing in the dark,
Or waters in a dream!

and,

Young and radiant, he is standing
As he stood at Salem's shrine;
Just a lad, a lad forever,
With a look and grace divine.

But he has also written a good hymn for airmen,

Mount up with wings as eagles,
Ye lovers of the sky, —

and his verses beginning,

The gray hills taught me patience,
The waters taught me prayer, —

while not quite a hymn in form, make a lovely little poem of meditation. While none of Mr. Cross's hymns are of the finest quality they are all helpful pieces of devotional verse.

In 1912 Rev. Jay T. Stocking,[8] while watching some carpenters at work in an Adirondack camp, wrote his hymn for young people on the theme of "The Carpenter of Nazareth":

O Master-Workman of the race,
Thou Man of Galilee,

1892–1896; Springfield, Mass., 1896–1901; (assoc. pastor) Old South Church, Boston, 1901–1912; Milford, Mass., 1916–1925; author of two volumes of poetry, *Pass on the Torch* (1929), and *Thunder over Jerusalem* (1936), from which about fifteen hymns have been taken for inclusion in various hymnals. The quotations from his hymns given in the text are made with his kind permission.

[8] Jay Thomas Stocking, b. Lisbon, N. Y., April 7, 1870; d. Newton Center, Mass., Jan. 27, 1936; educated at Amherst, Yale Divinity School, and the University of Berlin; ordained 1901; minister of several Congregational churches; moderator of the Congregational Council, 1934.

Who with the eyes of early youth
Eternal things did see;
We thank thee for thy boyhood faith
That shone thy whole life through:
'Did ye not know it is my work
My Father's work to do?'

Dr. George A. Gordon [9] was distinguished as a great preacher and an author of many books on religion. He occasionally wrote poems to be printed with his pamphlet sermons, and at Easter, 1915, wrote a hymn which first appeared in a hymnbook in *The Methodist Hymnal* of 1935. It is only incidentally an Easter hymn, and in the *Hymnal* is properly included under "God's Love and Mercy":

O Will of God beneath our life,
The sea beneath the wave;
From thee we rise in mystic strife,
In thee we find our grave.

Close akin in spirit to Dr. Stocking's, "O Master-Workman of the race," — is a hymn by Rev. Samuel Ralph Harlow [10] which also first appeared in *The Methodist Hymnal* of 1935:

O young and fearless Prophet of ancient Galilee:
Thy life is still a summons to serve humanity,
To make our thoughts and actions less prone to please the crowd,
To stand with humble courage for truth with hearts uncowed.

. . . .

[9] George Angier Gordon, b. Pitodrie, Oyne, Aberdeenshire, Scotland, Jan. 2, 1853; d. Boston, Oct. 29, 1929; emigrated to America 1871; studied at Bangor Theological Seminary and at Harvard; minister of Old South Church, Boston, for forty-three years.

[10] Samuel Ralph Harlow, b. Boston, July 20, 1885; educated at Harvard and Columbia Universities, Union and Hartford Theological Seminaries; ordained 1912; professor of religion and social ethics at Smith College. His hymn is quoted by permission.

O help us stand unswerving against war's bloody way,
Where hate and lust and falsehood hold back Christ's holy
    sway;
Forbid false love of country, that blinds us to his call
Who lifts above the nation the brotherhood of all.

The note of brotherhood is struck again, with more power,
in the verses by Professor H. H. Tweedy,[11] which in 1929
took the Hymn Society's prize for a new missionary hymn:

> Eternal God, whose power upholds
>   Both flower and flaming star,
> To whom there is no here nor there,
>   No time, no near or far,
> No alien race, no foreign shore,
>   No child unsought, unknown,
> O send us forth, thy prophets true,
>   To make all lands thine own.[12]

Professor Tweedy has also written a hymn of the Holy
Spirit in which he has made fresh and effective use of the
Pentecostal symbolism,

> O Spirit of the Living God,
>   Thou Light and Fire Divine;
> Descend upon thy Church once more
>   And make it truly thine!
> Fill it with love and joy and power,
>   With righteousness and peace,
> Till Christ shall dwell in human hearts,
>   And sin and sorrow cease.

Yet another of his hymns is one on prayer, beginning,

> O gracious Father of mankind,
>   Our spirits' unseen Friend, —

[11] Henry Hallam Tweedy, b. Binghamton, N. Y., Aug. 5, 1868; educated at Yale, Union Theological Seminary, and Berlin; minister of churches at Utica, N. Y. and Bridgeport, Conn.; professor of Practical Theology, Yale Divinity School, 1909–1937.

[12] Copyright by the Hymn Society of America. Quoted by permission.

in which he expresses the idea that our highest aspiration, thought, and work constitute our true prayer. Although these three hymns by Dr. Tweedy lack conciseness and any great distinction of phrasing, and are all written in common meter double which has a tendency to sing-song when carried on through several stanzas, they nevertheless represent the best contribution made by a Congregationalist to American hymnody in this century. Three more hymns which he has written are included in *Christian Worship and Praise* (1939), of which he was the editor, "under direction of the Commission for Christian Worship and Praise," but they are of less value than those already quoted. In its selection of tunes this book falls well below the best standards of today, representing the taste of the later Victorian period. Among the hymns the most striking single new item is the poem by Vachel Lindsay,

> An endless line of splendor,
> These troops with heaven for home,
> With creeds they go from Scotland,
> With incense go from Rome.[13]

Dr. Tweedy has also included a good many hymns by little known writers, too numerous to mention here, most of which have not hitherto come into use. Few, if any, of these have conspicuous merit, but they represent a wide search for new and fresh outpourings of worship song.

Rev. Shepherd Knapp [14] has written two hymns which have come into considerable use. The first was written in

[13] Quoted from Vachel Lindsay's "Foreign Missions in Battle Array," *Collected Poems*, N. Y., 1931. By permission of the publishers, The Macmillan Company, New York.

[14] Shepherd Knapp, b. New York City, Sept. 8, 1873; A.B. Columbia, 1894; B.D. Yale, 1897; ordained Congregational ministry, 1897; pastorates at Southington, Conn., (asst. minister) Brick Presbyterian Church, N. Y. City; Central Congregational Church, Worcester, Mass. The hymn, "Not only where God's free winds blow," is quoted by permission of the author.

1907, while he was assistant pastor of the Brick Presbyterian Church in New York, for the men's association of that church:

> Lord God of Hosts, whose purpose, never swerving,
> Leads toward the day of Jesus Christ, thy son,
> Grant us to march among thy faithful legions,
> Armed with thy courage, till the world is won.

His second, written a year later — a "hymn of the city" like Frank Mason North's "Where cross the crowded ways of life" — is sometimes printed with the first stanza omitted, but that stanza is an essential introduction to his thought:

> Not only where God's free winds blow
>   Or in the silent wood,
> But where the city's restless flow
> Is never still, his love we know,
>   And find his presence good.

> Dear God, the sun whose light is sweet
>   On hill and plain and sea,
> Doth cheer the city's busy street,
> And they that pass with weary feet
>   Give thanks for light from thee.

> . . . .

> But in the city's grief and shame
>   Dost thou refuse a part?
> Ah, no; for burneth there the flame
> Of human help in Christ's dear name;
>   There, most of all, thou art.

A little poem by Howard A. Walter,[15] a young man too early dead, has come into some use among young people.

[15] Howard Arnold Walter, b. 1884; d. Lahore, India, 1918; A.B. Princeton, 1905; Hartford Theological Seminary; a teacher in Japan, and Y. M. C. A. secretary in India; his poem was written in Japan at New Year's 1907, and appeared in *Harper's Magazine* in May of that year.

It is not a hymn in form but it does express the idealism of youth:

> I would be true, for there are those who trust me;
> I would be pure, for there are those who care;
> I would be strong, for there is much to suffer;
> I would be brave, for there is much to dare.
>
> I would be friend to all, the foe, the friendless;
> I would be giving, and forget the gift;
> I would be humble, for I know my weakness;
> I would look up, and laugh, and love, and lift.

Rev. J. Edgar Park,[16] president of Wheaton College, has written a hymn on a theme seldom used by hymn writers — the Temptation of Jesus:

> O Jesus, thou wast tempted,
> Alone in deserts wild, —[17]

and a more widely used one on the life of Jesus beginning,

> We would see Jesus, lo! his star is shining
> Above the stable while the angels sing.[17]

Rev. James Gordon Gilkey [18] wrote in 1931 a good hymn for Palm Sunday, which is also a modern hymn of the city,

> Outside the Holy City,
> Unnumbered footsteps throng,

[16] John Edgar Park, b. Belfast, Ireland, March 7, 1879; educated at New College, Edinburgh; Royal University, Dublin; and Princeton Theological Seminary; minister of The First Congregational Church, West Newton, Mass.; president of Wheaton College since 1926.

[17] Copyright 1913, by Congregational Sunday School and Publishing Society. Used by permission.

[18] James Gordon Gilkey, b. Watertown, Mass., Sept. 28, 1889; A.B. Harvard, 1912; B.D. Union Theological Seminary, 1916; asst. minister, Bryn Mawr (Pa.) Church, 1916–1917; pastor South Church, Springfield, Mass., since 1917; author of several books.

And crowded mart and streets of trade
Fling back a swelling song,

.   .   .   .

A distant music mingles
With all our songs today,
The chorale from a city fair
Where sin has passed away.

There rides the Christ triumphant
And victor songs ring clear;
O God, give us the strength to build
With Christ that city here.[19]

In this century no denominational group has produced a larger number of new hymns of good quality than the Congregationalists, although only a few of them have attained a conspicuous degree of excellence.

The Baptists have produced but one hymn writer of distinction thus far in this century, Rev. Harry Emerson Fosdick.[20] His noble hymn beginning,

God of grace and God of glory,
On thy people pour thy power;
Crown thine ancient church's story;
Bring her bud to glorious flower.
Grant us wisdom,
Grant us courage,
For the facing of this hour, —

was written for the dedication of the Riverside Church, New York, Oct. 5, 1930. It is one of the finest of modern

[19] Quoted by permission of the author.
[20] Harry Emerson Fosdick, b. Buffalo, N. Y., May 24, 1878; A.B. Colgate University, 1900; B.D. Union Theological Seminary, 1904; A.M. Columbia, 1908; ordained Baptist ministry, 1903; instructor in homiletics, 1908–1915; professor of practical theology since 1915, Union Theological Seminary; minister Riverside Church, New York; author of many books. His hymns are quoted with his permission.

utterances about the ideals for which the Christian church should stand, and has passed into several of the recent hymnals. Two other hymns by Dr. Fosdick have come into some use. One is a hymn of peace for the world,

> The Prince of Peace his banner spreads.

The other, beginning,

> O God, in restless living, —

is a prayer for inward peace, but neither of these reaches the high standard of excellence of his first-named hymn.

The Methodists in this century have been more prolific and have been zealous to improve their hymnody. It is significant of the rapidity of change of modern religious thought that few hymnbooks today remain in use for more than twenty-five or thirty years. This is illustrated among the Methodists by the fact that the first official and authorized hymnal for American Methodism was published in 1836 (with no American hymns included); revised in 1849 (with about fifty American hymns included); and was reissued in 1876, in 1905, and in 1935.[21] All these books, except the latest, had to compete with other publications, especially of the gospel-song type. *The Methodist Hymnal* of 1935 is the joint product of the Methodist Episcopal Church; The Methodist Episcopal Church, South; and the Methodist Protestant Church. While it makes some concession to the popularity of the gospel songs by including a considerable number of the better ones in its section headed "Songs of Salvation," its general standard of words and music is abreast of the books of other American churches, and is far higher than the Methodists have hitherto had. Its value is enhanced by the scholarly and

[21] B. F. Crawford, *Religious Trends in a Century of Hymns*, Carnegie, Pa., 1938, p. 20.

well-edited handbook prepared to accompany it.[22] For the first time the hitherto divided Methodists have a common hymnal of a high order.

The book includes several hymns by recent Methodist authors. The earliest, in order of composition, is the noble hymn by Richard Watson Gilder,[23] written in 1903 in connection with the observance at Wesleyan University of the 200th anniversary of the birth of John Wesley, and included in the *Methodist Hymnal* of 1905:

> To thee, Eternal Soul, be praise,
> Who, from of old to our own days,
> Through souls of saints and prophets, Lord,
> Hast sent thy light, thy love, thy word.[24]

Less adequate is another hymn,

> God of the strong, God of the weak, —

but his choral-like response, set to *Finlandia*,

> Through love to light! O wonderful the way, —

has great beauty.

Harry Webb Farrington's [25] Christmas song,

> I know not how that Bethlehem's babe
> Could in the Godhead be;
> I only know the manger child
> Has brought God's life to me, —

[22] R. G. McCutchan, *Our Hymnody: A Manual of the Methodist Hymnal*, N. Y., 1937.

[23] Richard Watson Gilder, b. Bordentown, N. J., Feb. 8, 1844; d. Nov., 1909; largely self-educated, he became editor of *The Century Magazine*, and a noted man of letters; author of five volumes of poems.

[24] "To Thee, Eternal Soul," copyright by Houghton Mifflin Company, quoted by permission.

[25] Harry Webb Farrington, b. Nassau, Bahama Islands, July 14, 1880; d. Nov. 1930; A.B. Syracuse University, 1907; Boston University School of Theology, and Harvard University. His Hymn for Airmen, copyright 1928, is included in *Valleys and Visions*, New York, 1932, copyright by Dora Davis Farrington, and is quoted by permission.

was written in 1910 while the author was a graduate student at Harvard, and took the prize which had been offered for the best Christmas hymn written by a student. It has since found its way into several hymnbooks. Mr. Farrington has written a number of other hymns, including an excellent one for airmen:

> O God Creator, in whose hand,
>   The rolling planets lie,
> Give skill to those who now command
>   The ships that brave the sky.
>
> Strong Spirit, burning with mankind
>   On missions high to dare,
> Safe pilot all who seek to find
>   Their haven through the air.
>
> Enfolding Life, bear on thy wing
>   Through storm, and dark, and sun,
> The men in air who closer bring
>   The nations into one.

Rather more traditional in thought and form is Dean Tillett's [26] hymn on the Incarnation,

> O Son of God incarnate,
> O Son of man divine, —

which thus far appears only in *The Methodist Hymnal* and in *Christian Worship and Praise.*

[26] Wilbur Fish Tillett, b. Henderson, N. C., Aug. 25, 1854; d. Nashville, Tenn., June 4, 1936; educated at Randolph-Macon College and Princeton Theological Seminary. In 1882 he went to Vanderbilt University as Chaplain and afterwards held professorships there; was Dean of the Theological Faculty until his retirement in 1919; was Vice-Chancellor of the University; an author of note, and an authority on hymnology.

Another of these writers is Dean Earl Marlatt[27] of Boston University School of Theology. He has written much poetry and a number of hymns. One of them was written in an endeavor to make clear to a student the doctrine of the Trinity, and it is an "explanation" which even a Unitarian could understand and perhaps accept:

> Spirit of Life, in this new dawn,
>   Give us the faith that follows on,
> Letting thine all-pervading power
>   Fulfil the dreams of this high hour.

> Spirit Creative, give us light,
>   Lifting the raveled mists of night:
> Touch Thou our dust with spirit-hand,
>   And make our souls to understand.

> Spirit Redeeming, give us grace
>   When crucified to seek thy face;
> To read forgiveness in thy eyes,
>   Today with thee in Paradise.

> Spirit Consoling, let us find
>   Thy hand when sorrows leave us blind;
> In the gray valley let us hear
>   Thy silent voice, 'Lo, I am near.'

> Spirit of Love, at evening time,
>   When weary feet refuse to climb,
> Give us thy vision, eyes that see,
>   Beyond the dark, the dawn and thee.[28]

[27] Earl Bowman Marlatt, b. Columbus, Ind., May 24, 1892; A.B. De Pauw University, 1912; S.T.B. Boston University, 1922; later studied at Harvard; Oxford, England; the University of Berlin. An officer in the World War, in 1923 he became Professor of Philosophy at Boston University. He is a poet of distinction and was associate editor of *The American Student Hymnal*, 1928.

[28] This and the following passage are copyright by Earl B. Marlatt and are quoted by permission.

A second hymn by Dean Marlatt is also included in *The Methodist Hymnal*, a hymn of consecration written for the Boston University School of Religious Education in 1926:

> "Are ye able," said the Master,
> "To be crucified with me?"
> "Yea," the sturdy dreamers answered,
> "To the death we follow thee."

One of the best recent missionary hymns reflecting the modern spirit is that by Mrs. Laura Scherer Copenhaver [29] beginning,

> Heralds of Christ who bear the King's commands,
> Immortal tidings in your mortal hands,
> Pass on and carry swift the news ye bring,
> Make straight, make straight the highway of the King.
>
> .   .   .   .
>
> Lord, give us faith and strength the road to build,
> To see the promise of the day fulfilled,
> When war shall be no more and strife shall cease,
> Upon the highway of the Prince of Peace.

Mrs. Copenhaver is a member of the United Lutheran Church.

Mention has been made of the small number of hymns written in the nineteenth century by the Presbyterians, in proportion to the size and generally high cultural standards of that body; and the inferior quality of most of the hymn-books used by the Presbyterians, prior to the publication of the *Presbyterian Hymnal* of 1895, edited by Dr. Benson,

---

[29] Laura Scherer Copenhaver, b. Marion, Va., Aug. 29, 1868; professor of English Literature at Marion College; author of several hymns, pageants, and magazine articles. Her hymn is quoted with her permission.

has been pointed out. For forty years he rendered distinguished service to his denomination, and to all students of hymnology. He prepared the revised edition of the *Hymnal* published in 1911, which amply justified the purpose announced in the preface,

to bring the book abreast of the latest developments of hymnody, and of the present state of Christian thought and belief; especially to meet the demand for the recognition of God's nearness to every-day living, the coming of the Kingdom in the sphere of common life, the spirit of brotherhood and of manly and resolute Christian life and service, social betterment and evangelistic work.

Far more important was the publication in 1915 of his great book, *The English Hymn*, which has no rival as a mine of accurate information about the development and use of English and American hymns and hymnbooks. Its range of knowledge and breadth of view marked its author as the preëminent hymnologist of his day. It is, however, a book for the student to use as an authority, and not for the casual reader. The present *Hymnal* of the Presbyterian Church, published in 1933, which he did not live to edit, while perhaps better suited to the needs of today, hardly maintains his editorial standards, and the *Handbook to the Hymnal*, issued in 1935 to give information about it, while useful within limits, contains some features which would have put a very severe strain upon his conscience as an editor.

The *Hymnal* contains eight hymns by Dr. Benson, besides one of his translations from the Latin. Several of his hymns were written before the nineteenth century ended, and one of them has already been mentioned. Almost all that he wrote are to be found in a little book containing thirty-two original hymns, written over a period of forty-seven years, and sixteen translations from the Latin, privately printed by Dr. Benson in 1925.[30] Several of them are of a quality to give them wide use and permanent value. His Christmas carol,

> O sing a song of Bethlehem, —

is unusual in that the succeeding stanzas sing of the later life of Jesus, in Galilee, and at Calvary. His post communion hymn,

> For the bread, which Thou hast broken,
> For the wine, which Thou hast poured,
> For the words, which Thou hast spoken,
> Now we give thee thanks, O Lord, — [31]

has unusual excellence. Perhaps most widely known is his noble song of brotherhood:

> The light of God is falling
> Upon life's common way;
> The Master's voice is calling,
> "Come, walk with me today":
> No duty can seem lowly
> To him who lives with thee,
> And all of life grows holy,
> O Christ of Galilee.
>
> . . . .
>
> Where human lives are thronging
> In toil and pain and sin,
> While cloistered hearts are longing
> To bring thy kingdom in,
> O Christ, the Elder Brother
> Of proud and beaten men,
> When they have found each other,
> Thy kingdom will come then.

[30] *Hymns, Original and Translated*, [with musical settings]. Philadelphia, 1925.
[31] Acknowledgement is made to Mrs. Robert E. Jeffreys, owner of the copyright, for permission to reprint Dr. Benson's hymns.

One of his latest poems is an exquisitely tender and trustful song of sunset, comparable to Tennyson's "Crossing the Bar," and Whittier's "When on my day of life the night is falling." It was written in 1923, and first appeared in his privately printed collection. It already has had widespread acceptance, having been sung at a music festival in Canterbury Cathedral, and translated into French:

> O Love that lights the eastern sky
>   And shrouds the evening rest,
> From out whose hand the swallows fly,
>   Within whose heart they nest!
>
> O life, content beneath the blue!
>   Or, if God will, the gray,
> Then tranquil yet, till light breaks through
>   To melt the mists away!
>
> O death that sails so close to shore
>   At twilight! From my gate
> I scan the darkening sea once more,
>   And for its message wait.
>
> What lies beyond the afterglow?
>   To life's new dawn how far?
> As if an answer, spoken low,
>   Love lights the evening star.

No other American author of the twentieth century has made any contribution to our knowledge of hymnody comparable to Dr. Benson's, and only two or three have written as many hymns of fine quality.

The most distinguished of this Presbyterian group was undoubtedly Dr. Henry van Dyke,[32] a man who played

[32] Henry van Dyke, b. Germantown, Pa., Nov. 10, 1852; d. Princeton, N. J., April 10, 1933; A.B. Princeton, 1873; Princeton Theological Seminary, 1877; ordained 1879; pastor of the United Congregational Church, Newport, R. I., 1879-1883; of the Brick Presbyterian Church, New York,

many parts in life as preacher, poet, professor, and diplomat. Two of his hymns are in the Presbyterian *Hymnal* and in many other recent collections. The first was written in 1907 while the author was on a preaching visit to Williams College. His purpose was to provide suitable words for the great "Hymn of Joy" in Beethoven's Ninth Symphony, which had for many years had some use as a hymn tune without finding any very satisfactory words. Dr. van Dyke succeeded admirably. His words from beginning to end express the mood of the music, and constitute one of the most joyful hymns in the language:

> Joyful, joyful, we adore thee,
> God of glory, Lord of love;
> Hearts unfold like flowers before thee,
> Opening to the sun above.
> Melt the clouds of sin and sadness;
> Drive the dark of doubt away;
> Giver of immortal gladness,
> Fill us with the light of day! [33]

Dr. van Dyke's second hymn, printed in *The Continent* in 1912, and in *Songs of the Christian Life* the same year, is a hymn for America:

> O Lord our God, thy mighty hand,
> Hath made our country free;
> From all her broad and happy land
> May worship rise to thee.

1883–1900; professor of English Literature at Princeton University, 1900–1923; U. S. Minister to The Netherlands and Luxemburg, 1913–1917; chaplain in the U. S. Navy in the World War; author of many books; chairman of the Committee of Revision of the Presbyterian *Book of Common Worship*.

[33] For permission to use this and following quotations from Henry van Dyke's hymns acknowledgement is made to Charles Scribner's Sons, New York, owners of the copyright.

> Fulfil the promise of her youth,
>   Her liberty defend;
> By law and order, love and truth,
>   America befriend.

It has a dignity and strength which place it among the other fine patriotic hymns of which so many have been written in the last half century. Several other of Dr. van Dyke's hymns are found in a few other hymnbooks. The two best are his,

> Return, dear Lord, to those who look
>   With eager eyes, that yearn
> For thee among the garden flowers;
>   After the dark and lonely hours
>   As morning light return, —

and his fine hymn of labor,

> Jesus, thou divine Companion,
>   By thy lowly human birth
> Thou hast come to join the workers,
>   Burden-bearers of the earth.
> Thou, the Carpenter of Naz'reth,
>   Toiling for thy daily food,
> By thy patience and thy courage,
>   Thou hast taught us life is good.

Another Presbyterian writer, Rev. Maltbie D. Babcock,[34] was a man of strong, vigorous, and attractive personality, who died at the height of his powers in 1901. His work was, indeed, done in the closing years of the nineteenth century, but his hymns were not published until a few months after his death, when they appeared in a little

[34] Maltbie Davenport Babcock, b. Syracuse, N. Y., Aug. 3, 1858; d. Naples, Italy, May 18, 1901; educated at Syracuse University and Auburn Theological Seminary; pastor of churches in Lockport, N. Y. and Baltimore, Md., and of the Brick Presbyterian Church, New York.

book of verse by him entitled *Thoughts for Every-day Living* (1901). From one of the poems has been taken a cento to form his best-known hymn:

> This is my Father's world
> And to my listening ears,
> All nature sings, and round me rings,
> The music of the spheres.
>
> This is my Father's world:
> I rest me in the thought
> Of rocks and trees, of skies and seas;
> His hand the wonders wrought.[35]

And from the same volume comes his rugged, vigorous hymn:

> Be strong!
> We are not here to play, to dream, to drift,
> We have hard work to do, and loads to lift;
> Shun not the struggle: face it. 'Tis God's gift.

These two hymns have come into considerable use. The Presbyterian *Hymnal* (1933) also includes one evening hymn,

> When the great sun sinks to his rest, —

but omits Babcock's other tender evening lines,

> Rest in the Lord, my soul,
> Commit to him thy way;
> What to thy sight seems dark as night,
> To him is bright as day.

Rev. Milton S. Littlefield,[36] an honored Presbyterian minister who was the editor of two hymnbooks, wrote two

[35] For permission to quote from this and the following hymns by Maltbie D. Babcock acknowledgement is made to Charles Scribner's Sons, New York, owners of the copyright.

[36] Milton Smith Littlefield, b. New York, Aug. 21, 1864; d. June 12,

serviceable hymns of good, though not of exceptional, quality which are found in several books, though neither is in the Presbyterian *Hymnal* (1933). The first, written in 1916, is a hymn of work:

> O Son of Man, thou madest known,
> Through quiet work in shop and home,
> The sacredness of common things,
> The chance of life that each day brings.[37]

The second, written in 1927, is a hymn of life's day,

> Come, O Lord, like morning sunlight,
> Making all life new and free;
> For the daily task and challenge
> May we rise renewed in thee.[38]

Another writer of distinction is Rev. William Pierson Merrill.[39] His two fine hymns were written in the same year, 1911. The first is a great summons of the Christian life, in the terse, vigorous lines of the short meter,

> Rise up, O men of God!
> Have done with lesser things:
> Give heart and mind and soul and strength
> To serve the King of kings.

No recent hymn has been more widely and eagerly accepted, in England as well as in this country. The Bishop

---

1934; educated at Johns Hopkins University and Union Theological Seminary.

[37] From *The School Hymnal*, copyright 1920 by A. S. Barnes and Company. Quoted by permission.

[38] From *The Hymnal for Young People*, copyright 1928 by A. S. Barnes and Company. Quoted by permission.

[39] William Pierson Merrill, b. Orange, N. J., Jan. 10, 1867; A.B. Rutgers College, 1887; Union Theological Seminary, 1890; held pastorates in Philadelphia, Chicago, and from 1911 to 1938 was minister of the Brick Presbyterian Church, New York; an outstanding preacher and religious leader.

of Ripon told the author that he used it at every confirmation service in his diocese when young people were received into the church. Dr. Merrill's second hymn, which first appeared in *The Continent*, a Presbyterian paper formerly published in Chicago, is less well-known but is a hymn of the higher patriotism which glories "Not alone for mighty empire," nor "for battleship and fortress," but "for conquests of the spirit . . . and the heritage of freedom" which have made America great. It is, perhaps, a weakness in any hymn to begin on the negative note, as this one does in the opening lines of its first two stanzas, but the vigorous affirmation quickly follows.

Another of this group of Presbyterian writers was Dr. Calvin W. Laufer.[40] He wrote a number of hymns, and the tunes for them, and through his editorial work and his book *Hymn Lore*, made a useful contribution to the hymnody of his church. His best and most generally used hymn is that beginning:

> We thank thee, Lord, thy paths of service lead
> To blazoned heights and down the slopes of need;
> They reach thy throne, encompass land and sea,
> And he who journeys in them walks with thee.
>
> . . . .
>
> We've seen thy glory like a mantle spread
> O'er hill and dale in saffron flame and red;
> But in the eyes of men, redeemed and free,
> A splendor greater yet while serving thee.

[40] Calvin Weiss Laufer, b. Brodheadsville, Pa., April 6, 1874; d. Philadelphia, Sept. 21, 1938; A.B. Franklin and Marshall College, 1897; Union Theological Seminary, 1900; held pastorates at Long Island City, N. Y., 1900–1905; West Hoboken, N. J., 1905–1914; from 1914 on was associated with various Presbyterian educational and editorial boards; was associate editor of the Presbyterian *Hymnal* of 1933, and of the *Handbook* of 1935. His hymns are quoted by permission of his son, Edward B. Laufer.

Another of Dr. Laufer's hymns is one for Palm Sunday,

> O thou eternal Christ of God,
> Ride on! ride on! ride on!

and a third is his,

> Thee, Holy Father, we adore.

A fine hymn on the theme of shared blessings, which closely parallels Theodore Williams' hymn,

> When thy heart with joy o'erflowing, —

was written in 1908 by Rev. Robert Davis,[41] who was at the time assistant minister at the Brick Presbyterian Church, New York. It is characteristic of the altruism of youth which is eager to bear its part of the world's burden of need and sorrow:

> I thank thee, Lord, for strength of arm
>   To win my bread,
> And that beyond my need is meat
>   For friend unfed:
> I thank thee much for bread to live,
> I thank thee more for bread to give.
>
> . . . .
>
> I thank thee, Lord, for lavish love
>   On me bestowed,
> Enough to share with loveless folk
>   To ease their load:
> Thy love to me I ill could spare,
> Yet dearer is the love I share.

[41] Robert Davis, b. Beverly, Mass., July 29, 1881; A.B. Dartmouth, 1903; Union Theological Seminary; assistant minister, Brick Presbyterian Church, New York, 1908–1910; minister Presbyterian Church, Englewood, N. J., 1910–1917. With the American Red Cross in Europe during the Great War, he has not returned to ministerial life in this country, but lives in France.

The last of this notable group of Presbyterian hymn writers is Miss Emily S. Perkins of Riverdale-on-Hudson, New York, who has been one of the most active and influential members of the Hymn Society of America and has privately printed two collections of hymns which she has written and tunes which she has composed. From one of these collections a hymn was taken for the Presbyterian *Hymnal*, beginning,

Thou art, O God, the God of might.

Taken as a group these Presbyterians have furnished American hymnody with the most distinguished new hymns written in the first four decades of the twentieth century.

The Protestant Episcopal Church issued its *New Hymnal* in 1918. It was ready for publication in 1916, and was copyrighted in that year, but, after the plates were made, a demand arose for a revision of the music, and the book was held back for two years during which a good many changes of settings were made. It was the first Episcopal *Hymnal* to be published with authorized tunes, and no other editions with different music have been permitted, as was the case with its two immediate predecessors. The revision to which it was subjected before publication undoubtedly raised its musical level, but hardly increased its popularity, which has never been great. Musically the book is overloaded with the now obsolescent tunes by the English "cathedral school" of nineteenth-century composers, so that it has fallen far behind the standards of the best recent English hymnals. And as a collection of hymns *The New Hymnal*, like all its predecessors, represents a rather timid compromise between conflicting tastes which has not greatly pleased anybody. It was surprisingly little influenced by the *Yattendon Hymnal* (1899) in England, including only one of the dozen or more fine hymns by the Poet Laureate Robert Bridges, which, with the music, had made that collection so notable, or by the *English Hymnal* of 1906, which for the first time seriously threatened the supremacy of *Hymns Ancient and Modern* in the Church of England. Apparently the Anglo-Catholic emphasis of the *English Hymnal* so frightened the editors of the *New Hymnal* that they failed to perceive its many excellencies, both in the new hymns which it introduced and, especially, in its tunes. On the other hand, they could not bring themselves to take much from the liberal wing of American hymn writers, venturing to include only four hymns by Whittier, two each by Oliver Wendell Holmes and Samuel Longfellow, and one each by Hosmer and by Samuel Johnson, and these not always of the best.

The fact is that the hymnbook editors of the Protestant Episcopal Church in this country have never had sufficient knowledge, independence, or courage to free themselves from the domination of the more conventional type of Anglican hymnbooks, especially *Hymns Ancient and Modern*, which, in turn, were so much under the spell of the rediscovered Latin hymnody that they were deaf to the singing voices of the new world. As Canon Dearmer puts it,

. . . while English compilers and translators were ransacking the material of the Dark Ages, and adding translations from hymns of the Counter Reformation to those of medieval origin, the modern American school was hardly consulted — if at all — by Anglican compilers; and, as it happened, it was just in America that the best hymns, and those most in accord with the convictions of the present age, were then being written.[42]

Under these circumstances it is not unnatural that the editors of *The New Hymnal* did not discover any writers of consequence within their own fellowship, beyond those

[42] Percy Dearmer, *Songs of Praise Discussed*, p. 5. Quoted by permission of the Oxford University Press, publishers.

whom we have already discussed, or that the impulse to write hymns should be very weak. In fact the only Episcopalian of the twentieth century whose hymns have come into some use is Rev. W. Russell Bowie.[43] He has written several, some of them too recently for inclusion in the *New Hymnal*, his finest and best known being his hymn for the nation, first printed in the *Survey's Social Hymns*:

> God of the nations, who from dawn of days,
> Hast led thy people in their widening ways,
> Through whose deep purpose stranger thousands stand
> Here in the borders of our promised land:
>
> . . . .
>
> Thy hand has led across the hungry sea
> The eager peoples longing to be free,
> And, from the breeds of earth, thy silent sway
> Fashions the nation of the broadening day.[44]

This, and his hymn of the heavenly Jerusalem, to be made real on earth,

> O holy city, seen of John,
> Where Christ the Lamb doth reign, — [45]

have come into considerable use.

The Universalists early in this century brought out two books, both wholly mediocre as to words and music, but

[43] Walter Russell Bowie, b. Richmond, Va., Oct. 8, 1882; A.B. Harvard, 1904; Theological Seminary, Alexandria, Va., 1908; rector Emmanuel Church, Greenwood, Va., 1908–1911; St. Paul's Church, Richmond, 1911–1923; Grace Church, New York, 1923–1939; professor at Union Theological Seminary; author of several volumes of sermons and Biblical interpretation.

[44] Copyright 1914 by Survey Associates, from *Social Hymns of Brotherhood and Aspiration*, copyright 1914 by A. S. Barnes and Company. Quoted by permission.

[45] From *Hymns of the Kingdom of God*, copyright 1910 by A. S. Barnes and Company. Quoted by permission.

one of their ministers, Rev. John Coleman Adams,[46] wrote in 1911 a notable hymn of the unfinished tasks of the world which has had far less use than it deserves:

> We praise thee, God, for harvests earned,
> The fruits of labor garnered in:
> But praise thee more for soil unturned,
> From which the yield is yet to win!
>
> . . . .
>
> We praise thee for life's gathered gains,
> The blessings that our cup o'erbrim;
> But more for pledge of what remains
> Past the horizon's outmost rim!

Some of the Unitarian writers who produced so many notable hymns in the latter part of the nineteenth century lived on into the twentieth, in which some of their later work, already discussed, was done. In 1911 Hosmer and Gannett brought out a revised edition of their *Unity Hymns and Chorals*. Besides their own contributions it contained a lovely hymn of winter by one of Dr. Gannett's parishioners, Mrs. Frances Whitmarsh Wile, beginning:

> All beautiful the march of days,
> As seasons come and go;
> The hand that shaped the rose hath wrought
> The crystal of the snow;
> Hath sent the hoary frost of heaven,
> The flowing waters sealed,
> And laid a silent loveliness
> On hill and wood and field.

[46] John Coleman Adams (son of J. G. Adams), b. Malden, Mass., Oct. 25, 1849; d. Hartford, Conn., June 22, 1922; A.B. Tufts College, 1870; B.D. 1872; ordained Universalist ministry, 1872; pastorates at Newton, Mass., 1872–1880; Lynn, Mass., 1880–1884; Chicago, 1884–1890; Brooklyn, 1890–1891; Hartford, Conn., 1901–1922.

In 1914 the American Unitarian Association issued its *New Hymn and Tune Book*, nominally a revision of the *Hymn and Tune Book* of 1877. The change of religious thought in the intervening thirty-seven years is indicated by the retention of only 242 of the 885 hymns which the earlier book had included. In reality the new book was based much more upon the later Unitarian collections of the eighteen-nineties, already referred to. The Unitarian hymn writers were, naturally, fully represented so far as their work still had living value, and the book was rich in hymns of public service and social righteousness. Musically it was less progressive, presenting the top musical level of about 1900, but paying inadequate attention to the new tunes which were coming into use in England, though they had not yet reached this country.

In 1937 a Hymn and Service Commission of the American Unitarian Association, collaborating with a similar Commission of the Universalist churches, brought out jointly a new book for use in both denominations, for which the title of Longfellow and Johnson's second book, *Hymns of the Spirit*, was revived. Like the *New Hymn and Tune Book*, it includes a very full presentation of the Unitarian hymn writers, and is even more pronounced in its emphasis on the "social gospel." It is greatly superior to the earlier book in its tunes, which are drawn from wider sources and are, on the whole, of a higher standard than those hitherto included in any other American hymn-book.

With the passing of the writers who made the last years of the nineteenth century so notable there has been a decided slackening in the number of hymns produced by the Unitarians, but several authors have made valuable contributions in recent years.

One of the finest hymns produced in this period is the revised version of the Yigdal, that great credal statement of the Jewish Articles of Faith formulated by Daniel Ben Judah Dayyan about 1400, a prose translation of which is to be found in the Jewish *Union Prayer Book*. As early as 1884 Rev. Newton Mann,[47] then minister of the Unitarian Church in Rochester, New York, at the request of a neighboring Jewish rabbi, put the Yigdal into metrical English. Early in this century Rev. William C. Gannett, who had followed Dr. Mann at Rochester, rewrote this metrical version to adapt its metre to the traditional Jewish melody, known as *Yigdal* or *Leoni*, to which the Hebrew words were sung. In view of Dr. Gannett's poetical abilities it is probable that the present form of the hymn owes much to his skill. It was included in the Jewish *Union Hymnal* (1908), and has thence passed into a good many other books, without either Mann's or Gannett's name attached to it. Sung to the traditional melody it makes a superb hymn for the opening of worship:

> Praise to the living God!
> All praisèd be his name,
> Who was, and is, and is to be,
> For aye the same!
> The one Eternal God,
> Ere aught that now appears;
> The first, the last; beyond all thought
> His timeless years!

With its inclusion in some evangelical hymnals it has undergone a rather curious transformation through its fusion — or confusion — with the well-known eighteenth-century hymn by Thomas Olivers, beginning,

> The God of Abraham praise.

[47] Newton Mann, b. Cazenovia, N. Y., Jan. 16, 1836; d. Chicago, Ill., July 25, 1926; educated at Cazenovia Seminary; ordained 1865; pastorates at Kenosha, Wis.; Troy and Rochester, N. Y.; and Omaha, Neb.

In 1770 Olivers, a follower of John Wesley, happened to hear the Jewish cantor Meyer Lyon, or Leoni, sing the Yigdal to the traditional tune in the Great Synagogue in London. Much impressed, he wrote his hymn, suggested, probably, by the words of the Yigdal but to which he gave an evangelical rendering quite alien to the original. His hymn, and the tune, were soon after printed in *The Pocket Hymn Book*, and from the Methodists passed into a widespread use which has continued until recent times.

Olivers' hymn, however, is far inferior to the modern version of the Yigdal, both in thought and form. The editors of both the Presbyterian *Hymnal* of 1933, and *The Methodist Hymnal* of 1935, wishing to use the Mann-Gannett version, yet reluctant to drop the long familiar hymn by Olivers, have resorted to the device of retaining Olivers' opening line,

The God of Abraham praise, —

but of following it with the modern words (with some minor alterations which are not improvements). The users of the books thus have a hymn of which the opening line is very familiar, but all the rest of which is quite new to them.

This arrangement raises some rather nice questions of editorial ethics. The hymn is not improved, from any point of view, and Olivers' opening line introduces a thought which is not in the original Yigdal. The authors of the modern version certainly did not intend to have their stanzas confused with those of Olivers. And to use Olivers' opening line has a tendency to mislead those who are looking for the familiar old hymn, and who think they have found it, when in reality they have got something quite different. The fact that they have been given something better than what they were looking for is hardly sufficient justification, and the *Handbook* to neither hymnal gives a sufficiently lucid explanation to enable puzzled minds to understand why the old hymn has suddenly taken on so different a meaning. Not to mince words, this unhappy mixture of two quite different versions of the Yigdal seems a peculiarly indefensible piece of hymn tinkering, and it will be unfortunate if this fine hymn gains widespread currency in a mangled form.

Rev. Marion Franklin Ham [48] and Rev. John Haynes Holmes [49] represent in a striking way two different but equally characteristic aspects of American Unitarian hymnody. Mr. Ham carries on the note of mysticism which was so marked a feature of some of the nineteenth-century writers:

> I hear thy voice, within the silence speaking;
> Above earth's din it rises, calm and clear;
> Whatever goal my wayward will is seeking,
> Its whispered message tells me thou art near.

Another hymn, written when blindness seemed to threaten, is one which allows of but infrequent congregational use, but which contains lines of great beauty:

> Touch thou mine eyes, — the somber shadows falling
> Shut from my sight the kindly light of day!
> Out of the depths my soul to thee is calling,
> Touch thou mine eyes, I cannot see the way!

. . . .

[48] Marion Franklin Ham, b. Harveysburg, Ohio, Feb. 18, 1867; minister of Unitarian churches in Chattanooga, Tenn., 1897–1905; Dallas, Texas, 1905–1909; Reading, Mass., 1909–1934; Waverley, Mass., 1934–; author of a book of verse, *The Golden Shuttle*, 1910; and of *Songs of the Spirit*, 1936, the latter of which contains most of his hymns. The quotations from his hymns are made by permission of the Beacon Press, owners of the copyright.

[49] John Haynes Holmes, b. Philadelphia, Nov. 20, 1879; A.B. Harvard, 1902; Harvard Divinity School, 1904; minister of the Third Religious Society, Dorchester, Mass., 1904–1907; and of the Church of the Messiah, now called The Community Church, New York, 1907–; author of several books. The quotations from his hymns are made with his permission.

Frail is the flesh that waits for thine appearing,
And blind the dust that turns to thee for sight;
Thy power must quicken earthly sight and hearing,
Thy word impart the Spirit's life and light.

Another hymn for the Communion Service begins:

O thou whose gracious presence shone
A light to bless thy fellow-men,
To thee we fondly turn again
As to a friend that we have known.

A fourth hymn is an exultant greeting to the Kingdom of God:

O Lord of life, thy kingdom is at hand!
Blest reign of love and liberty and light;
Time long foretold by seers of every land;
The cherished dream of watchers through the night.

Mr. Ham has also written two Christmas hymns,

Ring, O ring, ye Christmas bells,

for the music of Mendelssohn's *Festgesang*, and an original and moving interpretation of the significance of the birth of Christ, to go with the beautiful old French carol melody known as *Picardy*:

Heir of all the waiting ages,
Hope of ages yet to be;
Light to them that sit in darkness,
Living truth to make men free;
Stricken souls shall know the comfort
Of thy gracious ministry.

. . . .

Prince of peace, the warring nations
In thy name shall sheathe the sword;

> Justice, scorned of men and trampled,
>   By thy rule shall be restored;
> All the world with love shall follow,
>   And acknowledge thee as Lord.

Similar in spirit in his fine Palm Sunday hymn,

> From Bethany, the Master
>   Comes down Mount Olive's slope; —

and his hymn of church reunion,

> As tranquil streams that meet and merge.

These hymns constitute the choicest contribution to the "songs of the spirit" made by an American in this century.

Dr. John Haynes Holmes, on the other hand, carries on the tradition of independence and of eager social reform of which Theodore Parker and his sympathizers were the representatives in the nineteenth century. Indeed, like Samuel Johnson and Octavius Brooks Frothingham, although he is of the Unitarian heritage and training, Dr. Holmes has shaken off all denominational affiliations and taken an independent position. Nevertheless, as a hymn writer, he belongs with the Harvard school of hymnody. His finest hymn is his great call to the service of mankind:

> The voice of God is calling
>   Its summons unto men;
> As once he spoke in Zion,
>   So now he speaks again.
> Whom shall I send to succor
>   My people in their need?
> Whom shall I send to loosen
>   The bonds of shame and greed?
>
> . . . .
>
> We heed, O Lord, thy summons,
>   And answer: Here are we!

Send us upon thine errand,
　Let us thy servants be!
Our strength is dust and ashes,
　Our years a passing hour;
But thou canst use our weakness,
　To magnify thy power.

Others of his hymns stress the thought of human brotherhood and peace among men, as in his,

All hail, the pageant of the years, —

in his fine hymn for the nation,

America triumphant!
　Brave land of pioneers!

and in,

God of the nations, far and near,
　Ruler of all mankind,
Bless thou thy peoples as they strive
　The paths of peace to find.

Of a different type are his hymns of thankfulness for the
simple joys of life,

O Father, thou who givest all
　The bounty of thy perfect love,
We thank thee that upon us fall
　Such tender blessings from above, —

and,

O God, whose love is over all
　The children of thy grace,
Whose rich and tender blessings fall
　On every age and place: —

and his hymns of nature,

O God, whose smile is in the sky,
　Whose path is in the sea,

> Once more from earth's tumultuous strife
> We gladly turn to thee; —

and,

> O God, whose law from age to age,
> No chance or change can know, —
> Whose love forevermore abides,
> While aeons come and go;
>
> From all the strife of earthly life,
> To thine embrace we flee,
> And 'mid our crowding doubts and fears
> Would put our trust in thee.

While Dr. Holmes rather infrequently attains a distinction of phrasing which results in a memorable line, his hymns are all cast in vigorous and often stirring verse of high quality, expressive of a noble altruism and of a wholesome attitude towards life. Taken as a group they form one of the notable contributions to the hymnody of our day.

A number of other living Unitarians have each written one or more hymns which have, as yet, had only a limited use. Among them may be mentioned Rev. John Howland Lathrop's Palm Sunday hymn,

> Hosanna in the highest, —

Rev. Vincent B. Silliman's hymn of nature,

> Morning, so fair to see, —

and Rev. Jacob Trapp's vision of the future,

> Wonders still the world shall witness
> Never known by men of old,
> Never dreamed by ancient sages,
> Howsoever free and bold.

Evidently the stream of hymnody, which flowed with so strong and full a current in nineteenth-century Unitarianism, has not yet run dry.

Two writers without formal church affiliation should be noted here. The great hymn by Miss Katharine Lee Bates,

> O beautiful for spacious skies, —

has already been referred to. Early in this century she wrote a Christmas carol,

> The Kings of the East are riding
> Tonight to Bethlehem, —

which is fresh and lyrical in its beauty, and in 1928, for *The American Student Hymnal*, she wrote a profoundly moving one on the Divine Immanence:

> Dear God, our Father, at thy knee confessing
> Our sins and follies, close in thine embrace,
> Children forgiven, happy in thy blessing,
> Deepen our spirits to receive thy grace.
>
> Not for more beauty would our eyes entreat thee,
> Flooded with beauty, beauty everywhere:
> Only for keener vision that may greet thee,
> In all thy vestures of the earth and air.

In February, 1909 Rev. William M. Vories,[50] an independent missionary in Japan, published in the *Advocate of Peace* a good peace hymn, which has found a place in some hymnbooks:

> Let there be light, Lord God of Hosts!
> Let there be wisdom on the earth!

[50] William Merrell Vories, b. Leavenworth, Kans., 1880; founder of the Omi Mission, Province of Omi, Japan.

Let broad humanity have birth!
Let there be deeds instead of boasts!

. . . .

Let woe and waste of warfare cease,
  That useful labor yet may build
  Its homes with love and laughter filled:
God, give thy wayward children peace!

These American hymn writers of the first four decades of the twentieth century, whom we have been considering, are still too close for us to be able to judge their work in true perspective. There appear to be among them no individual writers as distinguished alike for the quantity and quality of their product as were a number of writers in the four decades between 1845 and 1885. But, as a group, they have given us a considerable body of noble worship song which is no less characteristic of the thought of our time. And during this period there has been a substantial improvement in the standard of hymn book editing, as regards both words and music, and an increasing appreciation of the treasury of Christian song on the part of hymn lovers which augurs well for the future of American hymnody.

CHAPTER X

Retrospect and Prospect

IN THE THREE CENTURIES since *The Bay Psalm Book* was printed the forms of thought and ways of living in western civilization have undergone a far greater transformation than took place in the sixteen previous centuries since the beginning of the Christian era. This stupendous development moved slowly down to the latter part of the eighteenth century, although the beginnings of modern science, the growth of constitutional government in England, and the settlement of the American colonies contributed to it, but in the last one hundred and fifty years it has gone forward with ever-increasing acceleration, until today we look out upon the world with very different eyes from those of our seventeenth-century ancestors.

That is the reason why the psalmody of the first English settlers in America speaks, for most of us, in what is almost an unknown tongue. We have moved so far from their ways of thinking and use so different a language that we marvel that they and their descendants for five or six generations could have found any joy or satisfaction in verses and music which seem to us so crude and uncouth. We are liable to the error of imagining that the people who sang and loved them must also have been crude and uncouth — quite different from their enlightened twentieth-century descendants. But if we push aside the veils of our self-complacent pride and prejudice and seek to enter with sympathetic understanding into the world in which our ancestors lived three hundred years ago, we discover that they were human beings who, in their essential characteristics of intelligence, emotion, purpose, and desire, were no different from ourselves. The differences which at first are so puzzling are to be found in the social order in which they lived, and in the world of thought which moulded their ideals and beliefs. They were simply the children of their age, even as we are of ours. They belonged to the later Reformation period, which was still freighted with the lingering influences of the Middle Ages, and the religious thought of which was still largely dominated by the theology of earlier centuries. But we have been reared in a new and vastly greater world of thought, dominated by science, and far more keenly alive to the social implications of religion.

In the field of religion the successive steps of the changing outlook can be traced more easily and illustrated more vividly in the hymnody of the passing generations than in almost any other way. Each generation has sung its songs of faith in the language which best gave utterance to its own highest vision, treasuring the songs of the fathers so far as they still seemed valid, but quietly discarding those that were outworn in thought and speech. It is easy to pick out lines or verses from these old psalms or hymns which amuse or appall us, and to draw a caricature of the people to whom they meant something, but it is far more worth while and important to understand the profound religious emotion which breathed in the old psalmody; the newly awakened faith which found utterance in the hymns of Watts and of Wesley; the stirring of the heart aroused by the camp-meeting hymns and gospel songs; the development of a fresh idealism and a new outlook on religion which speaks in the ever-widening stream of nineteenth-century hymnody. For beneath the archaic thought and the formal, pietistic words of songs which were the authentic utterance of now outgrown types of religious belief and

experience, there flows the uninterrupted stream of faith
and of idealism from generation to generation:

> From heart to heart, from creed to creed,
> The hidden river runs:
> It quickens all the ages down,
> It binds the sires to sons.

To know something of the forms of worship song which
moved the hearts of our forefathers enables us to understand them better, and to trace the development which
has taken place in America in these three hundred years
gives us a new appreciation of the more wholesome attitude towards life, the higher conception of religion, and
the broader view of Christianity into which we have
entered.

We have seen that down to the Revolution most religious
bodies throughout the English-speaking colonies clung
tenaciously to one or another form of their inherited psalmody, and that hymns were generally introduced into worship with hesitation and often against opposition. Even at
the beginning of the nineteenth century the Episcopalians
were still largely dependent upon Tate and Brady; the
Presbyterians on the versions of the psalms by Rous or
Barton; the Congregationalists on the psalms and hymns of
Watts, with small supplements of other eighteenth-century
hymns; the Methodists upon various Wesleyan collections,
supplemented, if not in some localities supplanted by camp-
meeting hymns; the Baptists either upon Watts or on popular collections of a very inferior type. There were almost
no hymns of American authorship in use in the churches,
but outside their walls the folk hymns and camp-meeting
songs were largely of native origin.

The nineteenth century saw the outburst in America of
a volume of religious song unequalled in any other country
during the same period except in Great Britain, where there

was a parallel development due to causes similar to those which prevailed here. In England the Nonconformists in the eighteenth century had to a large extent freed themselves from bondage to psalmody and had provided most of the hymn writers, the Independents following the lead of Watts, the Methodists eagerly accepting the hymns of the Wesleyan revival. But the Established Church clung to psalmody and paid little heed to hymns until near the end of the century, when in 1776 Toplady brought out his *Psalms and Hymns*, and in 1779 Cowper and Newton published their *Olney Hymns*. The movement from psalmody to hymnody in the Church of England, for which they were in considerable measure responsible, received a fresh impulse a generation later from Reginald Heber, and was profoundly affected by the Oxford Movement from about 1830 on, which awakened in its followers a new enthusiasm for the rediscovered heritage of Christian song. Thus it came about that while the eighteenth-century English hymn writers had been mostly Nonconformists of various types, those of the nineteenth century were predominantly Anglicans. Their hymns have been chiefly of the "objective," outward-looking type, with especial emphasis on the common life of the church. The Anglican hymnody is, therefore, in large measure ecclesiastical and liturgical in character.

In America, on the other hand, as we have seen, very few hymns were written by Episcopalians in the nineteenth century. There has been a larger product from other evangelical bodies here than in Great Britain, but the most prolific writers have been of the more individualistic and theologically independent type — Whittier the Quaker, and the Unitarians. Their hymns have been largely subjective and introspective, "I" hymns more often than "we" hymns — with a strong infusion of mysticism. Where they have given expression to aspects of a common religious life it has been in terms of human brotherhood, of "the goodly fellowship of the prophets," and of the Kingdom of God, rather than of "the holy Catholic Church." In this respect they struck a note which is the most characteristic feature of our hymnody today.

In the early part of the century the American hymn writers are most easily classified by denominational groups, because their hymns, and the hymnbooks in which their hymns were included, are often of quite distinctive types, and the inclusion of hymns produced by writers of one group in the hymnbooks of another group was a slow process. After the Civil War these denominational distinctions steadily shrink in importance, and by the end of the century are negligible except in so far as they are of interest as indicating the trends in hymnody in the several denominations. For a full understanding of the history of American hymnody, however, the influence of the various denominational groups, and of their respective contributions, is essential, for they represent diverse groups in our social order.

Thus the folk hymns, camp-meeting hymns, and gospel songs were, for a hundred years, largely the product of Methodists and Baptists, who made greater use of them than did other groups, although they also had their denominational hymnbooks for church use. Until the present century the Methodists made but slight contribution to American hymnody, but the Baptists produced an outstanding hymn writer in Samuel F. Smith. On the other hand, the Episcopalians, Presbyterians, Congregationalists, and Unitarians, who required higher educational standards for their ministry and whose congregations were accustomed to more staid and formal modes of worship, were influenced to a far less degree, or not at all, by the more popular types of worship song, and consequently have produced by far the larger number of standard hymns of enduring value.

It is an interesting and significant phenomenon that these

nineteenth-century hymn writers can also be classified by the educational institutions from which they graduated in groups which to a large extent run parallel to their denominational affiliations. Thus the Presbyterians have for the most part been associated with Union Seminary or with Princeton, either the College or the Theological Seminary, or both; the Congregational hymn writers in the nineteenth century were generally graduates of Yale and of Andover Theological Seminary; the Unitarian hymn writers were almost entirely graduates of Harvard College or the Harvard Divinity School, or both. The Episcopalian hymn writers, however, were educated in a number of institutions, mostly in the middle states. This grouping of writers by the institutions in which they were trained is not, however, applicable in every instance. Phillips Brooks, though an Episcopalian, was a graduate of Harvard and of Alexandria Theological Seminary, and Samuel F. Smith, a Baptist, was a graduate of Harvard and of Andover. And it applies in steadily lessening degree in the twentieth century to the great number of new writers, though it may be noted that some of the present-day Methodist writers come from Boston University.

Unquestionably the influence of these educational institutions upon the hymns produced by their graduates was considerable. It moulded the cultural standards of the writers and helped to formulate their thought and their religious outlook. This influence is most easily traced in the earlier writers. It was natural that the great missionary movement of the middle period of the nineteenth century should find its fullest utterance in the hymns produced by the graduates of Yale and of Andover, for both institutions were profoundly affected by evangelical zeal for foreign missions. The most remarkable instance, however, of the influence of an educational institution upon American hymnody has been that of Harvard, illustrated over a period of nearly one hundred and fifty years alike in the excellence of the hymnbooks which its graduates have compiled, in the number of writers, and in the quality of the hymns which they have written. In this respect no other institution in the English-speaking world can compare with Harvard, save Trinity College, Cambridge, England, which, for a much briefer period in the first half of the nineteenth century (1820-1845), was the nursing mother of a much shorter, though great, succession of Anglican hymn writers. It was recognition of this striking phenomenon which led W. Garrett Horder, an English Congregationalist who was a thoroughly competent hymnologist, to write, "Harvard, like our Cambridge, has been 'a nest of singing birds.' I was struck by this when editing *The Treasury of American Sacred Songs*. Harvard provided the bulk . . . of the verse I included."

It may, at first sight, seem surprising that an abundant stream of noble devotional verse should find its source at Harvard, where the atmosphere has been supposed to be coldly intellectual, where religion took on a more rationalistic form than elsewhere, and in an age when science was supposed to have destroyed spirituality. To some observers it has seemed still more strange that so large a proportion of the contributors to this Harvard school of hymnody should be Unitarians. Thus, just after the death of Canon Percy Dearmer, the noted Anglican hymnologist and editor of those outstanding books, *Songs of Praise* and *Songs of Praise Discussed*, the columnist in the *London Spectator* wrote,

Dr. Dearmer once observed to me how strange it was that some of the best modern hymns seemed to be by American Unitarians. He had in mind Samuel Johnson's "City of God," F. L. Hosmer's "Thy kingdom come," and, of course, O. W. Holmes' "Lord of all being." [1]

[1] Comment by "Janus," *London Spectator*, June 5, 1936.

The reasons are, however, abundantly clear. In the first place, the hymns of the nineteenth-century Harvard graduates are a part of the so-called "New England Renaissance," that literary revival of which Boston, Cambridge, and Concord were the chief centers in the nineteenth century. The writers belonged by blood, by education, and by social ties to the New England literary group. They were set down in Harvard as impressionable young men at a period when the spirit of the time was most favorable to the stimulation of poetic gifts. They had the culture, the familiarity with literary methods, and the warmth of atmosphere needed. And, happily, the greatest writers did not come first, to overshadow and check men with lesser gifts, as Watts overshadowed the Independents in England, and Charles Wesley the Methodists; nor were they dominated by the greater tradition of the Church of England, as were the American Episcopalians whose needs were satisfied by the Anglican hymn writers.

In the second place, the age was a stirring one. Grave national issues were at stake. A great transformation in the interpretation of religion was in process. These men were adventurers in faith; they were preparing to search out new habitations of the spirit; they needed new songs for the coming day, songs which should lift up their hearts in worship as they faced the dawn. The hymns of their fathers savored of a bygone period, and, as the free spirit of a prophetic faith took possession of them, they sang their own fresh songs of courage, trust, and service. It was indeed inevitable that they should do so, for practically every great epoch of spiritual awakening in Christian history has thus been marked by an outburst of hymnody.

And, finally, with their qualifications for literary work, and with this impulse in their souls, they found themselves in an institution singularly free from traditionalism and formalism. The very fact that their education was undogmatic, that they were under no bonds to keep within the limits of an established creed or ritual, meant the liberation of their hearts and minds to find outlet in fresh, untrodden paths. So they sang in no conventional piety, in no stilted phraseology, songs which were not echoes from ages of a greater faith, but which were fresh and pure expressions of their own deep experiences. They were sharers in a movement of deep significance towards a greater religious freedom, and they nobly interpreted one phase of the spiritual life of America. Thus it came about that, throughout the nineteenth century, Harvard produced by far the most notable succession of hymn writers in the English-speaking world coming from any single institution.

As we study the rise and development of American hymnody the trends of religious thought in the last century and a half stand out with increasing clarity. No more striking illustration can be found than in the provision of hymns for young people. The earlier American hymnbooks either contained none at all, or, in the collections of the folk hymn variety, only those of a monitory type. A good example of the latter is a little collection published in Boston in 1809 entitled, *The Young Convert, a collection of Divine Hymns or Spiritual Songs for the use of Religious Families and Private Christians.* It opens with this encouraging note:

> Wak'd by the gospel's joyful sound,
> My soul in guilt and thrall I found,
>   Expos'd to endless wo;
> Eternal truth did loud proclaim
> The sinner must be born again,
>   Or else to ruin go.

Almost all of the hymns strike a similar note, and in the entire collection there is but one,

> How firm a foundation, ye saints of the Lord, —

which is familiar today, or possible for modern use. To young people brought up on such a heavy and tasteless diet, or on hymns like another already quoted,

> Remember, sinful youth, you must die,
> You must die, —

the *Rollo Books* must have seemed like thrilling tales of adventure and romance, though the modern child would find them unbearably didactic and insipid. The monitory and depressing hymns which were thought suitable for young people a century and a quarter ago were well calculated to make religion seem a gloomy and somber affair. One has only to contrast them with collections like Prof. Augustine Smith's *New Hymnal for American Youth* (1930), or with *Hymns for Worship* (1939), prepared for the Student Christian Movement, to see how immense a change has come about in our conception of the religious life. In these latter books, as in many other collections for school and college use, and in the sections for children and young people in all modern standard hymnals, we do find, as we should expect, hymns which face the problems, difficulties, sorrows, and temptations of life, but the emphasis is on faith, courage, and hope, and the great majority of the hymns are joyful calls to the service of God and man.

This disappearance from modern hymnbooks of the old hymns "calculated to impart fear to the sinful" by a vivid portrayal of the imminence of death and the day of judgment is one of the most notable changes which came about in the course of the nineteenth century. At the beginning of that century even Unitarian collections still included Watts',

> Hark, from the tomb a doleful sound, —

but when the century ended it was no longer possible for any book to include, as did *The Methodist Hymnal* of 1835, what is surely the most morbid hymn in the English language, Charles Wesley's,

> Ah, lovely appearance of death!
> What sight upon earth is so fair?
> Not all the gay pageants that breathe,
> Can with a dead body compare:
> With solemn delight I survey
> The corpse, when the spirit is fled;
> In love with the beautiful clay,
> And longing to lie in its stead.

This is but the worst example of a great number of hymns of similar type which cluttered the evangelical hymnbooks of the first half of the century and gave to worship an unhealthy tone. There were, it is true, noble hymns of heaven like Watts',

> There is a land of pure delight
> Where saints immortal reign, —

and many others, some of them with a long ancestry which may be traced far back into the Latin hymnody of the medieval church. In the middle of the nineteenth century some of these hymns still drew pictures of the glories of heaven in terms which are rather too literal for the taste of the modern worshipper, but by the end of the century they were giving way to songs of faith and trust like Whittier's,

> When on my day of life the night is falling, —

or Hosmer's,

> O Lord of life, where'er they be,
> Safe in thine own eternity,
> Our dead are living unto thee, —

or Chadwick's,

> It singeth low in every heart.

There is another notable change in emphasis in the view taken of this earthly life. At the beginning of the nineteenth century many hymns still pictured humanity as lying under the curse of God and living in a vale of tears until a supernatural redemption should save the elect. People, at least in some churches, were still asked to sing,

> Plunged in a gulf of deep despair
> We wretched sinners lay,
> Without one cheering beam of hope,
> Or spark of glimm'ring day, —
>
> Grov'ling on earth we still must lie,
> Till Christ the curse repeal;
> Till Christ, descending from on high,
> Infected nature heal.

Nowadays we sing instead van Dyke's,

> Joyful, joyful, we adore thee,
>   God of glory, Lord of love;

or Longfellow's,

> God of the earth, the sky, the sea,
>   Maker of all above, below,
> Creation lives and moves in thee;
>   Thy present life through all doth flow.

And we do not any longer sing hymns in which we speak of ourselves as "worms." "Hymns with worms in 'em," — what Canon Dearmer calls "vermicular hymns," — seem to have appealed strongly to the English taste in the eighteenth century, and were, of course, imported into this country, but their production almost entirely antedated the rise of American hymnody and few, if any, specimens originated here. In England, however, the Roman Catholic F. W. Faber wrote "a hymn with a worm in it" as late as the middle of the nineteenth century.

Frequent reference has been made to the great number of missionary hymns produced in the nineteenth century, some of them notable examples. In these, too, we note a changing emphasis. In the earlier ones the appeal is usually to bring a gospel of personal salvation "to souls benighted" in heathen lands, but the later ones tend to become songs of human brotherhood, and of universal peace and goodwill in the light of the gospel. Indeed, in the last third of the century, and still more in the present era, the new hymns of the social gospel are the true successors both of the missionary hymns and of the early hymns inculcating Christian charity of a more personal type.

This change of emphasis in missionary hymns is in line with the lessening production and use of doctrinal hymns which seek to embalm theological formulas in verse. Such hymns have seldom been very successful. The noblest in all Christian hymnody are probably those of St. Thomas Aquinas for the feast of Corpus Christi,

> Pange lingua gloriosi
> Corporis mysterium, —

and

> Lauda Sion Salvatorem, —

in which the author succeeded in putting into superb verse a concise statement of the doctrine of transubstantiation. No Protestant has ever been able to write a doctrinal hymn approaching the standard which St. Thomas Aquinas attained, and most such Protestant hymns, though they may express a generally accepted belief at the time when they are written, carry within themselves the seeds of decay, because Protestant theology is not static, but a constantly moving and changing development of thought. Hence the disappearance from modern hymnbooks of a large proportion of the older doctrinal hymns. And new ones are seldom now produced, both because the field is already occupied and because the thoughts of men are turned as never before to the practical application of religion to life. This decline in doctrinal emphasis is illustrated in the *Pilgrim Hymnal* (1931), in its inclusion of but five hymns addressed to the Trinity, and to the omission of any reference to that doctrine in the Table of Contents. And *Christian Worship and Praise* (1939), edited by Professor Tweedy, includes but four in its Index of Subjects, and has altered Heber's,

> Holy, holy, holy! Lord God Almighty, —

so as to omit the Trinitarian formula with which his first and fourth stanzas ended.

In the hymns about Jesus or addressed to him there is also a marked change. Where the earlier hymns were addressed to him as enthroned in heaven and presently to come to judge the quick and the dead, — a thought in which fear was largely mingled with joy — the modern hymns are almost entirely concerned with his earthly life, example, and teaching. Cennick's hymn (as amended by Charles Wesley),

> Lo! He comes with clouds descending,
> Once for favoured sinners slain, —

has disappeared from many hymnbooks, and in its place we sing Washington Gladden's,

> O Master, let me walk with thee, —

and Frank Mason North's,

> Where cross the crowded ways of life.

A still more recent note connects Jesus with the labor of mankind. The fine hymn by the English writer Studdert-Kennedy,

> When through the whirl of wheels, and engines humming, —

is echoed in America by Jay Stocking's,

> O Master-workman of the race, —

and Milton Littlefield's,

> O Son of Man, thou madest known,
> Through quiet work in shop and home,
> The sacredness of common things,
> The chance of life that each day brings.

It is a very great gain in our hymnody to have the social aspect of religion thus emphasized in terms of our common human life, in the relations of man with man, and of nation with nation. That, in fact, is clearly the dominant note in our twentieth-century hymnody with its songs of social service, of peace among men, and of a patriotism which rises above a narrow love of country to include the whole brotherhood of man.

A different trend is to be observed in the Anglican communion, though more markedly in England than in this country, in the increasing use of translations of the Latin hymns from the Offices of the Roman Church. This is clearly associated with the liturgical, as distinguished from the homiletical use of hymns. The Roman use of these hymns is, of course, wholly liturgical, the hymns being fixed parts of the Breviary offices. When psalmody was adopted by the reformed Church of England as an unofficial substitute for the Latin hymns which had not been translated for the *Prayer-Book* the Psalms were probably sung in rotation, as a sort of compensation for what had been omitted. But when hymns came in the preacher found it convenient to select such as illustrated and reinforced his theme, and the early hymnbooks were arranged with more or less regard to the topics of the hymns, and were provided with topical indexes to aid the preacher in his selection. For example, the *Sabbath Day Hymn Book*, edited by Professors Park and Phelps of Andover, had a most elaborate and intricate table of topics, mostly theological. In Heber's *Collection*, published in England in 1827, the hymns were for the first time arranged according to the Christian Year, and this device, so convenient for a liturgical church, has been followed ever since in Anglican books, the hymns for the Christian Year being generally followed by a large section headed "General Use." In the liturgical use of hymns, those are sung on any given Sunday which are appropriate to the season of the church year, and the homiletical use of hymns is largely abandoned. The use of the office hymns translated from the Latin naturally fits into a liturgical scheme, hence their increasing adoption today by the High Church party.

It is, of course, an enrichment of English hymnody to have available good translations of the Latin hymnody, in meter which makes it possible to sing them to the ancient plain-song settings, but the fact remains that many of them reflect a mode of thought even more archaic than that of the early psalmody, and equally inadequate as an expression of the religion of the modern man. Not many, therefore, are likely to find wide currency except in those Protestant groups which like to follow the Roman model of worship as closely as they can. In such groups there is a natural tendency to regard them with a reverence akin to that which our seventeenth-century ancestors accorded to the metrical psalms, and to seek for "close-fitting" translations which shall reproduce the meaning of the originals as accurately as possible.

The trends of American hymnody in the nineteenth and twentieth centuries have, in general, been towards a far wider inclusiveness of theme, an application of religion to life, and a truer understanding of the relation of God to man, so that today our better hymnbooks on the whole reflect adequately the highest religious idealism of our day. Yet, so potent is the power of association with the hymns and tunes of one's youth, these changes have distressed some faithful souls, brought up in the hymnody of the past and hardly aware of the moving tide of religious thought. Thus, as late as 1903 Professor David R. Breed, of the Western Theological Seminary of the Presbyterian Church, at Pittsburgh, published his *History and Use of Hymns and Hymn Tunes*, based on the lectures on hymnody which he had given his students. The latest writer whom he names is the English bishop, W. W. How, who was born in 1823 and whose latest hymn in general use was published in 1872. Breed says of the second half of the nineteenth century that

the decadence of this period is marked in the large preponderance of translations and it would almost seem as though the ability of original utterance in sacred song of high character were departing from the church.[2]

And again,

In hymnody it is distinctly a period of decadence, a decadence which has continued to become more pronounced until the present day. . . . The reason . . . is found in the absence of a fresh impulse. . . . Therefore our later hymns are of the sentimental kind, and no writer is found the equal of some of the past periods. . . . Very few attempt to write hymns. And so we wait for a fresh outpouring of the Holy Spirit, involving some new struggle with the powers of darkness, some new development of spiritual life which shall stir the heart of Christendom and evoke again its noblest melodies.[3]

And this from a teacher of hymnody, writing about a half-century notably marked by "a fresh outpouring of the Holy

[2] D. R. Breed, *History and Use of Hymns and Hymn Tunes*, Chicago, 1903, p. 230, quoted by permission of the publishers, Fleming H. Revell Company.
[3] *Ibid.*, pp. 80–81.

Spirit" in song, and which saw the introduction of the hymns of Whittier, Longfellow, Hosmer, Phillips Brooks, Washington Gladden, and a host of others of whose very existence he was apparently ignorant! And most lovers of hymnody would regard the translations of German, Latin, and other hymns as an enrichment of our hymnbooks, rather than as a mark of decadence. They are one aspect of the immensely wider range of hymnody available today, as compared with the very narrow limits of the field a century and a half ago. This enlarging inclusiveness, with a steady winnowing-out of outworn and anachronistic religious verse, has gone steadily on in the twentieth century, until it becomes increasingly true that "in the hymnbook is the true key to the doctrine of the communion of saints, for here the saintly ones of all ages meet in their saintliest moods."

This great enlargement of the field of hymnody has been accompanied by a considerable, though much less notable, improvement in the quality of the music included in many standard hymnbooks. Lowell Mason's tunes which, for two generations in the nineteenth century, had played a notable part in raising the musical level of American worship song, but which had remained almost unknown in England, were slowly giving way by the end of the century before the rapidly rising popularity of the cathedral school of English composers. The *Presbyterian Hymnal* of 1895, which Professor Breed called "severely critical" in its standards of music, and which did well represent the better taste of its time, still included thirty-three of Lowell Mason's tunes, but it had thirty-four by Barnby, and forty-three by Dykes (including several repetitions in each case). By comparison, the recent *Christian Worship and Praise* (1939), edited by Professor Tweedy, has eleven different tunes composed or arranged by Mason, with three repetitions; nineteen by Barnby, with six repetitions; and twenty-four by Dykes, with seventeen repetitions. But *Christian Worship and Praise* still leans heavily upon the music of the Victorian English composers and has drawn but little on the wider resources now available. For example, it includes but one of Bach's chorales. The recent *Hymns of the Spirit* (1937), which draws upon a much more extensive range of music, old and new, including twenty-two of the Bach chorales, while retaining seventeen tunes by Mason, has only six by Barnby, three of them as alternative tunes, and fourteen by Dykes, seven as alternative tunes, with four repetitions.

In England, where there has been a great forward movement in church music since the opening years of this century, there has been a much more drastic elimination of the Victorian tunes from the recent hymnals. *Songs of Praise*, which is an outstanding example, includes but one by Barnby; five by Dykes, of which four are alternative tunes; and one by Sir Arthur Sullivan; with a similar reduction in the number of tunes by less popular but often superior Victorian composers. Their music has been replaced by various types of older music revived after long disuse — plain song; folk tunes; some of the Genevan psalm tunes; English tunes of the seventeenth and eighteenth centuries; hitherto overlooked Welsh tunes; and by a considerable number of modern compositions which have yet to prove their lasting value.

This reaction against the tunes of the Victorian era, now in full sway in England and already felt here in some measure, is easily explained. Taste in hymn tunes, as in all the other ways in which human beings give expression to their thought and feeling, changes from generation to generation. Just as the psalm tunes came to be regarded as old-fashioned in the eighteenth century, and the eighteenth-century tunes seemed old-fashioned in the Victorian era, so the Victorian tunes in turn are now out of style. To be old-fashioned is to be dowdy, a subject for mild ridicule, to be retained for the sake of sentiment, perhaps, but not because of outstanding merit, whereas to be a genuine antique, two or three hundred years old, is to be admired and respected. It is quite true that a great many of the Victorian tunes, and those the most popular, were very sentimental; pretty rather than strong; feminine rather than virile; and our generation is not at all sentimental in the Victorian way, but is quite hardheaded, if not "hard-boiled." Yet there is little doubt that the elimination of the Victorian tunes from the English hymnbooks has been too sweeping. A generation or two hence they will be rediscovered, and the best of them will be restored to use.

In the meantime we must recognize that most American hymnbooks lag twenty-five years behind their English contemporaries, so far as their music is concerned, as they generally have done in the past. They cannot afford to do so for long, for musical taste is rapidly improving in this country, and with it the ability to sing music which an earlier generation would have thought quite too difficult because utterly unfamiliar. The young people in our churches, trained in school and college to sing much finer music than their elders, are not likely to be content to sing hymn tunes which they regard as weak, trivial, or slightly ridiculous.

Unfortunately most of this finer music is outside the hymnals which they use. In the nineteenth century most schools and colleges used the standard books of the denominations with which many of them were affiliated. In the present century a good many books for school and college use, or for young people in general, have been published, most of which have no especial merit, being often but little more than abridged editions of the larger books for church use. A few, like the [Harvard] *University Hymnbook* (1890), and its successor *The Harvard University Hymn Book* (1926), while edited with meticulous scholarship and admirably annotated, have been far too doctrinaire in their selection of both words and music of a severely classical type to be satisfactory for practical purposes, and the same criticism may be made of *The Oxford-American Hymnal* prepared for use at Phillips Academy, Andover. The book prepared for use in the college chapels at Yale and Princeton is a good working compromise between the rigid standards of the present Harvard hymnbook and more popular tastes, though with a good deal more emphasis upon evangelical theology and the older type of hymns, and a good deal less on the social aspect of religion and the present-day thought of God than is needed for the most effective appeal to the religious views and altruistic idealism of modern youth.

Professor H. Augustine Smith, who has done conspicuous work for the improvement of forms of worship, especially among the Methodists, in his *New Hymnal for American Youth* (1930), produced one of the best recent books for young people, the music of which is generally of good quality, though not of exceptional excellence, and in which he included poems or centos from such writers as Sidney Lanier, Walt Whitman, John Masefield, Margaret Sangster, and Edna St. Vincent Millay. The use of such poems is an interesting experiment, and occasionally results in the discovery of a fine hymn. It was in this way that most of Whittier's hymns were introduced. It must, however, be remembered that, although hymns are religious poetry, a great deal of religious poetry is impossible to use in hymnody because it is not suitable for congregational singing either in thought or in verse form. A still more recent book, which, like Professor Smith's, has been referred to earlier in this chapter, is *Hymns for Worship* (1939), prepared for the Student Christian Movement, and published by the Association Press. It is smaller, and less experimental in its inclusion of poetic material, but its hymns are very well chosen for use by modern young people, and its music is of a high order. If it proves acceptable for the groups for whose use it has been prepared it may do much for the improvement of the taste of the rising generation.

It has been possible in this bird's-eye survey of American hymnody to name only the more important hymnbooks of the great number which have been printed in the last one hundred and fifty years, and only those writers whose hymns have either come into considerable use or have a degree of excellence which would seem to entitle them to wider use than they have yet attained. Hymn writing was, down to a generation or two ago, limited to a rather small number of people. Today, a far larger number are trying their hand at it, and are discovering that it is almost as difficult a task to write a really good hymn as it is to write a good sonnet. But here and there, out of a mass of mediocre productions, there appears some admirable hymn which sings with beauty and power the song of a new day, giving utterance to the faith and hope and love of the modern man. There is no reason to believe that the stream of American hymnody, which began as a slender rivulet in *The Bay Psalm Book* three hundred years ago, and which in the last century and a half has become a broad and noble river of song, will not continue to grow in strength and beauty in the years to come. And in our day we may well echo the words with which *The Bay Psalm Book* ends, even though we put our own interpretation into the archaic phraseology, and declare that we will go forward upon our way singing,

in Sion the Lord's songs of praise according to his will, until he take us hence, and wipe away all our tears, and bid us enter into our Master's joy to sing eternal Hallelujahs.

APPENDICES

APPENDIX A

The Controversy over the Practice of "Lining-Out" the Psalms

THE PRACTICE of "lining-out" the Psalms in the service of worship, to which we find such frequent references in the eighteenth century, is now so completely obsolete and seems to us so grotesque that it is difficult for us to understand the conditions under which it arose or the motives which led to its retention long after those conditions had passed away. In as much as the practice inevitably made any good singing almost impossible it became a cause of controversy when the introduction of "regular singing" led to the revival of music which has been described in Chapter III. This controversy did not, indeed, engender quite so much heat as did that over "regular singing," but it was long drawn out. It is, perhaps, only a side issue in the story of American hymnody, but is worth some attention because of its unfortunate influence in retarding the improvement of psalmody in the churches.

The custom originated in England, probably soon after the introduction of metrical psalms in common worship in the early years of Elizabeth's reign, and arose from the fact that the congregations in many, perhaps in most parish churches either did not possess a sufficient supply of psalm-books or were unable to read. Therefore, if they were to sing a psalm, it must be read to them, in passages sufficiently brief for them to be able to repeat them. So arose the practice of having the clerk, whose duty it was to "set" the psalm, read one or two lines, lead the singing of what he had read, then read the next line or two and sing, and so on, alternately reading and singing to the end of the psalm. The method was obviously cumbersome and disjointed, and must from the beginning have been very unsatisfactory to any good musicians, but it was the only practical one in churches which either lacked books or included any large number of illiterate persons. That it was regarded as a temporary expedient is clear from the Ordinance of 1644, which abolished the Prayer Book, and ruled, as regards singing,

That the whole congregation may join herein, everyone that can read is to have a psalm-book, and all others, not disabled by age or otherwise, are to be exhorted to learn to read. But for the present, where many in the congregation can not read, it is convenient that the minister, or some fit person appointed by him and the other officers, do read the psalm line by line, before the singing thereof.[1]

Three years later Rev. John Cotton published in Boston, Massachusetts, his *Singing of Psalms a Gospel Ordinance* (1647), in which he briefly refers to the "scruple" concerning "the order of Singing after the Reading of the Psalms."

We for our parts easily grant, that where all have books and can reade, or else can say the *Psalme* by heart, it were needlesse then to reade each line of the Psalme beforehand in order to singing. [But when this is not the case] it will be a necessary helpe, that the lines of the *Psalme*, be openly read beforehand, line after line, or two lines together, that so they who want either books or skill to reade, may know what is to be sung, and joyne with the rest in the dutie of singing.

These citations indicate that the practice was, both in England and in New England, regarded only as a temporary expedient to meet an immediate condition. Furthermore

[1] Quoted in Scholes, *The Puritans and Music*, p. 265.

there were churches in New England which did not follow it. In Plymouth the Pilgrims presumably brought with them a sufficient number of copies of Ainsworth's *Psalter*, or came to know the Psalms by heart, for "lining-out" was not introduced there until about the time that the Plymouth church abandoned Ainsworth for *The Bay Psalter* in 1692.[2] It was, apparently, the introduction of a less familiar version, and perhaps an insufficient supply of books, which, together with the deterioration of the singing, led the church to adopt "lining-out." The newly organized Brattle Square Church in Boston, voted on December 20, 1699, "that ye Psalms in our public Worship be sung without Reading line by line," and a few other churches may have followed its example. At least Cotton Mather in his *Church Discipline; or Methods and Customs in the Churches in New England*, published in 1726, says,

In some, the assembly being furnished with Psalm-books, they sing without the stop of reading between every line. But ordinarily the Psalm is read line after line, by him whom the Pastor desires to do that service; and the people generally sing in such grave tunes, as are the most usual in the churches of our nation.

When "regular singing" came in, and the singing schools were established in which the young people sang with enthusiasm from printed music, and presumably with psalm-books in their hands, so that "lining-out" was unnecessary, they quickly became dissatisfied with the retention of the old practice in public worship. Why should not the better way be introduced into the churches? An expression of this dissatisfaction appeared in the *New England Courant* in connection with the controversy in the church at South

[2] Thomas Symmes, *Concerning the Reasonableness of Regular Singing*, says that until about that time "their excellent custom was to sing without reading the line."

Braintree described in Appendix B. In the *Courant* of February 17–24, 1724, which contains the last fling against singing "by rote," is a "Letter to Janus," signed with the fanciful name of "Jeoffrey Chanticleer," in which the undesirability of the practice is set forth at considerable length:

> I have often wonder'd that the Spirit of Singing, and the great Care taken to regulate it in our Congregations throughout the Country, has not been attended with some Endeavours after the Removal of that indecent, unwarrantable, and unedifying way of *reading the Psalm Line by Line*. 'Tis true, Custom, and the Practice of our Forefathers, are the most convincing Arguments with most, for the Practice or Non-Practice of any Mode of Worship; and perhaps this may be the chief Reason why this of reading the Psalm, has not been more frequently declar'd against. However, I will venture to offer a few Reasons agains this Practice, tho' I expect to be proclaim'd a Roman Catholick throughout the Country for so bold an Attempt.
>
> It is certain, that this way of praising God by Peace-meal, between the Deacon and the People, was first introduc'd out of Condescension to ignorant People, who attended the public Worship. . . . [But] it *ought* to be laid aside in *New-England*, since there is not (I presume) one in a Thousand among us that have not been taught to read. . . . In the next Place I would observe, that in many of the Psalms, there is no Meaning (to say no more) in many of the Lines, if we take them by themselves; so that we are often oblig'd to *sing without a Meaning* (which is like *praying in an unknown Tongue*) till the Deacon is pleas'd to give us the next Line, or perhaps two or three more. I need not spend any Time in proving this Assertion, because it is obvious to every one, that even Blasphemy may be pick'd out of the Bible by leaving out a part of a Sentence. I confess, I was at first surpriz'd into an Aversion to reading the Psalm, by coming to the publick Worship in the Time of Singing, and just

before the Deacon read that Line of the 119th Psalm,

"Like Dross thy Laws I love therefore." [3]

Here I would willingly have join'd in the Worship, but I
consider'd, that if I sung that Line without knowing what
came before, or what follow'd, my own Voice would have
been a Witness against me that I *lov'd the Law like Dross*,
and yet could not tell for what reason. And what makes
this part of Divine Worship the more unedifying, is, That
the Readers are generally such, whose only Qualification for
parcelling out the Psalm to us, is, that they sustain the Office
[of] a Deacon; and if we now and then meet with a Line
which is a compleat Sentence of it self, the Words are often
murder'd or metamorphos'd by the *Tone* of the Reader. By
this Means it happens in some Churches, that those who
neglect to carry Psalm Books with them, only join in Singing
like so many musical Instruments, piping out the Tune to the
rest: So that while we are exclaiming against *dead Instruments of Musick* in the Worship of God, we encourage
many *Living Instruments*, who are of as little Use in the Congregation. I have myself been present at a Country Congregation when three Staves were sung, without understanding
three words; and yet the Deacon had the Character of a
very *affecting Reader*: But if a *Noise without Meaning*
affects us, our Devotion may as well be rais'd by the *Sound
of an Organ*, or the *ringing of Bells*, as the *insignificant Tone*
of many of our Readers. . . .

I have but one thing more to observe, and that is, that the
same Person who sets the Tune, and guides the Congregation
in Singing, commonly reads the Psalm, which is a Task so
few are capable of performing well, that in Singing two or
three Staves, the Congregation falls from a cheerful Pitch
to downright *Grumbling*, and then some to relieve themselves mount an Eighth above the rest, others perhaps a

---

[3] Here "Chanticleer" has his tongue in his cheek. In *The Bay Psalm
Book*, Psalm 119: 119 reads,
> As dross th' earth's lewd ones off thou throw'st,
> thy laws I love therefore.

Fourth or Fifth, by which Means the Singing appears to be rather a confused Noise, made up of *Reading, Squeaking and Grumbling*, than a decent and orderly Part of God's Worship: Nor can I see but that the Arguments made use of against the Peoples *Praying after a Minister*, will ly as fairly against their *Singing after a Deacon*.

I am, SIR,
Your Humble Servant,
JEOFFRY CHANTICLEER.

The arguments thus advanced by "Chanticleer" had, however, a more authoritative backing than that of his own satirical voice, for the critics of "lining out" could cite undisputed masters of song on their side. John Playford, in the preface to his *Whole Book of Psalms* (1677), had objected to "the late intruding of the Scotch manner of reading every line by the Clerk before it is sung." He went on,

I shall be willing to grant this way of reading to be useful in some small Villages by the Sea, or in the Borders of Scotland, where it may chance not two in those Congregations are book-learn'd; but not here in London, where in all Parishes, great and small you have not three in a hundred but can read.

And Watts, thirty years later, in the preface to his *Psalms of David imitated* had expressed himself as follows:

Though the author has done what he could to make the sense complete in every line or two; yet many inconveniences will always attend this unhappy manner of singing. But where it can not be altered, these two things may give some relief. First, let as many as can do it, bring psalm books with them, and look on the words while they sing, so far as to make the sense complete. Secondly, let the clerk read the whole psalm over aloud, before he begins to parcel out the lines; that the people may have some notion of what they sing, and not be forced to drag on heavily through eight tedious syllables, without any meaning, until the next line comes to give the sense of them.

In spite of these protests the practice seems to have been generally adhered to in New England for fifty years more, by the sheer tenacity with which the people clung to an old custom to which they had been so long habituated that it had become sacrosanct. It gave way at last to a combination of three influences which undermined it, the first of which was the partial introduction of Watts' *Psalms* and *Hymns* at the time of "the Great Awakening," accompanied as it was by an outburst of popular singing.

The second was the gradual introduction of new tunes from England. The old psalm tunes of the sixteenth or early seventeenth century, which the Puritans drew from Sternhold and Hopkins, and from Ravenscroft's *Psalter*, and which had once been sung with vigor and at reasonable speed, had become flattened with usage into wearisome and dragging measures which had lost all their freshness and vitality.[4] When the new tunes of the period of Handel became known, they had the advantage of being new, flowing, and singable, and there were many such tunes produced in England in the eighteenth century, of which Croft's *St. Anne* is one of the earliest and best known. The melodies, especially those known as fuguing tunes, did not lend themselves to "lining-out." When the irrepressible William Billings got to work in his singing schools and produced his own lively and popular, if musically illiterate, fuguing tunes, he vehemently opposed "lining-out" because of its incompatibility with the type of music he was promoting.

The third influence was the introduction of choirs into the churches between the seventeen-sixties and seventeen-eighties, to take the place of the precentor, or of the two or three persons who had hitherto been appointed to "raise the tune," generally from the front gallery. Evidence as to

[4] The most available illustration is *Old Hundredth*, already referred to.

the introduction of choirs is scanty, being for the most part buried in old parish records, but the following excerpts from the records of a single parish illustrate the slow development of the volunteer choir in many places. At Rowley, Massachusetts, in 1762, the parish voted "that those who had learned the art of singing may have liberty to sit in the front gallery." They "did not take the liberty," probably because they would not sing after the clerk's reading. In 1780 the parish "requested Jonathan Chapman, Jr., and Lieutenant Spafford to assist Deacon Daniel Spafford in raising the tune in the meeting-house." In 1785 the parish desired "the singers, both male and female, to sit in the gallery, and will allow them to sing once upon each Lord's day without reading by the Deacon." About 1790 the "lining-out" of the psalm was discontinued.[5]

The choirs naturally preferred to sing the psalm straight through, rather than by the tedious method of "lining-out," but the innovation was sometimes bitterly opposed by an old deacon who resented being deposed from his office as precentor. At Worcester, for example, the town voted, August 5, 1779, to give the choir the front seats, and that the

mode of singing in the congregation here, be without reading the psalms line by line to be sung. The Sunday succeeding the adoption of these votes, after the hymn had been read by the minister, the aged and venerable Deacon Chamberlain, unwilling to desert the custom of his fathers, rose and read the first line according to the usual practice. The singers, prepared to carry the alteration into effect, proceeded without pausing at the conclusion. The white-haired officer of the church, with the full power of his voice read on, until the louder notes of the collected body overpowered the attempt to resist the progress of improvement, and the deacon deeply mortified at the triumph of musical reformation, seized his hat, and retired

[5] These citations are quoted from Hood, *History of Music in New England*, 1848, pp. 181–184.

from the meeting-house in tears. His conduct was censured by the church, and he was for a time deprived of its communion, for absenting himself from the public services of the Sabbath.[6]

The contest did not always, however, result in such a pathetic scene. In one church where the choir similarly refused to wait for the deacon to read beyond the first line, he rose again at the conclusion of the psalm, reopened the book, said, "Let the people of God now sing," and set a psalm, which the congregation had the good sense to sing in the old way out of respect for him.[7]

Sometimes the issue was of sufficient importance to require a sermon from the minister. Thus Rev. Lemuel Hedge of Warwick, Massachusetts, preached one "at a singing lecture in Warwick" in 1772, advocating the disuse of lining-out.[8] The old custom practically disappeared from the New England churches before 1800, but it lasted much later in other parts of the country. Hood, whose *History of Music in New England* was published in 1846, wrote,

Yet still, to this day, it prevails over three-fourths of the territory of the United States. In some churches it is wholly used, and in others, only in their more social meetings. And still may be heard the same perplexities, that must always be found where this custom prevails — its broken and retarded sense, and its spoiled melody. Still may be heard occasional incongruities, as absurd, as those recorded of our fathers, when they read, and gravely sang:

"The Lord will come, and he will not" —

and pursuing the contradiction to a climax of absurdity, read and sang on:

"Keep silence, but speak out."

[6] Hood, *History of Music in New England*, pp. 183–184. Quoted from *History of Worcester*.
[7] *Ibid.*, p. 190.
[8] *Ibid.*, pp. 190–199.

It is but a year or two, since the writer frequently attended church in one of the western states, where the clerk, a lawyer of some note, used to dole out the hymn two lines at a time — with a nasal twang that Ichabod Crane might have coveted, but could never have obtained — always having the good fortune to be able to run out of the tune into the words, and from the words into the tune, without stopping or changing either the pitch or time.[9]

It will be observed from this statement, written in the eighteen-forties by a competent witness living in Philadelphia and familiar with the musical usages in other parts of the country, that it was in supposedly conservative New England that the outworn custom, so detrimental to good singing, was first abandoned. In this, as in practically every other matter relating to music, New England was more progressive than most other sections of the United States. In Great Britain the practice of "lining-out" survived locally to an even later date. Scholes cites a Devonshire village where it was continued until about 1870, "The clerk reading out the psalm, line by line, in a strong Devonshire accent, and accompanying the singing on a violin." [10] With the substitution of a bass-viol for the violin, and of a Yankee twang for the Devonshire accent, that might be a description of the practice in a New England meeting house a century earlier. In Scotland "lining-out" was widely prevalent down to recent times, but it now probably disappeared everywhere from public worship.

[9] Hood, *History of Music in New England*, pp. 200–201.
[10] Quoted by Scholes, *The Puritans and Music*, p. 265, from C. F. Abdy Williams, *The Story of Organ Music*, New York, 1905.

APPENDIX B

The Controversy at South Braintree over "Regular" Singing

THE CONTROVERSY between Rev. Samuel Niles and his parish at South Braintree, Mass., referred to on p. 110, over the introduction of "regular" singing, is an excellent illustration of the petty squabbles which rent a good many parishes over this, and similar issues. Generally they were unrecorded and soon forgotten, so that the publicity given to the South Braintree episode by *The New England Courant* has some value as an historical picture. The record begins with a fictitious letter dated "Brantrey, March 20, 1722," and signed "Ephraim Rotewell":

We are so exceedingly troubled with the Spirit of singing Psalms *by Rule*, as they call it, that we are afraid the new Singers will bring in *Popery* upon us before we are aware of it. Truly, I have a great jealousy, that if we once begin to sing by *Rule*, the next thing will be to pray by *Rule*, and preach by Rule; we must have the Common Prayer, Forsooth, and then comes *Popery*. . . . I know a very honest Man in the Country, who has travell'd pretty much in the World, and been on a Man of War ten Years, who says, That all prick'd [printed] Tunes came from *Rome*, except those we have in our psalm-Books, which are the only *Protestant Tunes* fit for Christians to sing. I think this is enough to set any Christian Man against this new upstart way of Singing; but yet many of our People are so in Love with it, that I don't know where they'll stop, for they now begin to find fault with our Version of the Psalms, and would bring in that of Tate and Brady, which some of us never heard of before.

To this imaginary letter "Janus" replies,

> Chear up, Mr. *Rotewell!* There's no Danger of Popery yet.
> The Argument . . . of the *honest Man* who has *travell'd* so
> much *on board a Man of War*, will confound all the *Roman
> Catholick Singers* in the Country, especially if we keep close
> to our own Version of the Psalms, which is a sure Bulwark
> against Popery.
>
> > *But O these Lines of* Nic. *and* Nahum! [1]
> > *May no one sing or ever say 'um!*

By midsummer the controversy had reached a point at
which each party was trying to drown the singing of the
opposing group by making a louder noise. *The Courant* for
Aug. 12–19, 1723, reports the disturbance:

> *South part of Brantrey, Aug.* 15. By this Time every one
> may see the hand of the Devil in the new Way of Singing, as
> they call it. It is impossible to tell what Disturbance it has
> made in our Congregation for more than a Year past, and in
> particular, the Disorder & Confusion it caus'd the last Lord's
> Day, cannot be easily related. No sooner was the Psalm set,
> than the bawling Party made such a hideous Noise, that the
> Minister forbid the Deacon reading any farther, upon which
> they carried on their Noise without reading, whereupon the
> Minister solemnly charged them to forbear; but notwithstand-
> ing they persisted in their Disturbance (with unaccountable
> Yells) to the End of the Psalm.

The scandal naturally resulted in a council of the neigh-
bouring churches which tried to settle the dispute. *The
Courant* of September 9–16, reports:

Last Week a Council of Churches was held at the South Part
of Brantrey, to regulate the Disorders occasion'd by regular
Singing in that Place, Mr. Niles the Minister having suspended

[1] "Nic. and Nahum" refer to Nicholas Brady and Nahum Tate, *The
New-England Courant*, March 18–25, 1723.

Seven or Eight of the Church for persisting in their Singing by Rule, contrary (as he apprehended) to the Result of a former Council, but by this Council the suspended Brethren are restor'd to Communion, their Suspension declar'd unjust, and the Congregation order'd to sing by Rote and by Rule alternately, for the Satisfaction of both parties.

This reasonable arrangement did not last long, however, for in the *Courant* of December 2–9, we read,

We have Advice from the South Part of Brantrey, that on Sunday the First Instant, Mr. Niles the Minister of that Place, perform'd the Duties of the Day at his Dwelling House, among those of his Congregation who are Opposers of Regular Singing. The Regular Singers met together at the Meeting House, and sent for Mr. Niles, who refus'd to come unless they would first promise not to sing Regularly; whereupon they concluded to edify themselves by the Assistance of one of the Deacons, who at their Desire pray'd with them, read a Sermon, etc.

The climax came in February 1724, and is thus reported in the *Courant* of Feb. 10–17:

We have advice from Brantrey, that 20 Persons at the South Part of the Town, who are Opposers of Regular Singing in that Place, have publickly declar'd for the Church of England.

Poor Mr. Niles! His own supporters had deserted, and it appeared that it was the "old way" and not the "new way" of singing psalms which was leading to the Church of England, with Popery, no doubt, following close behind! The danger must have reconciled him to the "regular" singers in his flock, for we hear no more of the controversy, except for a last fling in a "Letter to Janus" in the *Courant* of the following week, which concludes with a parable of "a poor ass" which "was wonderfully gifted, and could bray an Hour together by Rote."

With this blast the battle over music in the church at South Braintree came to an end. It was one of several similar, though perhaps less extreme, episodes to which Mather refers in his letter to Thomas Hollis. But the unwelcome prospect of the establishment of a Church of England congregation at South Braintree drew from Mather another letter to Thomas Bradbury, of the Society for the Propagation of the Gospel, in London, dated August 22, 1724. He writes:

It would amaze you to hear of the Occasions on which the Ch. of E. is here declared for. But I will mention One. . . . Very Lately, a Little Crue at a Town ten miles from the City of Boston, were so sett upon their old Howling in the public Psalmody, that being rebuked for the Disturbance they made, by the more Numerous Regular Singers. They declared they would be for the Ch. of E. and would form a Little Assembly for that purpose, and subscribed for the Building of a Chapel; and expect a Missionary to be sent and supported from your Society . . . for the Encouragement of half a score such Ridiculous Proselytes. But we suppose it will come to nothing.[2]

Mather was right in his supposition, for the plan to establish an Episcopal church at Braintree on so unstable a foundation came to nothing. But the episode gives us an interest and amusing glimpse into a parish squabble of the early eighteenth century.

[2] *Diary of Cotton Mather*, Mass. Hist. Soc. Coll., Seventh Series, VIII, 1912, 796.

INDEXES

INDEX OF NAMES AND SUBJECTS

INDEX OF PSALM BOOKS AND HYMN BOOKS

INDEX OF FIRST LINES OF PSALMS, HYMNS, AND SPIRITUAL SONGS